Class, Tax, and Power

The distribution of the total amount appropriated among the several branches of municipal administration is the central element to be considered in budget making, for this is the point at which the demands for efficiency and for social services collide with the claims of the politicians to the spoils of office and with the protests of those who would reduce government activities to a minimum.

— Charles Austin Beard, 1912

Class, Tax, and Power

MUNICIPAL BUDGETING
IN THE UNITED STATES

Irene S. Rubin
Northern Illinois University

Chatham House Publishers, Inc.
Chatham, New Jersey

CLASS, TAX, AND POWER
Municipal Budgeting in the United States

CHATHAM HOUSE PUBLISHERS, INC.
Post Office Box One
Chatham, New Jersey 07928

PUBLISHER: Patricia Artinian
COVER DESIGN: Antler Designworks
MANAGING EDITOR: Katharine Miller
PRODUCTION SUPERVISOR: Melissa Martin
COMPOSITION: Bang, Motley, Olufsen
PRINTING AND BINDING: Versa Press, Inc.

LIBRARY OF CONGRESS CATALOGING-IN-PUBLICATION DATA
    Rubin, Irene.
        Class, tax, and power : municipal budgeting in the United
    States / Irene S. Rubin.
            p.   cm.
        Includes bibliographical references and index.
        ISBN 1-56643-062-3 (pbk.)
            1. Municipal budgets—United States. 2. Municipal budgets—United
    States—Case studies. I. Title.
    HJ9147 .R827   1998
    352.4'8214'0973—dc21   98-8975
                                                                       CIP

Manufactured in the United States of America
10   9   8   7   6   5   4   3   2   1

Dedication

To Edward Artinian, who built a company on optimism and solid belief that he could do it better; who made networking a verb and kept us all together, which was harder than herding cats; who loved good food, good friends, and grand opera; and who loved well-made books. To Ed, who named this book over lunch. Goodbye, my friend.

Acknowledgments

I would like to thank Northern Illinois University for sabbatical research support in 1989 for gathering data on the six case study cities. I have incurred many other obligations while doing this research. I am especially grateful to all the public officials—elected, appointed, and career—who took the time to teach me how they budget, and to the document librarians and interlibrary loan librarians who made this research possible. I would also like to acknowledge Professor Lana Stein of the University of Missouri–St. Louis, who worked with me on the St. Louis case and generously shared her insights and expertise.

Contents

I

Municipal Budgeting in Context

THE PAST twenty-five years have seen enormous changes in municipal budgeting in the United States. Survey after survey has documented the extent of the changes. Puzzled by such a successful and untouted set of reforms in the public sector, I set out to explore six U.S. cities to figure out which budget reforms they had adopted and why they had adopted them. The core of this book is based on these six case studies.

I found that I could not tell the story of these six cities without explaining the earlier history of municipal budgeting more generally. Current arrangements only made sense in the context of the past. Looking at how municipal budgeting developed helped explain contemporary budgeting practices and made the bizarre understandable. Looking at budgeting over time helped sort out patterns. Historical context highlighted trends and suggested future directions. I also found that I could not describe what the cities had done with their budgets without also examining what the states had required or forbidden them to do. Not all cities were free to choose whatever budgeting practices they wished.

Stripped of its past and its political and intergovernmental context, municipal budgeting is technical, dry, and difficult to understand. But municipal budgeting has had a rich and lively history in the United States, beginning just after the Civil War. Budgeting in the cities reflected the struggle to modernize: to tame epidemics and fires that emptied and leveled the cities; to pave the mudholes that passed for streets; and to provide safe lighting at night and mass transit by day. Budgeting also reflected the political battles between machine and reform governments, between the rich and the poor, between those who paid taxes and those who benefited from them. This book is not just about how six cities changed their budgeting; it is also about municipal budgeting in the United States, from its origins after the Civil War to the present.

While the story has its squalid parts, it is basically an optimistic tale. It shows the extent to which government officials have been able to diagnose and solve problems over time. If one stands too close, one may see only the failures and the shortcomings; by standing farther back, one can see the range of improvements over time as well as the messy process of reform. Reforms that failed (e.g., the commission form of government) were followed by reforms that succeeded (e.g., the council-manager form of government). Negative impacts of generally successful reforms were later recognized and modified. For example, earlier efforts to disempower political machines often left the public without adequate control over local government. This problem contributed to a loss of confidence in government and to tax limits. These problems are now being addressed in a variety of ways, as the case studies illustrate.

Who Should Read This Book?

This book is aimed especially at three groups of people: those who study politics and public budgeting but have never focused on cities; those who study cities' politics and history but have not focused on budgeting; and those who manage cities or hope to do so in the future.

For those interested in politics and public budgeting who have focused on the national or state level, municipal budgeting is important for two reasons. First, municipal budget reforms generally preceded and influenced reforms at the state and national levels, and so they help explain historical and to some extent current practice at those levels. Municipal budget reforms continue to provide options to help reshape budgeting at state and national levels. Second, some important questions that have been obscured at national and state levels stand out at the local level.

One reason these issues stand out at the local level is that there are fewer distracting issues. Some of the issues that have dominated the research agenda at the federal level, for example, include the shift from laissez-faire to interventionist and regulatory government; the role of government spending and taxation in controlling cycles of the economy; the size and impact of deficits; the competition between the executive and legislative branches for control of budget processes and outcomes; the degree of interest-group or party domination of agendas and spending outcomes; and the growth of entitlements, which put government on autopilot and reduce the possibility of making choices among competing needs.

Many of these issues either are not relevant or are much less important at the local level. Cities have only a marginal role in influencing the economy; they have to, and generally do, balance their budgets; their regulatory role is minimal; separation of powers between the branches of government is much less rigid than at the national and state levels and hence competition between the branches is less noticeable; and cities provide almost no entitlements. Although political parties play some role, it is much smaller than at the national level, and ideological positions, when they are expressed, are unlikely to be stated in national political terms.

Stated more positively, cities primarily deliver direct services to citizens, which creates the image that taxpayers are spending money to buy something they want from government. Cities represent the first, most direct contact between citizens and their government. Moreover, direct democracy still exists, and to some extent thrives, at the local level. When government misbehaves, citizens have the tools to take control and fight back; the occasions on which they have done so have been warnings for government officials at all levels.

Because of these characteristics of cities, the research agenda at the local level has been, and can be, somewhat different from that at the national and state levels. The questions of what it means when government misbehaves and what kinds of controls can be imposed have been carefully scrutinized at the local level, with particular attention to machine governments. Also important at the local level has been the scope of services performed, including issues of municipal ownership, public-private cooperation, and contracting out. In the absence of party aggregation of interests, questions have arisen about how interests will be expressed and which ones will gain a hearing. The politics of taxation has been especially important. At the local level, observers can watch the circumstances that encourage or discourage taxpayers from paying the bills. Issues of accountability are particularly salient because of the tools of direct democracy available at the local level. The answers hint at the broader issue of how the legitimacy of government can be achieved and maintained or lost.

Variation between cities and across time makes some of these issues easier to follow at the local level than at the national or state level. At the national level, once a major reform has occurred, a problem may be resolved and fall out of view; but at the local level the problem may occur in different cities, at different times, and with different resolutions, keeping the issue in the forefront.

For those who study local politics and history, but who have never focused on budgeting, a historical survey of municipal budgeting allows a new angle on an old subject. For example, the powers of the mayor are most easily interpretable in the light of mayors' extensive budget veto powers and mayors' responsibilities to evaluate departmental requests and to make budget proposals to the council. The meaning of political reform is difficult to define absent a budget process because budgeting and finance are often seen as such a large part of what is to be reformed. During the Progressive era, the goal of reform shifted from changing the people who governed to changing the system of governance so that reform would be self-perpetuating. Budget processes were a substantial part of the shift. The change from dominance by an older commercial elite to a broader set of interest groups making demands on and opening up government is also seen clearly in budget and spending decisions. The relation between government and the citizens, now closer and now farther apart, is well illustrated in the budget process, which has been designed sometimes to keep the public at bay and sometimes to bring the citizenry on board.

This book is intended to be of use not only to scholars but also to practitioners, who are probably less used to looking for historical answers. At the same time, they may need history the most, to understand the world in which they operate. At the simplest level, a number of odd practices in municipal budgeting make sense only in historical context.

For example, Illinois has a law mandating balanced budgets at the local level but does not require cities to have a budget. Cities can use an appropriation ordinance instead of a budget. An appropriation ordinance is a law passed by a city council that says, if this amount of revenue comes in, it is appropriated, or approved to be spent. The state law, passed in the 1800s, made the numbers in the appropriation ordinance very difficult to change once the ordinance was passed. The intent was to prevent cities from passing an appropriation and changing it so many times that the original passage was meaningless. In addition, reformers feared that if the appropriation was easy to change, supplemental appropriations would put the city in debt. Cities that used the appropriation ordinance adapted to the rigidity that prevented them from changing revenue or expenditure estimates by estimating their expenditures high, well above revenue estimates. That way, they had council approval to spend whatever level of revenue showed up, without changing revenue or expenditure estimates. The appropriations ordinance had almost no useful information in it because the spending estimates were unrealistic and the revenue estimates unreliable, but the ordinance did not need to be changed. To city clerks and other public officials dealing with this system today, appropriations ordinances must seem odd, though very flexible.

A second historical peculiarity allowed cities to begin a budget year without a budget. It used to be very common for cities to pass the budget sometime in the first quarter of the fiscal year. If the current year's budget estimates were to be based on the previous year's spending, waiting until the previous year was over may have been necessary, as estimates were not at all reliable. The practice must seem strange today, but a number of jurisdictions still have budget deadlines in the first fiscal quarter.

Among the more bizarre remnants of the past are fractional assessments for the real estate tax. The real estate tax for residences is based on an estimate of what the property would sell for, but some states use some portion of the sales value of property, rather than the full price, as the value for tax purposes. The practice stems from the days when state governments taxed local governments. State governments levied this tax on cities based on the value of property. The greater the assessed value, the more the cities owed the state governments. So city officials invented fractional assessments, reporting the value of property for taxation at a proportion of the sales value instead of the whole amount. Fractional assessments lowered the amount of money cities owed the state governments, without affecting their own revenues, because they could raise tax rates to compensate for the lower assessments. Now that the states no longer collect property taxes from local governments, the system should be abolished. Some states have eliminated fractional assessments, but in others, because citizens fear that elevated assessments would not be matched by reduced tax rates and their bills would increase, the state government has been unable to change the unnecessarily complex system.

In short, some of the strange things we do are explicable only in historical context. Moreover, by looking at them historically, and seeing why they were passed and what their function was supposed to be, we can decide if these practices still make sense or whether the system is unnecessarily clumsy and hard to understand. For example, do we need so many prior constraints on budgeting as well as after-the-fact controls? The executive budget reforms were intended to replace the need for powerful vetoes; prior mayoral control was considered more effective and was supposed to reduce or even eliminate the need for powerful vetoes. Instead, in some cities, mayoral control over proposing the budget was added to powerful vetoes, giving the mayor almost total control and the council almost none. A second example of over-control resulted from the investments that cities made in railroads, often characterized more by enthusiasm than by judgment. The railroads in which cities owned shares often went bankrupt, resulting in the loss of public investment. State governments stepped in to limit cities' borrowing privileges and often forbade cities to buy equities in private companies. These constraints still exist, frustrating some cities in their efforts at economic development and encouraging adaptations such as special district government and off-budget enterprises to increase the level of borrowing within the law. The result is complex and nearly impossible for citizens to follow or control.

Sometimes the history of a practice explains not only why we do something that appears absurd but also what that practice means, what it represents, both in its pure and its deteriorated form. For example, practitioners often wonder why state laws specify that the city hold budget hearings, when few citizens come and city decision making does not depend on anything that is said during the hearings. The current practice needs to be put in the context of the battle between the Progressives and the Taft conservatives in the early part of this century.

The Progressives felt that citizens had a right to be heard on the budget, that every step of budget making should allow for citizen input. Further, Progressives felt the government was obliged to rouse public interest and inform citizens so that they could make meaningful and useful comments. In contrast, the Taft conservatives felt that citizens should have no direct role in the budget. They felt that legislators should be able to ask members of the executive branch to explain the budget proposal and that the questioning should replace any public hearing. Neither view won the day; a position partway between them was soon worked out. Citizen hearings stayed, but they became pro forma. At the same time, attempts to interest and inform the public were generally dropped. Hence the often heard complaint, "We had a hearing, and nobody came." If public officials today understood the real purpose of hearings, they could put life and meaning back into them.

Knowledge of the variety of ways that budgeting has operated over the years can provide practitioners with a quiver full of alternatives when they are looking for solutions to current problems. Program budgeting, which became popular twenty years ago, and performance budgeting, which is now becoming popular, were prominent budget alternatives in the early 1900s. Many problems faced in budgeting today have been confronted before, and many solutions have been worked out, adopted, and modified or dropped when the problems disappeared. These solutions are still available should current problems resemble those faced earlier.

The record of municipal budgeting makes it clear what each reform movement was trying to accomplish. Budget reforms are not neutral, technical choices but the embodiment of political and often ideological programs. They mean something, and it is important to understand what we are doing when we adopt one or drop one.

For example, as is related later, the city of Tampa, Florida, recently abandoned a comprehensive planning process that measured city needs and government performance for a strategic planning process that linked community groups loosely to budgetary goals. What was going on there? How can this change be understood? Similarly, what did it mean when the city of Dayton, Ohio, faced with declining revenues and a citizenry reluctant to vote new taxes on themselves, created a planning process that brought citizen priorities directly into the budget? Both these changes occurred in this generation, but they are best understood in terms of what went on nearly a hundred years earlier.

If we are lucky, history not only explains the meaning of things we deal with on a daily basis but also tells us something about how to deal with them. If we can see the current tax revolts in historical context, we can understand what makes tax revolts happen and how to avoid them. The history of tax revolts can remind all of us of the constraints on government in a democratic society, especially when our expertise makes us cocky or our commitment to government programs makes us deaf.

History provides many benefits for the practitioner: it helps explain oddities, it provides options, it puts reforms in their political context, and it suggests which aspects of budgeting are crucial and which are accretions of the past that no longer serve much purpose. Budget history can serve as an antidote to arrogance because it reminds us that the citizens have and should have final budget control. Equally important, no practitioner should be able to read this history without a feeling of pride. Local government budget reforms generally have preceded and influenced those of the state and national governments. Academics and government practitioners together have examined the best of existing practice and devised solutions to financial management problems. Municipal budgeting continues to be an important laboratory for solutions not only to technical but also to political problems of resource allocation in a democracy.

Organization of the Book

Chapter 2 presents municipal budgeting in the context of tax revolts, the negotiation of consent to taxation, and what happens when that consent breaks down. Chapter 3 is an overview of municipal budgeting history. Chapter 4 introduces the early years of budgeting from the post–Civil War period to roughly the Great Depression of the 1930s. Chapter 5 examines the modern period of budgeting from the 1950s through 1990, with three original case studies, and chapter 6 covers the same years with three additional cases. Board of Estimate, council-manager, and strong-mayor cities are all represented: Rochester, New York; Boston, Massachusetts; Dayton, Ohio; Phoenix, Arizona; Tampa, Florida; and St. Louis, Missouri. These chapters combine historical, documentary information and interviews. Chapters 7 and 8 describe the historical and current role of state government in changes in budgeting at the local level—cities operate within the constraints of state requirements that have sometimes facilitated and sometimes hindered the development and improvement of municipal budgeting. Chapter 9 offers a brief conclusion.

2

Tax Limits, Protests, and Revolts:
The Erosion of Consent

SOMETIMES MAJOR problems in municipal budgeting really are new. More often, they are only new to a particular generation. They have occurred before, often many times before. These precursors of current problems leave a residue in law and a record of information about what happened, why it happened, and, potentially, how it can be avoided.

When Proposition 13 was passed in California, it seemed to usher in a new, less pleasant world of public administration. Everything that happened after it was different, colored by citizen unrest, taxpayer revolt, and revenue limits. Revenue limitations and tax protests are not new, however. Studying them in their historical context helps explain the circumstances that erode popular consent to taxation. If citizens do not agree to taxation in a democracy, government loses not only its revenues but also its legitimacy. The ability to address collective problems collectively is reduced, if not destroyed.

The pressure for state tax and expenditure limits that accompanied Proposition 13 in California abated by the early 1980s, but feelings of discontent with tax levels, especially with the property tax, have continued in some places. For example, in 1992 the State of Illinois imposed a tax cap in Dupage County, outside Chicago, in response to popular demand. What happened? How did local taxation get out of line with what people were willing to pay, and why was local government less than responsive?

Dupage County is one of the wealthiest counties in the country. It is also growing rapidly. Middle- and upper-class residents of Chicago have moved out to the suburbs in Dupage for years. These residents left Chicago to find better schools, safer neighborhoods, and lower taxes. Some believed that as the number of poor in Chicago increased, the remaining middle and upper classes would increasingly be drained to pay for the poor, who constituted the voting majority. In the suburbs, these outmigrants would be the decision makers. They expected that total costs of government would be less than in Chicago, but more important, they would be spending their tax money only on public services they wanted.

Reality did not turn out exactly as some of these new suburbanites anticipated. The continued demand for suburban housing pushed up the price and hence the assessed value of housing. New infrastructure, including water, sewage treatment plants, schools, streets, and parks, was expensive; improved services such as fire protection, police, and education also cost more money. The local governments did not reduce the tax rates as assessed values grew. Tax bills rose faster than the paychecks of some of the new suburbanites.

Growth was, and still is, an ideology in Dupage. There has been difficult even to discuss it as a potential cause of increasing taxes. A county planning department report suggesting that the form of growth might be a problem was roundly condemned and remained highly controversial for its implications. Because local governments refused to identify, let alone control, the source of the problem, some citizens pressed the state for tax relief. The state eventually granted relief in the form of a tax cap that allowed slow growth in property tax yields. The tax cap has major implications for management, especially in school districts that have been unable to accommodate increasing enrollments; it also has major implications for citizen control of government.

In a sense, the Dupage tax cap was a success. Irate citizens took control of public revenues, if not of public spending. But in a broader sense the tax cap represented a series of failures. The mechanisms that normally keep the level of taxation in line broke down. The citizens were unable to influence their local officials, and so they bypassed their local governments. In the process, they hamstrung their local officials. The citizens made an end run to the state and forced local government compliance, but they were unable to fix either the communication problem or the expenditure problem that had generated the situation. Moreover, with the cap in place, citizens who moved to the suburbs to get better schools found their children attending class in trailers because there were not enough classrooms. Streets were clogged with traffic because infrastructure improvements lagged behind population increases. Lack of planning resulting from a gung-ho growth model exaggerated the discomforts. Pressure for spending increases remains, forcing cities to look for additional revenues. Because revenue sources available to local governments are generally regressive, such a search is likely to end in higher tax burdens for those least able to pay.

The tax cap in Dupage is best understood in historical context and in the context of the larger question of how tax levels are controlled in a democracy. In a sense, the Dupage case represents the failure of the traditional mechanisms that have controlled taxation at the local level in the United States. What are these mechanisms? How do they normally work? Under what circumstances do they fail? What are the implications for government officials, for policymaking, and for the budget process?

The question of how taxes are controlled in a democracy is one of the most fundamental connections between political theory and actual practice. Is government controllable? Are the bureaucrats or the interest groups in control? Are the citizens as taxpayers adequately represented, or are they overrepresented, preventing societal needs from being addressed because they do not want to pay for them?

Many political conservatives have visualized government in terms of continuous and uncontrollable growth. The size of the federal deficit has for years reinforced this notion of government spending out of control. The continual focus on government out of control has obscured the more important question: why does taxation *not* always grow? What keeps it in balance with citizen willingness to pay? There have been episodes of public rebellion against taxes, but generally, taxes have been paid voluntarily, if not with pleasure. The record has been one of success, punctuated by occasional flamboyant failures.

Taxation in a democracy must be based on consent, not force. In the face of widespread opposition to taxation, government falls apart. Some level of consensus must be achieved, even if only at intervals. One way of examining the process of achieving and maintaining a balance between what government wants to spend and what citizens are willing to pay is to watch what happens when the balance breaks down and has to be renegotiated or readjusted.

Breakdowns often occur during or just after a lengthy period of rapid increase in government spending. This increase can occur because of a growth in population, an expansion of government functions, rapid inflation, gross mismanagement and patronage, or some combination of the above. The expansion may be accompanied by or funded by large amounts of borrowing, in the belief that growth will be assured by the investment and will pay off the debt. When the economy falters or falls into recession, a city may find itself without enough revenues to pay off debts and provide services. Taxpayers hurt by the recession cannot afford at that time to bail out the city with additional taxes. Tax burdens that were carried comfortably during a period of general prosperity become intolerable when recession reduces the ability to pay the greatly enlarged taxes. This pattern of expenditure growth followed by recession has contributed to tax protests and tax and expenditure limits and has characterized both the 1870s and the 1930s. This pattern may also help account for the more recent round of tax and expenditure limitations in the 1970s and early 1980s.

Citizens have often endorsed or even demanded rapid expansion, but when the projects fail, when citizens' incomes lag and they no longer feel that they can afford these projects and programs, or both, they withdraw their support for additional taxation or try to reduce their tax burden.

Assessment practices have also been an important contributor to the breakdown of consensus on the appropriate level of taxation. In earlier years, assessment practices were political and irregular. Citizens were thus buffered from increases in assessed valuation both by the political process and by infrequent assessments. As assessment practices improved or threatened to improve, they created pressure on taxpayers.

For example, personal property was supposed to be taxed in many states at the same rate as real estate, but most personal property escaped reporting. People who had money in the bank or who owned stock or bonds just did not tell the government about their wealth. Real estate was harder to hide. Real estate tax rates had to be higher to compensate for the lower personal property tax rolls. The threat of applying this high real estate rate to personal property and forcing personal property onto the tax rolls suggested near confiscation of profits, motivating frantic efforts to limit taxes. Also, efforts to bring property tax assessments up to 100 percent of sales value created fear that property tax rates would not be reduced to compensate for the increased assessed valuation, creating pressure to mandate property tax rate limits as a condition of reforming the assessment practices.

The reform of assessments was often done in a clumsy way. In Chicago in the late 1920s, assessment was challenged by taxpayers, resulting in the suspension of collections for several years, followed by efforts to speed up payments thereafter, threatening taxpayers severely, and contributing to a widespread tax revolt. Rapid growth in population and rapidly increased assessed valuations contributed to the Proposition 13 tax limitation movement in California in the 1970s. More honest reassessments led to greater burdens on homeowners compared to businesses and exaggerated the pain from rapidly increasing assessments.

Growth in spending is more likely to get out of balance with people's ability to pay in the realm of property taxes, rather than other revenue sources, because property taxes are a tax on wealth, rather than on income. A person may own a nice house and suddenly find himself or herself unemployed, or may lose income during a divorce and no longer have enough income to pay the real estate taxes on that house. Other forms of taxation are more dependent on income than wealth, and thus they go up and down more automatically with people's ability to pay. As a result, as more people in the country can afford houses, the popular base for a tax revolt increases. In contrast, as cities diversify their tax base and reduce their dependence on property taxes, they reduce pressure on this politically sensitive tax.

Though it seems counterintuitive, sometimes an imbalance between government spending and citizen willingness to pay occurs because the government is spending less than the public demands in the way of projects and services. For example, political parties may outbid each other to reduce taxes, cut waste, and win voter support. If one party offers a low tax, the other feels that it has to match the offer or risk losing votes. A tax reduction bidding war was characteristic of San Francisco in the late 1800s. Also, governments can spend too little in comparison to need during recessions, creating a pent-up citizen demand for services and projects when growth resumes. Sometimes the demand for additional spending comes from those who pay little in the way of taxes, but sometimes it comes from taxpayers themselves.

Three broad mechanisms can be used to help restore the balance when government wants to spend more or less than taxpayers want. One is an internal model, in which the existing government identifies and addresses the problem, in response to actual or anticipated complaints or in response to problems observed in other cities. In the second model, groups or individuals bring pressure on city hall through lobbying and protest activities, and, failing those, take over city hall through electoral politics. These reformers then remake the city's financial policies to serve their interests. The third model involves groups of actors who have given up trying to make the local system work for them. They either make end runs around local government, pressuring the state government to mandate their preferred policies, or they take direct action through binding referendums and tax revolts.

Direct action often results in some long-term constraint, such as a charter requirement or a state constitutional limit. The efforts of the protesters are necessarily temporary and fragmentary, only occasionally reaching the level of organization and power necessary to bring about change. Knowing that they cannot keep up constant pressure, protesters set up mechanisms to ensure their accomplishments will last long after the movement has dissolved. The goal may be to shift taxes to another group, to ensure the equity of assessments, or to limit overall taxes. Because these external actors typically lack government experience, they often phrase their petitions crudely, doing more damage than necessary to credit ratings, borrowing costs, administrative efficiency, and service levels. By circumscribing the power of local governments, they not only make it more difficult for such governments to manage but they reduce the capacity to solve problems. They may make it impossible for local governments to respond to legitimate demands in the future.

When direct action takes the form of tax resistance, the impact on government can be devastating. A sharp reduction in current revenues may force reductions in staffing and service levels and encourage higher levels of unfunded debt. Tax protests take legitimacy away from local government; protesters who withhold tax payments are saying government is not worth what they are paying for it, and so they would rather do without it.

What follows is a selection of historical cases of tax limitation and revolt. They illustrate the causes of imbalance between citizen willingness to pay and government readiness to spend, as well as the responses that restored balance. The examples also illustrate the shift from a property-owning elite that both directs city financial policy and pays the taxes to a set of competing interest groups or classes that have different contributions to and dependence on city hall. By presenting cases from different periods of time, the chapter suggests the political dynamics that characterized each period.

The cases chosen are Houston and San Francisco in the late 1800s; the state of Ohio from 1910 to 1925; the city of Chicago in the late 1920s and early 1930s; and California in the 1970s. These illustrations were picked because they represented the problems and solutions of different eras and because each case has been well described in the literature. These cases were prominent in their own time, and stood out as examples of what to do or what would happen if appropriate action were not taken.

Houston was chosen in part to illustrate the impact of post–Civil War growth followed by the recession that began in 1873. Houston represents an internal model of response; the business elite was the governing and taxpaying elite; it worked out its own solutions insofar as it was able. San Francisco was less extensively affected by the recession of 1873 and more influenced by the alternation of machine and reform governments and by party competition. San Francisco illustrates the pattern of outsiders taking over city government in order to implement the financial policies of their choice. Ohio in 1910 represents a reaction to the growth of expenditures during the Progressive era combined with assessment problems; it also represents the model of the state intervening to control local governments. Chicago in the 1930s represents both a reaction to growth followed by severe depression and a reaction to totally fouled-up assessment procedures. These problems resulted in an acute tax revolt. California in the 1970s represents the pattern of rapid growth in population and assessments resulting in tax bills that outstripped people's ability to pay, leading to an end run around local government for a statewide solution.

Houston, Texas

Houston's public finances were in a mess after the Civil War, as the desire for public projects outstripped the city's tax base.[1] The government issued scrip (a sort of IOU in lieu of money) in payment of debts. The scrip was increasingly discounted by those who accepted it, resulting in a downward spiral. By 1868, many of the town's civic elite and large property owners got together to work out a solution. They agreed to tax themselves to pay off bonds, but in exchange they in-

---

1. The material on Houston is from Platt 1983.

sisted that whoever ran city hall had to follow their priorities and implement their plans, "without deviation." Under this agreement, there was no split between what the taxpayers wanted and what they were willing to spend, since the same people made both sets of decisions.

The city had overborrowed with respect to its tax receipts, and when the recession of 1872 hit, the city was hopelessly in debt. Hard-pressed taxpayers revolted en masse. Not having enough money to pay off bonds and provide city services, the mayor in 1874 gave priority to police and fire protection, street lighting and repair, and public health and sanitation. Instead of equating the legitimate purposes of the municipal corporation with the enhancement of the taxpayer's estates, the mayor demanded that property owners contribute to the support of essential public services in spite of personal sacrifice. Rather than try to increase taxes, however, which was not likely to be successful in the poor economic environment and the general tax revolt, he tried to compromise with the city's creditors. He lost his next election, and his proposals were not implemented.

When the economy began to improve, the resistance of taxpayers diminished. Payment resumed when it was felt to be less burdensome, and when the taxpayers wanted particular projects they could not fund without the restoration of the city's credit. In 1880 the civic commercial elite reassumed direct command of city hall.

The Houston case represents most closely the type of government in which the civic elite are the taxpayers and simultaneously control municipal expenditures. Because these members of the civic elite were paying the taxes, they felt they had a right to demand what they wanted from government in the way of development projects to expand their business opportunities. The recession that began in 1873 ruptured this agreement; not only were members of the elite unwilling and unable to continue to pay for bonds they had supported in the past, but their withdrawal of support created the idea that services had to continue, that city hall served some other purpose than the developmental goals of the city's business elite, namely, to serve a broader public. The tension between service delivery, taxpayer pressure, and bondholder pressure made it clear that there were at least three distinct groups arguing for different public policies, where before there had been only one group and no splits. As soon as the financial situation improved, the elite resumed support for public projects, and the cleavage that had become apparent in the 1870s became less prominent.

San Francisco, California

Unlike Houston, where the commercial elites had run the government and made little distinction between public and private, in San Francisco in the 1850s the elites were on the outside of government.[2] These members of the elite felt that corrupt, heavy spenders were running government. The reformers in the 1850s started out with the notion that taxes were squeezed from the people but not spent on them.

When a crusading editor of a reform newspaper was shot by a local politician he had been attacking in the newspaper, local notables formed a vigilante committee, captured the accused murderer, tried him, and hanged him. Leaders of the vigilante committee formed a political party (called the People's Reform Party), nominated candidates, and were elected to office in 1856. The People's Party defined politics in terms of the people versus the professional politicians who feasted at the public crib. As far as the People's Reform Party was concerned, only those in the elite could have the necessary background and integrity to manage the city safely.

The People's Reform Party controlled San Francisco politics continuously until 1866 and maintained considerable influence for a number of additional years, when other political parties took up its platform. The People's Reform Party represented the city's merchant elite and pushed a policy of fiscal conservatism. They cut government spending dramatically, from an estimated $2.6 million in 1855 to $353,000 in 1857. The party also made a concerted effort to reduce the level of debt and contract no new debt. In order to keep new debt levels down, municipal improvements were on a pay-as-you-go basis; projects were done piecemeal. Mayors vetoed proposals to subsidize railroads with the argument that keeping taxation light would cause the city to grow.

Decreases in debt service and growth in assessed valuation paid for moderate incremental growth between 1860 and 1875. No party advocated growth, but because the tax rate was under control, there was no pressure to prevent slow spending increases. After 1875 pressure grew to keep taxes down, in part the result of the weak economy that characterized the commercial sector from 1875 to 1880. Between 1875 and 1882, political parties competed to see who could lower taxes more and passed the dollar limit on property taxes.

---

2. The material on San Francisco is from McDonald 1986.

The result was a continual cutting of services, with the exception of increasing the staffing level in the police department, which required an increase in the tax rate in 1880. The increase in police was a result of riots in the Chinese section of the city and the resulting vigilante movements that sprang up. City officials defended the increase in police, while school administrators argued they needed more money to deal with increased enrollments. Realtors, however, protested the increases. In a very contemporary-sounding argument, real estate representatives argued that increased taxes reduced the price of real estate. A Republican supervisor argued back that it was the poor condition of the streets, not the tax rate, that depreciated the value of real estate. The initial outcome was more cuts in nonpolice services.

The city had more than doubled the police force. To pay for the increase, the city had to raise the property tax, contributing to a tax revolt and the dollar limit on property taxation. The dollar limit appeared in the platforms of the major parties from 1882 to 1899, and in 1900 it was embodied in the new charter. The parties actually pushed spending down below what the citizens and taxpayers wanted in the way of services.

The support for continuing low services and low taxes began to erode in the late 1880s under the pressure of demands from neighborhood and businessmen's groups for municipal improvements. Beginning in 1891, representatives of newer neighborhoods appeared at finance committee meetings, demanding that services be extended into their areas. By 1894 these groups formed into a citywide organization and were joined by the Merchants' Association, a citywide group of high-status businessmen. The businessmen's group urged greater efficiency in municipal government. These pressures contributed to a change in policy. Before 1892, the goal was just to keep taxes down; afterward, the aim was to get the most for each tax dollar.

A major recession from 1892 to 1897 put pressure on government to keep taxes down because taxpayers could not afford to pay more despite pressure for government-sponsored relief from the depression. At this point, reformers proposed new government-financed projects that would help provide jobs for the unemployed, arguing simultaneously for increased efficiency to keep costs down. They also suggested borrowing for some projects. When the state took over the assessment process, it immediately increased assessments, providing funding for some of the projects.

The State of Ohio

The Ohio Tax Limit of 1910 was imposed by the State of Ohio after years of spending growth that characterized the Progressive era.[3] The limit was also a response to a change in assessment practices. The limit was harsh and imposed on rapidly growing cities. A mismatch was put in place between what the local residents wanted and what state law allowed. The initial result was a growing gap between revenues and spending, a gap filled in by floating debt (debt without a planned source of repayment) and covered over by poor budgeting. Gradually, however, the state relented, allowing citizens to override the limits at the polls and providing for repayment of debt to please both bankers and business people who wanted improvement projects.

In 1908 property was supposed to be listed at 60 percent of full market value, but the average was close to 45 percent, with rural realty listed at only 39 percent of its actual value (Atkinson 1923). In 1909 a law was passed requiring reassessment every four years (instead of every ten years) and setting the next appraisal for the year 1910. As the appraisal approached, great popular opposition arose to the assessment of property at its full value, as required by the state's constitution. If property tax rates were not reduced, the reassessment would increase people's real estate tax bills by a huge amount and would have a disproportionate impact on those whose assessments had been lowest with respect to sales value. For people who owned intangible property, such as bank accounts or bonds, that bore interest of 4 or 5 percent, a 3 percent tax rate practically amounted to confiscation.

To handle the public's fear, the state passed the One Percent Law, capping the property tax rate at 1 percent (Wilcox 1922). Sinking funds and debt repayment were outside the 1 percent limit, but the total limit was 15 mills, or 1.5 percent. The law was a promise to citizens that their tax bills would not go up as assessments went up. The law drastically curtailed the spending power of public officials.

Ohio's 1 percent tax limit fell heavily on larger, rapidly growing cities. Expenditures continued to increase because the rapid expansion of population required such improvements as city water and paved streets and because rapid inflation necessitated wage increases. The

---

3. The material on Ohio is from Atkinson 1923; Wilcox 1922; and Atkinson 1936.

expansion and modernization of governmental functions that characterized cities across the country during the Progressive era continued to characterize Ohio cities from 1910 to 1920, exaggerating their spending problems (Atkinson 1923). To make matters worse, the State of Ohio applied workers' compensation to municipalities, established a maximum eight-hour day on public work, and sometimes mandated water and sewage purification projects. The financial problems of the cities were made worse by slow reassessments. Only thirty of eighty-eight counties had been reassessed between 1910 and 1920.

While per capita revenues dropped, per capita expenditures rose almost throughout the period from 1910 to 1919. Expenditures were $5.42 in 1911, $5.91 in 1915, and $6.86 in 1919. The corresponding revenue figures were $5.01, $4.97, and $4.97. The gap was filled by floating debt.

By 1916, cities had so much floating debt that they had to hold elections to get support for bond issues to pay it off. The campaigns for these bond elections helped educate the public about the consequences of the tax limit and helped build support for loosening the limits. Chamber of commerce representatives from around the state and the State Board of Commerce supported a change in the One Percent Law to permit the electorate to place levies for debt purposes outside the act. Note that the concern of these business representatives was with the cities' ability to borrow and pay off debt. Such a concern reflects, on the one hand, the interests of the bankers and other holders of city debt, and on the other hand, the interests of those who wanted the cities to make more capital improvements. Only the real estate interests continued to oppose any changes in the tax-limit law.

Unfortunately, as often happens in such cases, neither the governor nor the legislature was willing to take the lead in changing the law, and so the state response to the fiscal stress of the cities was delayed. It was 1919 before the cities received any substantial relief from the state. Among the relief provisions were alternative sources of revenue and an earmarked tax for road repair. Debt payments were excluded from the tax limit. During the next legislative session, the state empowered citizens to suspend the operation of the One Percent Law for three years by a 60 percent majority vote. Even with the requirement for a supermajority, citizens often voted to increase the property tax rate. During the 1920s, rates rose, with citizen approval, from 1.5 to 3 percent, more in line with the rest of the nation.

After amendment, the law allowed citizens to vote every five years to renew the levies they had approved; if not reapproved, the levies would lapse. That put public finances in an unstable situation, especially when confronting the Great Depression of the 1930s. Some jurisdictions were threatened by a fallback to the 1.5 percent level written into the statutes. The problem became worse as the depression deepened. "Having failed to secure temporary tax relief at the hands of the 1933 legislature, the farmers and city real estate boards took the bit in their teeth, initiated a constitutional amendment cutting the tax limit from fifteen to ten mills, and all the king's horses and all the king's men could not prevent its passage under existing economic conditions. The amendment went over by an immense majority, carrying every county" (Atkinson 1936, 72). Thus a 1 percent limit was written into the constitution. Levies voted by the citizens were exempt from the limit, but average rates still declined considerably, from a state average of 22.42 mills (2.24 percent of the assessed value) before the limit to 18.79 mills after the limit was put into effect. The levy was reduced about 20 percent (calculated from data in Atkinson 1936, 73). The reduction in property tax revenue hastened the development of alternative revenue sources, in this case, the sales tax. This change shifted the burden of taxation from rural to urban areas and from richer to poorer taxpayers.

The Great Depression and
the Chicago Tax Strike

Pressure for tax cuts became acute during the Great Depression of the 1930s. If the state government did not grant sufficient relief soon enough, citizens, often led by real estate interests, took matters in their own hands. In Ohio, the voters passed a binding referendum. In Chicago, citizens organized and refused to pay their taxes.[4]

Many of those who pushed for tax and spending reductions developed an ideology to support low taxes and low spending. This ideology had several elements: (1) politicians, bureaucrats, and municipal bond holders were not trustworthy; (2) bureaucrats and politicians were tax spenders, those who received government funds were tax eaters; and (3) governmental power should be reduced because small, decentralized government was best. These sentiments were so widespread, they raised questions of governmental legitimacy.

---

4. The material on the Chicago tax strike is from Beito 1989.

Government and its supporters did fight back. Supporters "conceived of government as the cooperative manifestation of society's will. Government, especially if efficiently administered, was a necessary, positive tool to fight poverty, ensure public health, provide sanitation, and promote economic planning. For them, expanded government and advancing civilization were inseparable" (Beito 1989, xiv).

Most tax resisters were more skeptical of the state's expansion beyond police and national defense. "They feared that, unless limited in its power to tax, government would become the protector of entrenched special interests, retard economic recovery, and sap individual autonomy.... Tax resisters argued that government could best fight the depression by deflating to the same level as the economy. Indeed, many resisters blamed excessive taxes and spending for causing the depression in the first place" (Beito 1989, xiv).

In Chicago from 1930 to 1933, many taxpayers refused to pay their taxes. The cause of the protest was mainly the assessment process and efforts to reform it. Assessments had been corrupt and politicized. Pressure built for a reassessment. While the city was doing the reassessment, it suspended taxation. Taxes for 1928 would be due in July 1930; taxes for 1929 would be due in February 1931; and taxes for 1930 would be due in November 1931. Taxpayers had to pay three years' worth of tax bills in sixteen months, and the 1930 tax collection was about 24 percent higher than the 1928 total. This schedule contributed to the tax revolt. A group of wealthy real estate operators took the lead in beginning the protest, and others later joined in.

The possibility of a broad-based tax revolt had increased with the proportion of homeowners. In 1930, 42 percent of immigrants and 28 percent of second-generation families owned homes. In 1908, the figures had been 15 and 20 percent respectively. In 1930, half of all the owner-occupied homes in the city showed a value of less than $8,250. The group of real estate operators who organized the protest signed up people of modest means and gave them legal services. They had two goals, a massive real estate tax reduction (in excess of 50 percent) and a delay in tax sales until economic recovery restored the ability to pay. (A tax sale occurs when a unit of government takes over a property from owners who have not paid their taxes and sells the property, keeping the profit to compensate for unpaid taxes. During the depression, tax sales were more of a threat than a reality because no one would buy the properties.)

The protesters' initial tactic was to shift the burden of taxation away from real estate taxes on to the personal property tax and on to an income tax. When these efforts failed, the group encouraged property owners to appeal their assessments. As a result, the appeals process collapsed. The group advised their members to withhold their payments until the appeals process could be fixed.

The leaders of the tax protest held that taxes should be levied in proportion to the services that an individual receives from government. They argued that if taxes reflected the benefits people received from government services, spending reductions would quickly follow. No citizen should be required to pay for what any other citizen got. They divided the world into two classes, those who paid taxes and those who did not. They noted that the real estate of Cook County (in which Chicago is located) was held by 22 percent of the voting population; the other 78 percent voted but paid no taxes. The tax protesters felt that only those who paid taxes should have the right to determine how the money should be spent and how heavily property owners should be taxed. This argument assumes that landlords do not pass property taxes on to renters.

The strike was initially successful. In 1931 only 55 percent of total tax levies were collected prior to 15 May, the penalty date. The depression deepened. By 1932 unemployment was higher than 40 percent. People just could not afford to pay their mortgages and taxes. The city's revenues continued to slide, and its dependence on the banks for loans gave bankers a disproportionate voice in city financial dealings. The bankers insisted on more service cuts. Chicago's city budget declined by 35.4 percent between 1930 and 1933. These reductions in spending did not result in much tax relief because increased debt service canceled out the effect of service cuts. The bankers' main concern was that the city's debts be paid off.

The city's efforts to persuade people to pay their taxes had relatively little effect. The strike was initially weakened by court decisions that finally went the city's way and by internal squabbling within the tax strikers' organization. The faction that supported ending the strike won, and the organization terminated itself in 1933. While the tax strike eventually collapsed and the organization disbanded, the strike succeeded in shifting the burden of taxes to other taxpayers. The strike resulted in lower property taxes while other tax sources grew, especially after 1933.

The Chicago tax strike is significant in part because it shifted the burden of taxation; it also represented an intense threat to the legitimacy of government that was barely beaten back. Many protesters could not afford to pay their bills; equally important, many protesters were disgusted with the level of government corruption and believed that government should be smaller and perform fewer services. The tax strike represented both groups.

The tax strike was pivotal because its major supporters were blue-collar workers who had struggled and finally owned property and now found it in jeopardy. In the past, this group would not have been property owners, and they might have been consumers of and supporters of governmental services. As this threatened group of homeowners grew, it became a potent voice against property taxation.

As Chicago became more dependent on loans to pay bills, bankers increased their influence over fiscal policies as a condition for granting those loans. The financiers chose to cut service costs to ensure that the city would be able to pay back loans; neither tax relief nor social services interested them.

The strike was supported mainly by blue-collar workers and small merchants; wealthier businesses never bought into the coalition. Part of the reason was that at least some of their wealth was in the form of personal property, such as stocks and bonds. The tax protesters wanted to shift the burden of taxation more on to personal property. Another part of the reason was that many of them did business with the city and wanted the city to be able to pay its bills.

The Chicago tax strike thus shifts focus away from the taxpayers and tax eaters toward cleavages within the business community—small merchants and independent contractors such as carpenters versus the larger and richer businesses and the bankers. The strike also set up tensions between those working people who owned property and those who did not. Many of these same elements reoccur in the California Proposition 13 tax revolt.

Proposition 13 and California

By the mid-1930s, the financial picture had changed at the local level. The Great Depression continued, but the federal government had become an active participant in finding and funding solutions at the local level. World War II followed the depression, keeping the costs of local government down as the nation funded the war. After World War II, and after long years of neglect, cities began to fund capital expenditures and renew the older cities. Massive migrations to the suburbs began, with increased spending on infrastructure and expansion of government personnel. The 1950s and 1960s were periods of local government growth. The 1970s, in contrast, were marked by a deep recession, followed by rapid inflation and relative stagnation in the economy. The 1970s ushered in a period of tax and expenditure limitations and tax protests.

The most dramatic of these protests and one of the most severe of the limits occurred in California with the successful citizen initiative called Proposition 13.[5] In some ways, the conditions leading up to Proposition 13 were similar to those leading to tax protests in the Great Depression, but in other ways the causes were somewhat different.

Proposition 13 was supported by a grassroots, citizen-based political movement. The stage was set for protest beginning in the 1960s. Elected tax assessors were accused of accepting bribes to adjust assessments for business properties. The legislature passed a bill in response to the scandal requiring reassessment of all property at 25 percent of sales value within three years and frequently thereafter. The unintended outcome was to increase the burden on homeowners. Businesses had been assessed at a higher rate than private homes, so an across-the-board assessment ratio lowered business assessments and raised that of homeowners. "In addition, A.B. 80 [the state legislation requiring assessment reform] transformed property tax assessment into a nondiscretionary, administrative function. In the 1970s, as a result, 'political discretion could not act as a buffer between homeowners and inflation' " (Sears and Citrin 1985, 20).

This pressure on homeowners contributed to a ballot measure to limit property taxes to 1 percent of market value and to earmark property taxes for property-related services. Supporters of the measure argued that the state should pick up people-related services such as health, education, and welfare. This citizen initiative lost support because it would have cost the state additional taxes. The governor and legislature acted to head off the revolt by proposing a constitutional amendment for a homestead exemption, that is, the first $750 of assessed value was to be exempted from taxation for owner-occupied homes. This measure passed, while the more radical property tax limit failed at the polls.

---

5. The Proposition 13 material is from Sears and Citrin 1985 and Lo 1990.

A second citizen initiative that attempted to shift taxes to the state level and away from the property tax failed in 1972. Instead, and in response to citizen pressure, the state increased the homeowners exemption to $1,750 and placed limits on city and county tax rates.

Up until this point, the main focus of tax protesters was to shift the burden of taxation away from themselves and the property tax, but in 1973 the focus turned more to an antigovernment spending approach. Governor Ronald Reagan proposed an amendment to the state's constitution to limit the size of the public sector. His proposal would have limited annual growth of state expenditures to the increase in state income, tightened the limits on local tax rates, and required a two-thirds legislative majority for state tax bills. The vote was closer than the previous ones, but the measure lost, 54–46 percent.

The boom in California real estate that began in 1974 pushed up housing prices. With the new mechanics of reassessment, the new sales prices were automatically translated into higher assessments and often into higher tax bills. Property tax bills went up 80 percent in three years in Los Angeles. These tax increases generally exceeded the rate of growth of people's incomes. The ballot measure Proposition 13 addressed these problems by rolling back sales value for assessment purposes to 1975 or, if the property was sold after 1975, to the price at sale, limiting increases in assessment to 2 percent a year and holding tax rates down to 1 percent of full cash value.

Local government had grown over the previous decades, and the public did not have much confidence that government was honest, professional, or efficient. Thus the public in general was not inclined to defend government against the attacks of antitaxers. Moreover, this time the state government failed to respond to the threatened opposition until it was too late. By the time the legislature acted on a moderate proposal, angry citizens rejected it in favor of Proposition 13.

The origins of Proposition 13 were like those of Chicago in the early 1930s in the sense that they involved the modernization of assessment practices, making them less political and more automatic, and hence more threatening to some groups. But while assessments were in fact dropping in Chicago, they were increasing in California. In Chicago, tax rates did not drop as fast as people's incomes; in California in the 1970s, people's incomes did not grow as fast as their tax bills. The effect in both cases was a tight squeeze on citizens. In Chicago in the 1930s, the result was an illegal, broad-based tax strike. In

California, the result was an alternation between threats of drastic action posed by citizen initiatives and more moderate state-level pre-emptive action, a pattern that broke down when the state could not act quickly enough to forestall Proposition 13.

In the Chicago tax strike the lines of cleavage between supporters and opponents were relatively clear and narrowly based on interests —blue-collar workers and small merchants in a coalition opposed to bankers and more successful businesses. In the Proposition 13 cam-paign, the lines of cleavage were drawn somewhat differently. For one thing, instead of trying to shift the burden of taxation to the wealthy owners of personal property, supporters of Proposition 13 wanted to shift the burden of the poor to the state government and limit prop-erty taxes to property-related services.

Proposition 13 was primarily a movement of homeowners, who gradually came together across class lines because of their shared problems. For the blue-collar homeowners of lower-middle incomes, rising assessments threatened their homes; for the upper-income pro-fessionals, rising assessments threatened their lifestyles. In both kinds of communities, however, homeowners often opposed further devel-opment because it threatened their neighborhoods. They wanted more, not fewer, city services; they wanted more regulation to keep polluting plants and heavy traffic out of their subdivisions; and they opposed the developers' schemes for high-density apartments, condos, and malls. Local communities had to pay for the consequences of growth, such as more roads, street signals, schools, police, and fire services. Growth pushed up the tax burden and pulled down the qual-ity of life. Many business people opposed Proposition 13, especially in its early stages, because it would hamper growth (Lo 1990).

Those business people who did support Proposition 13 came at tax limits from a different angle. They sought less regulation on busi-ness and wanted to cut services, not merely reduce the tax burdens on themselves. The homeowners who supported Proposition 13 had nothing in common with these business people. But even more pros-perous homeowners found they had little political clout in their own communities when it came to tax limitation. Local officials often ig-nored citizen demands, sometimes rudely. In order to gain some politi-cal power, some of the wealthier homeowners formed a coalition with business people who wanted to reduce their own tax burden and de-cided to press a statewide campaign, rather than a local one, using their local organizations as a base. This combination proved the win-

ning one, but a disproportionate amount of the tax relief that resulted
went to business instead of homeowners.

Proposition 13 in California represents a redefinition of the context and causes of tax protest. In earlier years, taxpayers resented paying for services for the poor. This idea was captured in the distinction
between taxpayers and tax eaters, where tax eaters included government officials who lived off government, businesses that supplied
government, and renters who benefited from services but presumably
paid no property taxes. By the time of Proposition 13 in 1978, the
property-owning class had expanded to include many moderate-
income people, obscuring the link between taxpaying, landowning,
and social class. As this happened, the burden of property tax payment shifted at least in part to those with more moderate incomes.
The idea that they were paying for the poor against their will remained, but more dominant was the idea that they were paying for
economic development, the burdens of growth, from which they did
not benefit. Development pushed up taxes beyond what they could afford; the beneficiaries were the developers, builders, bankers, realtors,
professional service providers, and merchants who profit from an expanding population. When these moderate-income homeowners,
joined by wealthier homeowners with similar though less acute problems, confronted local government to curtail growth and tax burdens,
they were unable to make any headway. Frustrated, they joined a
business coalition with some different but overlapping goals. As Clar-
ence Lo summarized, "The triumph of the tax revolt annihilated the
corporatist complacency that the unrepresented could be taxed to pay
off the interest groups. But the winning alliance also saw to it that the
spoils of victory went to both homeowners and businesses, the latter,
in fact, receiving most of the benefits" (Lo 1990, 197).

Conclusions

What caused tax revolts? Citizens' willingness to be taxed decreased
when the burden of taxation suddenly increased substantially. In some
cases that increase in burden resulted from a sharp decrease in income, for example, during a recession. If the preceding period was one
of rapid growth in spending and taxation, then a drop in income may
have made the tax burden too heavy to bear. Changes in assessment
practices, even efforts to improve assessments, sometimes had the
same effect or created the fear that the tax burden would suddenly

and dramatically increase. In more recent years, the costs of suburban infrastructure and the increases in assessed value from continuing growth have combined to push up property taxes, in some cases more quickly than people's incomes.

Tax revolts were not inevitable. California had dodged them successfully for years. More thought about the impacts of reassessment could have derailed tax protest in Chicago. Controlled growth policies might have been helpful, not only in California but also in Dupage County. More realistic estimates of the costs of infrastructure in new suburbs might also have drained some of the frustration with tax increases. If outmigrants from the inner cities had expected higher tax burdens, they might have bought less expensive homes and put themselves under less financial pressure. If tax increases had followed more closely voters' ability to pay, there would probably have been fewer citizen-initiated tax limits, and those passed would probably have been less draconian.

But the breakdown in the consent to be taxed had another, more troubling dimension, the unwillingness to be taxed for services or projects for someone else's benefit. The dollar tax limit in San Francisco insulated property owners not only from the apparently limitless financial demands of building city infrastructure but also from the costs of service to the poor. Over time, the model has changed from the rich property owner's unwillingness to pay for services to the poor to all taxpayers' unwillingness to pay for services and projects from which they do not benefit. More specifically, in recent years, as homeownership has spread to larger percentages of the population and as the taxes have diversified from property to sales taxes, a broader group of taxpayers is arguing that economic development projects are redistributive, taking from ordinary people and giving to developers and large property owners. Unless their neighborhoods benefit, they don't want to pay for the costs of economic development. Moreover, they want services to their neighborhoods, such as police and street repairs.

The need to consult the public more widely on what to spend taxes on is one consequence of the breakdown in consent to taxation. A second consequence is the need to improve budgeting and make it more meaningful to the public. How much money is being spent on police? What is happening to the crime rate? The budget has to answer citizen concerns. Waves of tax revolt have often been followed by waves of budget reform.

A successful tax revolt may ultimately stimulate more responsive budgeting, but in the short run it is likely to make financial management worse. City staffs have to cope with limited resources and seemingly unlimited demands. Needs and demands do not go away because revenues are curtailed, as demonstrated in the Ohio example. Cities may raise a lot of little fees that are expensive to collect or borrow for operating expenses because their main sources of revenues are curtailed, but the pressures pushing for higher expenditures are still in place.

When citizens initiate a tax limit, they are taking control of a government they have been unable to influence in other ways. But tax limits are not necessarily good for democracy. Constitutional tax limits represent democratic movements and public control of government only to the extent that they represent the common will, rather than that of a small minority who temporarily takes control and locks in its preferences and its reduced tax burden indefinitely. Requirements for a tax referendum are more flexible than tax limits written into constitutions. If citizens want more taxes for specific services, they can vote for them. The campaign becomes a kind of negotiation of consent, with the city offering to provide what it thinks the public wants for its tax dollars, and the citizens rejecting some and supporting other proposals. But in some states, in order to pass, the tax measures have to gain supermajorities, not just a simple majority of voters. Such requirements allow a minority to block tax increases that the majority would prefer—which is undemocratic.

Tax revolts have had impacts not only in the states in which they have occurred but also in states that have looked on and fear the same kind of heavy-handed limits. Such states often take preventive action. As a result, those who have supported reductions in property taxes have often been successful in shifting the burden of taxation elsewhere.

Those who have opposed the property tax did not curtail the causes of increased spending but did shift the burden of taxation. As a result, their power over spending decisions was diluted. They were no longer the only or even the major taxpayers. Their ability to funnel spending in ways that would benefit only themselves may have decreased proportionately. Newer policies—and newer budget processes—take into consideration a broader base of taxpayers. Cities have diversified their revenue bases; the consequences of this diversification are still playing themselves out.

3

Evolution of Municipal Budgeting:
An Overview

Taxation is one issue that links budgeting and politics. Others include the degree of openness and accountability in the budget; the degree to which budget allocations favor one group or another; and the degree to which budgeting enhances municipal activism in solving collective problems or makes such activism more difficult. In one sense, budgeting has been cyclical, shifting back and forth between supporting collective problem solving and emphasizing balance and cutback. But in another sense, budgeting has developed over time, responding to and resolving major problems of process and control. From its first tentative steps as a way of estimating how much property tax to levy, budgeting has developed over 125 years into a major, integrated tool for management, policy, and financial control.

The development of municipal budgeting in this country can be crudely divided into four periods. The first is roughly from the end of the Civil War to the beginning of the Progressive era in about 1895. The second is the Progressive period, from about 1895 to about 1915. The third is the post-Progressive era, from 1915 to the end of World War II. The fourth and current period began after the Second World War.

These periods are not uniform or totally distinct from one another. The post–Civil War period and the current period include governmental growth and cutback; the Progressive period was primarily one of government growth; and the post-Progressive and depression eras were primarily those of governmental shrinkage. Some periods are known for one budget innovation, while others are known for several key reforms. Reforms developed in one period often bloomed many years later, creating some overlap between periods. The categorization is therefore not neat, but it is useful.

The earliest period of budgeting occurred just after the Civil War in response to a burgeoning municipal population, causing dramatic collective needs for clean water, sanitation, paved roads and bridges, street lighting, and market facilities. Urged on by municipal boosters, cities borrowed money for projects, only to find themselves caught short in a major recession beginning in 1873. The combination of municipal needs and constrained revenue sources gave rise to budgeting as a control device.

As cities continued to grow and machine politics came to characterize a number of cities, reform movements grew up to curtail corruption and at the same time try to solve collective problems. This second period, called the Progressive era, was focused on creating activist government that would also be accountable, honest, and responsive to reformers' agendas. Initially characterized by reforms in accounting, the Progressive era also generated the first program and performance budgets and executive budgeting reforms. The executive budget gave policy initiative to the chief executive, to get projects accomplished, while examining the departments' requests and creating a rough prioritization based on citywide needs. It also disempowered the councils, which were seen at the time as seats of corruption.

The developments of the Progressive period contradicted themselves, creating a rich and complex legacy for later periods. Emphasis on efficiency and accountability generated line-item controls, detailed lists of items to be purchased and personnel to be paid, with costs attached to each item. The executive budget reforms rejected line items because they curtailed the discretion of the executive. Beginning at the turn of the century, executive budget reforms tried to disempower councils. The slightly later council-manager reform gave the councils more power but reorganized them so that they were smaller and less representative of the neighborhoods and ethnic groups whose demands reformers feared.

The post-Progressive period, including World War I and the Great Depression, emphasized budgetary balance and fiscal control. This was not an activist period. Many cities were caught short during the Great Depression when called on to provide relief for their citizens. They were, with few exceptions, unable to do so. Popular resentment against taxation grew, resulting in reduced services and lower salaries. Pressure also built for reforms such as cost accounting and performance measurement that could simultaneously improve efficiency and demonstrate to the public how efficient cities were. World War II prolonged the period of delayed capital expenditure and low levels of service delivery.

The period after World War II was initially characterized by an economic boom. Cities tried to address a long backlog of delayed capital projects. Shortly after the war, some cities and counties began to implement the performance budgeting that had been recommended by professional societies during the Great Depression, but a growth and planning emphasis won out with the creation and dissemination of Planning and Programming Budgeting Systems (PPBS). With the waning of economic growth later in the period, however, PPBS and its planning orientation faded, to be replaced by budgeting systems more oriented to prioritization for cutbacks. Zero-based and target-based budgeting were adopted and implemented in the 1970s, 1980s, and 1990s. Performance budgeting has also become much more popular in recent years.

Budget Beginnings: After the Civil War

As cities grew in population after the Civil War, the functions of city government became more complex, and spending began to increase. In an effort to constrain expenditures, municipalities began to experiment with primitive budgets. Frederick Clow (1901) examined the development of municipal budgeting from the end of the Civil War to 1900.[1] He noted that some cities used a simple tax levy, while others used a tax levy preceded by detailed estimates, and a third group used the tax levy accompanied by detailed appropriations. The first two

---

1. The cities Clow studied were basically those with a population of more than 80,000 at the time of the census of 1900; only eight having a population of more than 60,000 were omitted from his list. A few other cities were added for geographical representation, including some smaller cities such as Akron, Ohio; Augusta, Georgia; Bangor, Maine; Burlington, Vermont; Canton, Ohio; Chelsea, Massachusetts; Covington, Kentucky; and Dallas, Texas. I counted 102 cities. They do look representative. Clow visited twenty-three of the cities.

were not quite budgets, but they showed what cities were trying, the weaknesses they discovered, and how they corrected them.

Under the simple tax levy, the council would decide how much to raise in taxes without setting a formal limit on spending. The levy itself was the informal limit. The city councils felt the brunt of the taxpayers' aversion to paying taxes and increased the property tax rate only under dire necessity. The council would apportion money by granting contracts and authorizing the payment of bills. The simple tax levy characterized primarily the smaller cities.

The tax levy based on detailed accounts of prior receipts and expenditures provided a little more systematic basis for the allocations and provided a mechanism for limiting the requests for spending. This model reflected the efforts of the time to rein in public spending, since the implicit limitation on spending was what was spent in prior years, and the implicit limit on revenues was what was levied in prior years.

City council members were under no obligation to spend money in accordance with the estimates made for tax purposes. Clow (1901) argued that a "corrupt gang in control of the council can let the estimates distribute the funds wisely, at the time of year when the making of the budget attracts public attention, and later further their selfish ends by directing the funds to purposes not named in the estimates" (p. 28). It was in an attempt to control such nonapproved spending during the year that some cities adopted annual appropriations with the tax levy (Schiesl 1977, 89). When appropriations were combined with the tax levy, the plan for spending had the force of law. These combined appropriation ordinances and tax levies were intended to be hard to change during the year. Clow reported in 1901 that "this form of budget has been growing in favor the past thirty years and is now used by nearly all of the larger cities and many of the smaller ones" (p. 30).

Many cities had difficulty budgeting for a whole year; midyear updating was common. In a few instances there were regular updates. Troy, New York, made a preliminary budget just before the beginning of the fiscal year, intended to last six months. Then the final estimates were made and the levy issued. Atlanta, Georgia, issued the budget in January, but updated regularly in June and October, based on estimates from the departments. New Orleans and Cincinnati passed semiannual appropriations in addition to an annual levy budget. St. Louis passed a regular appropriation bill toward the end of the fiscal year to cover deficiencies. Louisville passed a final appropriation bill in the last month of the fiscal year. This disposed of all surpluses and deficiencies and ended the year with clean books. In Cleveland, the council could amend the budget three times during the year—in May, December, and September. Clow (1901, 59) objected to such procedures because they would make financial control difficult—everyone would know a revision was coming that would catch up with and ratify what they had already done. Moreover, at the end of the year, it would be less apparent which departments had overspent.

A problem that many cities had to face was keeping the departmental spending within budgeted levels. Frequently, severe penalties were attached to overspending, even forcing the department head to make up the differences from his own money. These penalties were generally ineffective. The most common way of funding overdrafts was to transfer money from one appropriation to another. Because such transfers were sometimes excessive, threatened the notion of annual appropriations, and made the budget hard to understand, the rule in New York, Wisconsin, and Iowa was to forbid transfers completely. Ohio, Michigan, and Minnesota forbade transfers for some cities. Boston allowed transfers on the written permission of the mayor with a two-thirds vote of the council. But the budget order always provided for transfers by the auditor and mayor between the items of any department and during the last two months of the year between departments.

The need for transfers could be eliminated by creating contingency funds for emergencies. This model was used in Boston, which reserved from one-quarter to one-half percent of appropriations for this purpose. When directed to do so by the mayor, and with the approval of the committee on finance, the city auditor was authorized to transfer from this fund. Cincinnati set aside $50,000 semiannually for reserve, to be used with consent of the mayor and two-thirds of the council. In Minneapolis, twenty out of twenty-six votes were necessary to spend from the contingency fund. Although a good solution to the problem of excess transfers, keeping such a balance on hand was politically difficult. The balance could become too large if all of a particular revenue source was earmarked for the fund. Clow (1901) stated that the pressure to spend the reserve on a variety of projects was often intense: "most officers who have had experience with such matters are unwilling to stand the pressure and prefer to have no reserved fund, notwithstanding the incontrovertible reasons for having one" (p. 62).

In a practice that still occurs, officials sometimes found unofficial ways to create contingency funds, such as by intentionally underestimating revenue or overestimating expenditure, or by keeping quiet about some surplus that was pledged but that they knew would not be spent. Officials could then challenge those clamoring for money to show where the money was to come from, although they knew where it might come from. "Here also may be a reason why some comptrollers do not wish the accounts to be too simple or easily understood: it would not then be so easy to plead poverty to the importunate alderman or department chief" (Clow 1901, 63).

Because municipal budgets grew out of the practice of estimating and appropriating property taxes, they were often incomplete with respect to other revenue sources. Some left miscellaneous revenue in the departments, others did not report it at all. Also, there was no guidance or uniformity in terms of how far to break down expenditures. The number of items in the budget varied enormously, Clow noted, from 13 in Youngstown, Ohio, to 2,071 in the appropriations of New York City.

Regardless of the level of detail, budgets generally did not break out capital expenditures from operating expenditures. The earliest reference to a capital budget was in Boston in 1897. Boston's Mayor Josiah Quincy drew up two budgets, one for ordinary expenses and revenue, and one for improvements paid for by borrowing. The mayor called on the departments for capital estimates, the same as for the ordinary appropriations, and transmitted the department requests to the council without change or recommendations of his own. The loan order was then prepared by the finance committee, in consultation with the mayor and the heads of departments. This procedure was not continued. Budgets for loans were often informally made, but Clow found no other examples of formal loan budgets.

Post–Civil War developments in budgeting were oriented toward control, to limit overall tax and expenditure growth and help assure that the budget that was passed was the budget that was implemented. By the late 1880s and early 1890s, as cities continued to grow, pressure for increased expenditures began to change the focus of budgeting toward greater efficiency in the managing of the accounts. This focus gradually shifted the activity of proposing budgets from the legislature to the executive.

As Clow reported: "Up to 1850, the councils were everywhere decidedly predominant. Since then, the executive departments have gained immensely" (Clow 1901, 21). As of 1901, most of the charters still gave more power to the councils than to the executive. The councils were split into standing committees, with an average of more than three that dealt in some way with finance and budget in thirty-five cities that Clow looked at. In large cities, however, the council normally accepted the proposal of the controller without important change. Financial administration in big cities is complex and delicate, Clow argued, and could be handled only by a man of above average ability who was willing to spend time on it. Few councilmen had the time and ability to do this, and this work could not be bungled, so it was handed to the executive.

The precise location of decision-making power depended more on the personality of the officials than on the city charters. In financial matters, sometimes the mayor was dominant, sometimes the controller, sometimes the treasurer, often the chairman of a council committee, and most often the head of the accounting department or his chief assistant. Executive budgeting, at this early stage, was not necessarily the prerogative of the mayor, nor was it necessarily a policy tool. The goal was still very much to keep expenditures down, and the structures invented to do this took power away from councils but were not designed for addressing municipal problems in any activist way.

In 1873 in New York City a structure for budgeting called a Board of Estimate and Apportionment was created. This structure was widely copied by other cities. Boards of Estimates were variously composed, but generally included the mayor, the comptroller, and the president of the board of aldermen, and sometimes the director of public works, the city attorney, or a citizen. Boards of Estimate were intended to bring some technical expertise to the creation of the budget and to take budget power away from councils, which were viewed as corrupt and undisciplined with respect to spending. The goal was to keep spending down. The composition of the board, requiring so many different actors with such different objectives to agree on spending proposals, necessarily slowed down ambitious or expensive projects.

The budget process was somewhat similar whether someone in the executive branch or the Board of Estimate presented the budget to the council. Clow argued that in 1901 the typical budget process began with a call to the department for estimates of needs. In cities that had a Board of Estimate, the departmental requests would go to the Board of Estimate. In most other large cities (more than 200,000

population in 1900), the estimates would be given to the head of the
Finance Department. In Massachusetts cities, the estimates would go
to the mayor, and in California, to the auditor. In legislatively dominated cities, usually below 100,000 in population, the estimates went
directly to the whole council or to the budget committee of the council.

The total of the departmental requests normally exceeded revenue
estimates and had to be cut back. When the budgets went to an executive officer like the mayor or controller, he ordinarily revised and compiled them. Rarely, as in Mobile, he used them only as a basis for his
own estimates, which he sent on to the council. Sometimes, as in Min-
neapolis, he transmitted them to the council just as they came to him,
"without adding any recommendations of his own" (Clow 1901, 38).
But ordinarily he sent both the departments' requests and his own recommendation, side by side. Sometimes he included a third column for
the previous year's appropriation.

When the budget requests went directly to a council committee,
the work of examining requests was usually done by one person or by
a small number of people. The budget was seldom changed by the
larger body because increases in services required unpopular increases
in taxes, and reductions in planned spending brought an outcry.

When the controller or mayor revised the estimates, he made the
budget. Only if the council ignored the mayor's recommendations and
began *de novo* could the council be much of a factor in the budget.
The council's role of budget approval was not very significant in shaping the budget, as councils often strained after gnats, debating at
length minor items and ignoring major ones. Moreover, Clow noted
that in most cities the mayor had a veto. Exceptions the author found
were Buffalo, Dayton, Charleston, Detroit, Norfolk, San Francisco,
Worcester, and Wheeling (West Virginia). The newer charters gave the
mayors item vetoes. Usually, a two-thirds majority was required to
overrule the mayor.

The Progressive Era: 1895–1915

The post–Civil War period was marked initially by expansion, followed by the recession of 1873. After a long period of cutback, however, by the middle of the 1890s the public mood had swung back in
many cities toward growth and the resolution of massive public problems. Not only was the mood more optimistic, but the period was col-

ored by an anti-laissez-faire philosophy that encouraged the growth of government services and regulation of industry. Municipal expenditures rose throughout the period.

The emphasis on budgeting shifted from holding down costs to maximizing efficiency so that savings could be spent on additional worthy causes, such as schools, milk inspection for infants, zoos, the construction of streets and sewers, and the improvement of public water supplies.

In Boston, the expansion of services and alterations in the budget process got under way earlier than in other cities. Population growth and demand for projects had contributed to an increased need for efficiency that was reflected in continuing demands from mayors for separating the executive business from the legislative and giving the mayor more budget power. By 1885 these pressures resulted in a charter change transferring executive powers to the mayor. The council was forbidden to employ labor, make contracts, or purchase materials. Departments were forbidden to exceed their appropriations, and the mayor could veto council increases in bills and appropriations. These powers were strengthened in 1907 (Huse 1916, 12–13).

The view that increased population meant more public responsibilities and hence a greater need for efficiency in spending was articulated by William H. Allen, who was concerned with how government could afford to take on new responsibilities, and Frederick Cleveland, who was more concerned about how a democracy could provide services in an efficient manner without losing its democratic nature. Both men were involved in starting and running the New York Bureau of Municipal Research in 1905–6. The New York Bureau was a research center supported by leading business people. The center promoted a variety of public budgeting reforms.

The bureau undertook scientific surveys to determine what services the public needed and advocated municipal performance of those functions. Allen took a new budgeting system invented by the controller of the Association for the Improvement of the Condition of the Poor and adapted it for cities. The new system included program and performance budgeting and emphasized efficiency. Most important, the New York Bureau advocated educating the public about budgeting, accounting, and reporting, so the public could play its role of electing responsible officials and throwing dishonest politicians out of office. In short, the New York Bureau advocated honest, efficient, and responsive government that solved public problems.

Allen summarized the bureau's budget program in an article published in 1908. He argued:

> The four cardinal weaknesses of American municipal budgets are: (1) lack of classification; (2) lack of segregation; (3) the mental reservation that excludes numerous items from the budget, with the idea that revenue bonds or corporate stock shall be issued to cover them during the year; (4) the undemocratic tradition that taxpayers, rather than city officials, are on the stand to answer questions and define their intention with respect to the amount and distribution of taxes. (Allen 1908, 193)

By "lack of classification," Allen meant that the budget was not divided up into meaningful categories, such as programs, and that the budget did not include goals for each of the programs in the budget. There were no lists of what each department was trying to do, how it was deploying its resources, and no information about what the planned accomplishments of each program were. The New York Bureau helped set up a program and performance budget for the Health Department in New York City. This was perhaps the most important and long-lasting original contribution of the bureau.

By "lack of segregation," Allen meant that budgets were often made in a lump-sum fashion or that strange groups of expenditures were clumped together. Such lump-sum budgets made it impossible to figure out if the departmental estimates were reasonable for the work the departments were expected to do: "... it has been easy in dealing with an ignorant public to ask for a barrel of pepper to season a pound of steak" (Allen 1908, 198). To prevent such padding, expenditures for each department should be itemized so that they can be compared to the work program and goals as well as costs for similar items in other cities.

Segregation of expenditures also had the very important effect of preventing open and widespread transfers between expenditures so that the disbursements approved by the Board of Estimate and the public would be the ones that were actually made. "Those familiar with budget making will recall that it has been a familiar ruse of clever, modest department heads to ask for money to increase the number of employees and then to use that money for increasing salaries without increasing services" (Allen 1908, 198). The goal of increased segregation in the budget was to help hold down costs for services and improve accountability.

Allen's third complaint was that budgets were often woefully incomplete, covering only a portion of expenditures. He mentioned in particular that anything to be funded with revenue bonds might be omitted from the budget, but he might have mentioned a number of other kinds of expenditures commonly excluded from the budget. His primary concern, however, was that operating items were being inappropriately put into long-term debt, in effect covering up deficits, burdening the city with millions of dollars of permanent debt.

His fourth criticism, based on observations of budget hearings in New York City, was that officials often acted in a high-handed way, not really listening to citizens and sometimes even trying to humiliate them. The first step in getting greater citizen involvement in budgeting was to treat citizens with respect. The second was to invite them to hearings at various stages of the budget process, so that the documents the public read and commented on were really the basis for decision making.

Frederick Cleveland, another founder of the New York Bureau, was later viewed as the inventor of public budgeting in the United States. That title exaggerates his accomplishments,[2] but he did make several arguments that turned out to be important. First, he insisted that the executive must control the departmental budget requests and must know what the departments were spending. To gain this knowledge and control, the executive needed consolidated rather than fragmented accounts and accurate accounting data. Second, to achieve efficiency and democracy at the same time, the executive would have to take over the role of preparing the budget, gathering up information from departments, weighing it, looking at the requests in the context of revenue estimates, and then presenting a revised request to the legislature. As far as Cleveland was concerned, if these steps were not followed, the government did not really have a budget process.

Cleveland repeated an argument that had been circulating since

---

2. Budgeting had been evolving since the end of the Civil War. Even the recommendation for executive budgeting, often attributed to Cleveland, emerged before he advocated it. Boston had been moving toward an executive budget before the turn of the century, and the National Municipal League advocated executive budgets in its model charter of 1898. Cleveland's original contribution was to emphasize the role of good accounting data in maintaining control over departmental spending. He was also an effective spokesperson for the executive budget reforms that had been emerging.

the turn of the century, that the increasing activities of government required that public affairs be managed by public servants with efficiency and economy. But while others suggested that it was appropriate for the controller or someone else in the executive branch to put together the estimates, Cleveland argued that it had to be the chief executive or his staff member. He reasoned that because the executive was responsible for carrying out the budget and implementing legislative will, the chief executive had to be the one to put the budget proposal together and present it to the legislative body.

> More concretely, the form of organization of our public corporation provides that the legislature as a representative deliberative body must decide what work is to be done; what personnel, organization, and equipment shall be provided; what funds shall be granted. The executive branch or administrative officers or agents must be relied on to execute these plans, subject, however, to review both by the legislature and by the courts. . . .
>
> The need for an exact statement of these [budget] proposals is to be found in the fact that the executive is the one responsible for carrying out the details of administration. In executing policies and administrating on the details of the business in hand, administrative officers are the only ones who fully understand the technical requirements of the services; they are the ones who are meeting the needs of the public; they are the ones who know what are the conditions to be met in order to perform public services with economy and efficiency. The officers who are in immediate charge of these details are the ones who must be looked to, to describe the needs of each branch of the administration as they see it. They cannot, however, consider the needs of the service as a whole; they cannot represent the executive branch of the corporation. This must necessarily fall on the chief executive. The chief executive is the only officer who can represent the government as a whole; he is the one who should be held responsible for submitting proposals based on a consideration of the proposals of his subordinates. (Cleveland 1913, 454–56)

Expenditures per capita rose from 1895 to 1915. Rising expenditures helped focus attention on the need for cost accounting to differentiate inefficiency from increased service levels. The New York Bureau of Municipal Research advocated a budget with segregated functions and cost accounting by function; one New York City department tried to implement it by 1908. But the major push for line-item budgeting came a little later, after the main burst of spending caused by Progressive era expansion. Line-item budgeting was associated with efforts to curtail political machines, keep costs down, and balance the budget.

The emphasis on efficiency and accountability that characterized the Progressive era gave rise to line-item budgeting, but the later emphasis on spending controls and budgetary balance led to its widespread adoption. Ironically, the reform may have resulted in greater, rather than less, expenditure. And line-item budgeting ran into opposition from supporters of executive budgeting.

Between 1907 and 1912, the general practice was to place large lump sums at the disposal of administrative officers, over whom there was little if any control. Line items were often grouped together oddly. In the Philadelphia budget in 1911, items were grouped as follows: postage, ice, files, incidentals, meals, repairs, advertisements, and entertainment of city and visiting officials, $25,000; rent, postage, horse keep, and miscellaneous expenses, $25,000 (Taylor 1925). A new proposal provided for itemization to curtail unauthorized expenditures. Instead of a lump sum for the operation of police wagons in the department, the amounts were broken down as personal services (permanent salaries), contractual services (repair of auto; other), and materials and supplies (gasoline, lubricants, metal products, rubber auto tires; other).

R. Emmett Taylor argued that the new practice had some merit but was too rigid. The lump-sum budgets that were typical of the period up to about 1907 invited abuses. Line itemization was adopted as a means of control. Rather than give an administrator a lump of money to spend on a variety of purposes, the purposes were to be specified and a sum of money for each one allocated; no more than that amount could be spent on any item.

Line items as a means of control spread widely, but before long many of their weaknesses were observed. The rigidity of the segregated budget led to overestimates of the sums required. Once the funds were obtained, many departments would spend whatever they had in the budget, preventing unused portions from reverting to the treasury. The result pushed up costs. In response to overly strong constraints, the line items began to be evaded through transfers. In some cases, poor administration reduced the segregated budget to a lump-sum budget (Taylor 1925).

Those who favored a strong executive budget argued against line-item controls. Supporters of executive budget reforms contended that line-item budgets were useful if there was no responsible executive in charge of the budget and the departments needed to be controlled, but they would hamper a responsible executive. Moreover, line items gave the legislature a way of controlling the executive and preventing him from exercising managerial discretion. Arthur Buck, quoting Frederick Cleveland, asserted:

> The best that can be said for the detailed appropriations of the past is that they are part of a system that has operated to prevent administrative action premised on infidelity and ignorance; that legislative control over the administration through detailed appropriation is a device adapted for use in a political institution, in which all the elements essential to administrative efficiency are lacking. Given a responsible government and a real executive, the legislative restrictions which go with detailed appropriations are a first obstacle to efficiency to be removed. (Buck 1934, 151)

In 1934 Buck argued that detailed line-item appropriations were a way for the legislative body to control the executive directly through detailed specifications in the granting of money (p. 151). The financial history of Boston offers some evidence for Buck's and Cleveland's point of view. The Finance Committee, representing reformers in Boston, supported strong powers for the mayor in 1909, including strong budgeting powers (Koren 1923, 14). To the chagrin of the reformers, however, the newly strengthened position of mayor was taken over by a machine politician, not a reformed one. In 1916 the Finance Committee successfully recommended the adoption of segregated, or line-item, budgeting. This reform presumably would give the council control over a financially irresponsible mayor. What Buck did not adequately note, however, was that a strong mayor was able to evade the line-item controls through transfers.

Line-item budgeting and its emphasis on financial control has lasted over the years. The persistence of a reform that seemed almost immediately not to be working may seem stunningly irrational, but it makes more sense in the context of struggles for power between the executive and legislative branches of government. Executive budget reformers treated councils as the seat of corruption and ineptitude and tried to disempower them with respect to budgets. They envisioned strong and reform-minded mayors, not corrupt or managerially inept mayors. But having strengthened the mayor's position, they had little control over whether the new position would be occupied by a reform mayor. If not, then line-item controls might help control departmental spending. Line-item controls contradict the broad grants of power embedded in executive budget reforms; where line-item controls are strong and active, skepticism about strong executives may persist. Moreover, line-item controls can provide council members with some budgetary power over a strong mayor; council members may be reluctant to give up these controls. To the extent that battles between the executive and legislative branches continue at the local level, line-item budgeting remains a politically salient issue. Line-item budgeting is more than a matter of emphasis on fiscal control, it is also a matter of how that fiscal control will be achieved.

The first decade of this century was a seminal period for municipal budgeting, not only for the origins and spread of executive budgeting and line-item reforms, but also for the invention and spread of the commission and council-manager forms of government. Both of these were changes in the structure of government that also affected budget processes.

Beginning in 1903 in the city of Galveston, Texas, the commission form of government was widely copied over the next decade. In the commission form, commissioners, or council members, were elected at large, and each one was simultaneously the head of a department and a member of the council. There was no separation of the branches of government. Department heads proposed their own budgets and collectively passed them.

The greater efficiency of the commission form was supposed to come from reorganization and simplification of the bureaucracy. Only a small number of departments were permitted, usually four or five. Each department had to report to a single commissioner, as opposed to a committee. Major efforts were made to ensure that machines did not control the commissions. Some of the charters contained requirements for direct primaries and nonpartisan elections as ways of breaking the back of the dominant party.

Perhaps most important, the commission form was sold to the public on its similarity to the governing board of a corporation.

> Much had been said and claimed for the plan on the score of its analogy to the governing boards of corporations. Literally hundreds of magazine articles had glowingly described the boards of commission-

ers of Galveston and Des Moines as groups of businessmen gathered about a table in conference to discuss the business problems of administration and to determine questions theretofore left to councilmanic committees or to irresponsible department heads. (Bruere 1912, 25–26)

The city commissioners did not in fact have similar responsibilities to a governing board of a corporation, but the appeal of the commission form to reformers was based at least to some extent on this analogy.

Most of the commission governments that sprang up before 1912 were in fact light on business techniques. There was little about budgeting in commission charters. The basic outline was for departments to draw up estimates, which were forwarded to the commission; the commission would scrutinize the requests, estimate revenue, and apportion the revenue to the departments.

Henry Bruere, a director of the New York Bureau along with William H. Allen and Frederick Cleveland, did a major study of the commission form of government. He commented on some of the budgeting requirements that were not included as charter provisions, but probably should have been. He noted that there was no provision for publishing budget proposals for the public to examine or for public hearings on the budget; that there was no requirement that one of the commissioners review the request, analyze it, and make recommendations to the commission; that there was no provision for budget allocations by function or program, only by departments; and that there was no requirement for estimates to be prepared on the basis of actual expenditures and experience of the previous fiscal year (Bruere 1912). Bruere hinted at what later became obvious as a weakness of the form, that is, that each commissioner represented a department and was reluctant to cut any other department's request lest the commissioner's own be cut.

The council-manager form of government, invented in 1908, helped shore up the weaknesses of the commission form. In council-manager government, the elected council hires a professional manager, whose job, among other things, is to request and examine budget proposals from the departments, balance these requests against expected revenues, and then submit this extensively reviewed proposal to the council for approval. This governmental form matched the emerging executive budget reforms.

The Post-Progressive Era: 1915–45

The Progressive era was characterized initially by efforts to improve efficiency and effectiveness, efforts that spawned line-item budget controls, program budgeting, and executive budgeting. By the end of the period, emphasis had shifted more toward controlling the level of spending and away from collective solutions to collective problems. As part of this latter thrust, state governments began to mandate budgets for local governments and require that budgets be balanced.

Massachusetts, beginning in about 1910, and especially in 1913, passed a series of laws affecting all local units except Boston. These laws were to attain the following: no borrowing for current needs, no unrestricted borrowing in anticipation of revenues, no diversion of trust funds, and sound management of sinking funds (money saved to pay off bonds when due). State certification was required to assure procedural conformity. Serial bonds (bonds with varied due dates that spread out repayment) were substituted for sinking funds because cities were not paying the required amounts into their sinking funds to repay bonds (Griffith 1974). Massachusetts passed the first law requiring all local governments to have a budget, although most of its provisions were ignored.

The New Jersey Commission for the Survey of Municipal Finance recommended in 1915 that local governments draw up a true budget, adopt a uniform fiscal year, prohibit the refunding of floating debt, limit the term of a bond to the life of the improvement, and borrow through serial bonds rather than sinking funds. The commission also recommended a debt limit of 10 percent and uniform accounting. Most of the recommendations were enacted within the next two years. North Carolina and New Hampshire passed municipal finance acts in 1917. The mood of the times was not only to balance the budget and control debt accumulation, but also to hold down taxation. Indiana in 1919 gave its Board of Tax Commissioners complete authority to review and reduce local budgets. In the same year the state instituted the first detailed supervision of municipal debt.

Between 1915 and 1940, many, if not most, cities adopted some form of budgeting, but in many cases the budgets were incomplete. Arthur Buck, surveying cities in 1929, found that the majority of budgets contained little more than operating budgets. Capital expenditures were often excluded, and sometimes utilities' operating expenses were omitted. The New York City budget was $475 million, but the controller said it should have been $530 million. Even the larger figure left out a great deal. In New Orleans, according to a study by the New York Bureau in 1921, of $16 million in annual spending, only $6 million appeared in the budget. The San Francisco Bureau of Municipal Research reported in 1928 that San Francisco's budget listed $25 million in expenditures, but the real figures were closer to $56 million. Outside the budget were some construction projects, operations and other costs of schools, municipal railroads, and nonbudgeted revenues, mostly tax levies for parks, playgrounds, libraries, and debt retirement (Buck 1929). Buck also reported that bond fund expenditures and agencies supported by earmarked money were often omitted from the budget.

Besides these frequently missing parts, each city put its budget together differently, some leaving out one part, others another. Some budgets virtually ignored revenues; others left out summaries of the totals, presenting masses of unaggregated details; and a number of cities included only a brief summary of revenues and expenditures, with no details.

The executive budget spread quickly in cities between 1915 and 1929, as a result of the adoption of the centralized mayor or manager form. Correspondingly, legislative budgeting was disappearing. As late as 1929, however, most cities did not have permanent budget staffs, although a few large cities had set up budget offices. Many more cities were in the process of creating budget staffs.

Buck noticed that most cities did not begin the budget process with a statement of policies that would guide decisions. Instead, the departments would set forth their spending requirements without any advance guidance from the executive. Policy choices, if they were made at all, were made when going over the departmental proposals or when the budget was being reviewed. Counter to the general trend, the city manager in Berkeley, California, and his budget director devised a system of setting limits for departmental proposals and giving those limits to the departments before they submitted their proposals. The departments were forbidden to request more than the maximum amount, but could prepare a supplemental list of what they wanted if additional money became available.

Buck observed in the late 1920s that very few councils had any kind of budget staff to help them understand or review the budget. He also noted that the councils were not generally prevented from changing the mayor's or manager's budget proposal, despite earlier efforts during the Progressive era to disempower councils.

Earlier efforts to disempower city councils with respect to the budget had occurred in New York City, Baltimore, and Boston. The Greater New York City Charter adopted in 1897 and revised in 1901 forbade the Board of Aldermen to add to the appropriation ordinance when adopting the budget; the aldermen were only allowed to reduce items, and even the reductions could be vetoed by the mayor. The Baltimore city charter, adopted in 1898, forbade the city council to increase the amounts fixed by the Board of Estimate or add any new item (Schiesl 1977). In 1909 Boston adopted a new charter that contained the following provisions: the city council may reduce or reject any item, but without the approval of the mayor it shall not increase any item in, nor the total of, a budget, nor add any item thereto, nor shall it originate a budget. A provision like this was later made applicable by general law to all cities in the state of Massachusetts. But these restrictions were not widely applied in local government, in part because the reconstitution of councils under the commission and council-manager form made them unnecessary.

Arthur Buck described municipal budgeting just before the Great Depression. The effect of the depression on cities' budgeting was to cut spending on the one hand, and to show up weaknesses in budgeting on the other. Overwhelming pressure from banks to cut budgets, along with antigovernment ideology promoted by tax protesters, stimulated efforts to show how well cities were managed financially. The pressure to reduce taxes during the depression was accompanied by a public belief that there was great waste in government and that a tax limit would squeeze out waste without cutting basic services. Public officials and their organizations responded by trying to reduce waste, cutting taxes without the pressure of limits, and conveying the image of greater efficiency to the public.

Public expenditures for the ordinary activities of government were reduced in the vast majority of municipalities. Salaries were slashed, some public services were abandoned, and school terms were shortened (Chatters 1935). Unemployment relief was a major new burden for many cities. The property tax system broke down, as evidenced by rising tax delinquencies, the movement for tax limitations, and cities' searches for new sources of revenue. The result was often piecemeal taxes, such as more business license taxes, charges for miscellaneous services, and increased municipal utility charges. Re-

portedly, only 820 cities and villages defaulted on their debt, less than
one-half of 1 percent of the total, but many more were paying a high
proportion of their total revenue for debt service.

The depression showed up weaknesses in city budgeting and accounting and brought pressure from investors and from state government, research organizations, and the federal government for improvements. The movement for unit cost accounting broadened. In
1935 nearly 100 cities maintained some form of cost accounting in
public works. Officials of professional organizations such as the International City Managers Association and the Municipal Finance Officers Association advocated performance budgeting as a form of cost
accounting. Reporting how much it cost cities to do particular tasks
might improve efficiency—and hence provide a buffer against continued cuts—and help explain to the public how well city services
were being managed (Ridley and Simon 1938).

The emphasis on budget reform waned during World War II.
Many municipal managers felt that it was their patriotic duty to keep
taxes low so that money could continue to flow to the war effort.
New federal facilities in many cities were tax exempt, further squeez-
ing revenues. Many services were cut back, and capital projects were
delayed. Firefighters and police had often been drafted into the army,
and such vehicles as squad cars were difficult to purchase because of
wartime controls (Buck 1943).

At the same time that services were being cut back and capital
projects delayed, officials began planning for the postwar period. They
envisioned returning soldiers, population surges, increases in the number of school-age children, and long-delayed capital projects. Management of resources became a post–World War II priority. Performance
and program budgeting, cost and program accounting, and performance auditing were all evidence of this goal (Petersen, Stallings, and
Spain 1979).

Post–World War II Municipal Budgeting

The problems of city budgeting were difficult during the period of
rapid population growth at the turn of the century, but many of them
were resolved. Health and sanitation were improved, and the political
machines that were anathema to reformers were weakened by council-
manager government and at-large elections. Political machines lost

strength as the level of popular education increased and dependence on machines for basic services and public-sector jobs decreased.

As the original problems that budgeting was designed to deal with were resolved, new ones appeared. Rapid growth and the funding of infrastructure remained problems in the expanding suburbs, but for the larger, older, central cities, population began to decline. Political problems became more complicated after the demise of political machines because there was little way to gain or influence mass support. Public acceptance of tax policy, which has often been problematic, became more acute as people's incomes failed to keep pace with the cost of living.

In the simplest of early governmental models, during the late 1800s, the elite paid property taxes for the projects they wanted to help expand business; when they could not afford to pay taxes during recessions, they withdrew their financial support, and the cities fell on hard times. Voluntary contributions by the elite resumed when the economy improved because the wealthy taxpayers wanted the projects that the city built for them, such as public markets and harbors.

This simple picture became more complex as cities expanded their functions to include services to the poor and to neighborhoods, services that wealthy taxpayers were not always willing to allow at what they perceived to be their expense. These elites often took over the machinery of government to assure that their spending goals were the ones to dominate the agenda and that others were not raising their tax bills to pay for benefits the wealthy would not enjoy. Toward the middle and end of the Progressive era, with the expansion of public services and a relatively broad definition of city services and projects, large taxpayers and newly wealthy businessmen promoted reforms to take power away from the relatively poor by closing off the power of city councils, and they began to run government like a business, for businessmen.

After World War II, after many years of low-profile, low-energy local government, business coalitions in many cities took over government again to mobilize economic rejuvenation, usually in the form of downtown renewal. But, as had happened many times in earlier years, a period of major borrowing and capital expenditure was followed by a period of relatively sharp contraction. Beginning in the mid-1970s, the economic problems of the cities were compounded by major recessions that were bigger, longer, and deeper than most earlier cyclical changes. With inflation raging and the number of jobs stagnating, the faltering economy put pressure on taxpayers to keep the level of taxes down. Whereas in the past a limited number of wealthy people had taxed themselves to pay for their own benefits, there was now a broad taxpaying public who wanted and needed to curtail the tax burden on themselves or face the possible loss of their homes. The result was a wave of restrictive tax limitations, with some states adopting new or more stringent tax limits, and other states, fearful of such limits, voluntarily circumscribing the growth of property taxes.

As property tax levels were controlled, sales taxes became more important, as did fees of various sorts. Taxes at the local level generally became more regressive, continuing to broaden the base of payers for public services and breaking the lock on spending held by the narrow groups of elites who had paid the bulk of property taxes in the last century.

The size and composition of the active electorate also changed. At the turn of the century, fear of the poor combined with a fear of blacks, especially in the South, to limit the number of poor people who could vote. Many southern states had prevented the poor— blacks and whites—from voting by means of poll taxes. Throughout the country, reformers tried to reduce the power of the poor in cities by reducing the power of the city council to make budget decisions or by making it difficult to elect poor people to the council by mandating at-large elections. Thus, the well-to-do taxpayers insulated themselves from the demands of the poor and the neighborhoods.

The civil rights movement of the 1960s had, with great pain, established fairer voting laws, changing the electorate and making it more inclusive. Further, the urban riots that followed the assassination of civil rights leader Martin Luther King Jr. in 1968 raised the question in the minds of many whether complete exclusion of blacks from the political process was a good idea, since it seemed to encourage political violence. As a result of both the civil rights movement and the riots, effort was made in many cities to make the councils more representative and, in some cities, to give minorities and neighborhoods some responsibility in budgeting.

In addition, the increasing pinch of tax limits often forced local governments to go to the public for tax referendums. Because of the difficult financial times, but also because so many people had been excluded from both decision making and from the benefit of city services, and because many of the formerly excluded people could now vote, city officials were often rebuffed when they went to the public for approval. Many taxpayers were reluctant to pay for services for anyone other than themselves. In desperation, public officials began to rethink their traditional patterns of decision making. In some cities, public officials tried to involve the public earlier in the decision-making process, to make sure the public approved the spending plans and understood the efficiency with which the city government operated. These pressures helped change both the process and the format of budgeting.

For many cities, despite their attempts to get more public approval, tight budgets were a fact of life. Living with limited resources became one of the problems that budgeting had to address. New budgeting systems were adopted that helped prioritize spending and created some flexibility for politicians to respond to public demands.

The main focus of budgeting during World War II was on keeping costs and taxation down. Interest in performance budgeting flared briefly after the Hoover commission report in 1949, which advised the federal government to adopt performance budgeting. Los Angeles was an early municipal adopter, beginning its performance budgeting in fiscal year 1953 (Terhune 1954; Eghtedari and Sherwood 1960).

Performance budgeting did not catch on in cities in the 1950s. Nevertheless, the number of adoptions of some type of performance measurement has increased over the past ten or fifteen years. The circumstances have changed to be much more like those of the late depression period, when there was considerable antitax sentiment and professional associations of government officials urged cities to explain to the public what a good and efficient job they were doing. Proposition 13 in California signaled a new and long-lasting antitax sentiment. Taxpayer revolts may have contributed to the more recent adoption of performance measurement.

As a measure of the acceptance of performance budgeting, the General Accounting Standards Board (GASB), the body that sets the standards for financial reporting for cities in the United States, has actively promoted Service and Efforts Accomplishment Reporting in cities' annual reports. In the 1990s debate has focused on whether "service and efforts accomplishment" should be required in annual reports or whether such reports should remain an optional part of the budget.

Of the cities reported later in this book, Dayton, Phoenix, and Boston had thoroughly incorporated performance measurement into their budgets. Tampa had incorporated a service-level analysis into its budget process. Service-level analysis funds the departments in return for a specified and measured level of service delivery. St. Louis is still developing its performance budget, and Rochester is trying to simplify its performance measures and weed out the useless ones.

Although performance budgeting has taken off recently, it did not suit the expansionary needs of the postwar period. During the period of rapid growth after World War II, the planning focus of the Planning and Program Budgeting System (PPBS) was more attractive. The orientation of PPBS was on linking the budget to goals that the government was trying to achieve (Schick 1966).

Rather than emphasize routine expenditures on routine services, PPBS asked, what are the goals the community wants to achieve and how can the budget best be harnessed to achieve those goals? Along with this goal orientation came a technical apparatus of analysis to see which programs could deliver more of needed services for the least cost. The aim was to figure out where additional funds could best be spent in order for those collective goals to be achieved. Underlying this budgeting system was a feeling of optimism and a belief in government. Collective problems could be solved collectively.

PPBS was initiated in the federal government and was spread to state and local governments in a federally sponsored experiment called the Five-Five-Five program because there were five states, five counties, and five cities chosen for the experiment. The experiment began in 1968 (Mushkin 1969).

Many local governments besides the ones in the experiment tried various aspects of PPBS, but in most cases the system did not succeed. Part of the problem was that PPBS relied on some form of merger between planning and budgeting, but it was difficult to get any kind of cooperation between the budgeting office and the planning office. A second part of the problem was that chief executives often gave the system only lukewarm support, generally viewing it as experimental, needing to prove its worth. Some city officials felt that the Department of Housing and Urban Development would require PPBS as a condition of grants, and when they found out that was not going to happen, they dropped the system. A third problem with PPBS is that it fit well with a growing economy; when the boom times of postwar growth yielded to slower growth and long, deep recessions, the optimism that characterized PPBS disappeared. It was hard to plan when making cuts. Various elements of the story of PPBS are told in the cases presented in later chapters.

Few cities practice PPBS today, but there has been a resurgent interest in various elements of the package. Rather than link the budget to a comprehensive planning process that includes population estimates and a systematic inventory of capital needs, a number of cities are engaging in various kinds of strategic plans and linking those to the budget process. This process requires much less of the planning model that provoked opposition earlier and much less analytical apparatus; it also offers more direct benefit to politicians and to the public. The public can help articulate selected goals for the community, and the politicians can use the budget to help demonstrate that these goals are being achieved. The emphasis in recent years on shifting from an input to an output focus is also reminiscent of the emphasis in PPBS.

PPBS was suited to a time of growth, but by the mid-1970s, a deep recession had hit the cities. In the late 1970s federal aid began to decline, and some taxpayers supported property tax revolts. A second deep recession hit in the early 1980s. Some cities began to experiment with zero-based budgeting (ZBB). For example, Oakland, California, drew up a zero-based budget to help handle anticipated cuts resulting from Proposition 13.

Zero-based budgeting aimed to examine and sometimes cut items that were part of the "base," or normally ongoing and unquestioned portion of the budget. The goal of zero-based budgeting was to examine the whole budget, from the first dollar to the last one. A second goal was to prioritize all those expenditures, having compared each one to every other one, in case massive cuts became necessary. Examining the whole budget from time to time seemed efficient, especially when a city was confronted with the possibility of major reductions in revenues.

While zero-based budgeting was focused on cutback rather than growth, it relied on concepts from earlier periods, such as program budgeting and cost accounting. Each department had to be broken up into programs and realistic costs associated with each program. Each department would rank its own programs and then a citywide list integrating each of the departmental lists would be drawn up. A crude form of cost-benefit analysis might be done to help compare programs and put some higher on the priority list than others.

Implementation of zero-based budgeting was difficult and wasted time making seemingly impossible and unnecessary comparisons. It did not make any sense to compare the Fire Department's fire-suppression program with the Police Department's crime-suppression program and come up with a ranking because it was clear that neither one of them was going to be eliminated. Threats to eliminate popular programs were unrealistic. To make the whole thing work, programs were divided into service levels, with each level associated with a cost. One program might be associated with three service levels: a basic, bare-bones level; a current level; and a beefed-up level. Each of these options became a decision unit, and the department would rank all the decision units in the department. This process required good cost data not only for each program but also for each level of service within each program. Fortunately this process did not have to be done every year.

Some cities and counties have used zero-based budgeting from time to time, but is it so clumsy and requires so much data that ZBB is rarely used. Many of the advantages of zero-based budgeting can be achieved with target-based budgeting without many of the drawbacks because target-based budgeting concentrates on prioritizing at the margins, where the real decisions are made. Target-based budgeting requires only one budget request from the departments—not three numbers for each program. It is both easier to establish and easier to maintain.

Target-based budgeting is a budget reform that requires the budget office to give targets, or maximum amounts, to the departments before they draw up their budget requests. The departmental requests must be within these targets. Target-based budgeting has several outstanding strengths that have added to its recent appeal: it is highly adaptable to unpredictable revenue levels; it provides an easy mechanism for elected officials to reduce revenue levels; and it decentralizes management control to the departments while maintaining fiscal control in the budget office.

Target-based budgeting reallocates some of the traditional functions of the budget office and the departments (Rubin 1991; Lewis 1988; Wenz and Nolan 1982). Under traditional budgeting, budget requests came up from the departments with few or no prior constraints from the budget office. The totals of the requests normally exceeded the revenue available, forcing the budget office to cut back the departmental requests. Such cutbacks could be across the board, requiring little knowledge of the department's operations, or could be detailed, giving the budget office the opportunity to micromanage the departments. In contrast, target-based budgets require the budget office to give ceilings to the departments for their budget requests. These ceilings are framed by the budget office's estimates of revenue and policy guidance from the budget office, mayor, manager, and council. If the department heads fail to keep their requests under this ceiling, the budget office returns their budget requests for revision until the requests come in either at or under the ceilings. The decisions of what to cut to get under the ceilings are made by the departments, not by the budget office. The responsibility for ensuring that budget requests do not exceed revenue lies with the budget office, while the responsibility for making managerially responsible cuts goes to the departments.

The earliest reference to target-based budgeting in the budget literature is in Arthur Buck's 1929 text, *Public Budgeting*. He described a system of budgeting in Berkeley, California, in the 1920s that would today be recognized as target based. After several years of experimenting with commission government and experiencing the logrolling and high rates of expenditure that came to be associated with that form, a budget reform group in Berkeley advocated the adoption of council-manager government. The requirement for more stringent budgeting was included in the new council-manager charter effective in 1923. The city had been running deficits in the early 1920s, just prior to the adoption of the council-manager form, at least in part because of war-induced inflation and resulting salary increases combined with tax limits and a citizenry unwilling to override the limits.

The new budget system was given life and form by the first city manager, John Edy, and his budget officer, J.H. Jamison. Their goal was to rebalance the budget within the tax limits by controlling the departmental requests while creating a little flexibility in the budget for capital projects and new or expanded services.

In 1929 budget reformer Buck described the system that Edy and Jamison had worked out.

> The manager, with the assistance of his budget officer, J.H. Jamison, makes a careful analysis of the current year's budget in the light of the work program and in this way decides upon the total budget for the forthcoming year, definitely allocating to each spending agency the maximum amount which it may spend during the budget year. Each spending agency is then notified of the maximum amount which it may spend and asked to submit its estimates so as not to exceed this amount. In the event that a spending agency desires to submit requests in excess of the amount allowed by the manager, it must do so on supplementary estimate sheets and arrange the requests in

the order of their importance. These additional requests are allowed only in the event and to the extent that revenue is found to be available to meet them at the subsequent date when the budget is formulated. Mr. Edy claims that this method has greatly reduced the work of preparing the city budget, since the estimates require very little revision and practically no redrafting. (Buck 1929, 307)

Target-based budgeting is highly adaptable to fluctuating or hard-to-predict revenues because it is relatively easy to budget for the worst-case scenario while maintaining a list of prioritized add-backs in case more revenue comes in than originally estimated. This procedure is fiscally conservative, helping to prevent deficits created by overestimates of revenue, but it puts the burden of uncertainty on the departments.

Politicians also find target-based budgeting useful for reducing taxes and gaining some popularity for themselves. They start the budget process with parameters for revenue, such as reducing the property tax rates by 10 percent. The targets to the departments are calculated with the new figure in mind; the departments have to say how they are going to use the lower amount and what will be unfunded as a result. Politicians presumably could back off from the most politically threatening of the cuts, or they could force the departments to cut in other areas instead.

Despite the difficulties that departments have in continually complying with reduced revenue levels, they tend to like the increased autonomy that target-based budgeting gives them to budget as they wish for greatest efficiency. Department managers experience way fewer limitations on how they can spend money. Target-based budgeting is fundamentally a lump-sum appropriation, not a detailed line-item control. As long as the departments deliver a negotiated amount of services at a negotiated level of quality, elected officials should not care whether $1,500 was spent on office supplies or a new photocopy machine was purchased. The department heads know the constraints they have to operate under and are unlikely to waste resources when there is so much to do and so few resources, and they are accountable for the results.

Many of the conditions that spawned target-based budgeting in the 1920s are similar to conditions today. It is not surprising, therefore, that target-based budgeting has become increasingly popular in cities over the past ten to fifteen years. Target-based budgeting has become so common in recent years that of the six case studies re-ported in later chapters, five have adopted target-based budgeting.

Conclusions

To some extent, later reforms have built on earlier ones. Zero-based budgeting assumed program budgeting and cost accounting, for ex-ample. Also, when conditions are similar, budgeting reforms devel-oped in earlier years come back. Target-based budgeting, designed for the post-Progressive era in Berkeley, California, has been widely adopted in the past twenty years. The performance budgeting urged as a response to taxpayer protests in the 1930s has been adopted, with modifications, in recent years that have been marked by widespread taxpayer resistance.

There is also an internal logic to budgeting evolution: budgeting has learned from its own failures. PPBS was not only suited more for growth than for decline, it was planning dominated, and cities were often not comfortable either with the planning model or with domina-tion by planners. But the idea of seeing the budget as a tool to accom-plish municipal goals was attractive. It has evolved into a strategic planning model that serves the politicians better. Contemporary bud-geting is not only related to the past, and incomprehensible without knowledge of the past, its current shape results from learning what worked and what did not.

4

The Early Years

AFTER THE Civil War, cities began to grow rapidly. Industrialization, immigration, and rapid population and areal growth brought problems of health, transportation, and education for cities to grapple with. At the same time, the freed slaves and immigrants who had been naturalized were given the vote, and women began to agitate for the franchise. The newly expanded electorate contributed to the perception of a division between those who paid the taxes and those who voted to spend the money.

Two distinct but related problems arose. First, city councils that had for many years been directing the business of cities were often overwhelmed with technical requirements they did not understand. Second, city councils came to include representatives of neighborhoods, immigrant groups, and the poor. Elites had been willing to pay taxes for expenditures they wanted, but now someone else was spending their money, and not always in the amounts or for the projects they wanted or with the efficiency they demanded. These taxpaying elites wanted to restore their control over taxing and spending decisions.

As one participant at the National Municipal League's 1907 meetings put it, "A man paying $5,000 taxes in a town is more interested in the well-being and development of his town than the man who pays no taxes. . . . Shall we be truly democratic and give the property owner a fair show or shall we develop a tyranny of ignorance which shall crush him?" (Glaab and Brown 1983, 221).

Reformers representing these taxpaying elites suggested a number of solutions over the period from 1870 to 1915 (Hays 1964). One approach was to shift budget power away from elected councils and toward the mayor or other specially created body. A second solution was to reorganize the councils so that members were elected at large rather than from districts, making neighborhood representation more difficult. Some reforms combined both approaches. A third strategy was to disrupt the power of political machines by giving citizens the information and interest to act as watchdogs and the power to disapprove effectively if they disliked what they saw. Machines were assumed to be corrupt and therefore wasteful of taxpayer money.

An example of the first approach, shifting budgeting power away from the legislative body to the mayor or other specially designated group, was the creation of the Boards of Estimate and Apportionment. First established in New York City in 1873, the Board of Estimate in that city overruled efforts on the part of the aldermen to increase spending and hence became a popular pattern for other cities to emulate. The New York City Board of Estimate and Apportionment included both the mayor and the president of the Board of Aldermen, but budget power was gradually ceded to the mayor. The birth and evolution of this odd structure is illustrated in the New York City and Baltimore cases, detailed below.

The second approach, reorganizing the council and/or electing it at large, is represented by the invention and adoption of the commission form of government. Between 1903 and 1912, 206 cities had adopted the commission form of government (Bruere 1912, 40). The commission combined often sprawling bureaucracies into a handful of departments. The department heads formed a commission, which served simultaneously as the executive and legislature. Thus council members, acting as department heads, proposed their own budgets, which were then approved by themselves acting as the council. In the unusual case of Houston, the commission form was combined with a strong mayor, who received and examined the budget proposals from the departments and revised them according to his plan before presenting the budget to the commission.

Commission members were elected at large, so the representation of neighborhoods was intentionally difficult or impossible to achieve. Moreover, the commission system was often combined with direct election in primaries and citizen referendums, techniques intended to short-circuit the powers of political machines and restore direct power to citizens. "Citizens" often meant the nonpoor, nonimmigrant, property-owning voters.

Efforts to shift power away from the legislative branch led eventually to the executive budget. In the earliest stages of municipal budgeting, departmental estimates would be presented to a controller or other executive branch official, who would gather the proposals, add other nondepartmental obligations, estimate revenues, and pass on the information to council committees. Gradually, this process was elaborated. The controller would first estimate revenues and require departments to justify their budget requests in detail. Then the comptroller or other executive would cut back the requests so that they fit the revenue estimates. This revised and summarized proposal would then be forwarded to the council.

This line of evolution eventually combined in some cities with efforts to centralize executive power in the mayor. This reform gave the mayor responsibility for the city's finances and disempowered the council, which continued to represent the poor and the neighborhoods. This line of evolution can be seen clearly in Boston, as its financial management evolved from 1885 to 1909. Initially oriented to the control of overspending, the reform as it evolved was more oriented to efficiency, the careful examination of requests coming from the departments, and the control or elimination of requests emanating from the council.

While some reforms traded off democracy for efficiency, others traded representative democracy for direct democracy, including the initiative, referendum, and recall. For budget reformers, direct democracy meant not only referendums on bonds and tax increases but also accurate public accounting and reporting. If public officials did not do their jobs properly, they could be recalled. As part of the budgetary and political process, citizens had to be educated to watch for waste and empowered to act against such waste when they saw it. A set of democratic reforms was embodied in the efficiency movement proposed by the New York Bureau of Municipal Research, beginning around 1907. As reformers pushed for centralized, executive budgeting, reporting and accountability became more important.

Council-manager reforms represented a combination of several different approaches. The council-manager form of government incorporated executive budgeting. A professional manager appointed by the council and responsible to it would draw up the budget based on analysis of departmental requests and present the proposal to the council. Unlike the strong-mayor form that gave mayors veto power over the council, the council retained real budgetary power in the council-manager form, although the council was reduced in size and elected at large. Like the commission form, the council-manager form was intended to introduce businesslike efficiency to city hall and take the politics out of government management. That meant taking the political machine out of local government; it also meant restoring the dominance of business and the propertied classes over spending decisions. Berkeley, California, and Rochester, New York, are illustrations of cities that adopted the council-manager form, with major implications for budgeting.

The cases presented in this chapter were chosen to illustrate particular reforms, to show why they were adopted and what impact they had on budgeting. The cases were also chosen to show continuity between one model and the next in a pattern of learning or dissemination of ideas and adaptation. A third reason for the selection of cases was to show continuity with chapter 2, on tax revolt, and chapters 5 and 6, on budgetary developments after World War II. Houston is included as an illustration of commission government because it was used in chapter 2 to illustrate tax revolt and because it reflected the influence of the National Municipal League in encouraging executive budgeting. Berkeley is included in this chapter because it was the earliest known example of target-based budgeting, which was adopted later in the cases presented in chapters 5 and 6. Rochester was picked as the example of council-manager government because it is also one of the cases presented in chapter 6. Because of the continuity of the examples, the reader should be able to follow general trends and to see how individual cities adapted as the definition of key problems changed over time.

New York City and the Board of Estimate and Apportionment: Making Spending Difficult

The New York City Board of Estimate and Apportionment was created by a charter reform in 1873, on the heels of revelations of the enormity of the graft of "Boss" Tweed's political machine. Tweed's machine had spent generously on city development projects and on corruption. Almost all power over budgeting and finance was transferred to the Board of Estimate and Apportionment. The mayor and the president of the Board of Aldermen were both on this board, but neither one was granted power to dominate the board. The goal was a kind of structural stalemate, to help hold expenditures down.

The Board of Estimate was initially used for quite different purposes than it ended up serving. In 1870, the Tweed Ring was in trouble in New York City, but the Ring took advantage of a rare Democratic majority in the state legislature (reportedly bribing many in the process) to push through some structural changes, including the creation of an executive branch Board of Estimate to control virtually all finances (Durand 1898). Because the members of the new Board of Estimate were Ring members, it was easy for the Ring to spend whatever it chose to spend. The disempowerment of the legislature was intended to facilitate, not end, corruption, and increase, not decrease, spending.

The Tweed Ring was finally brought down, and the city's fiscal condition was made public, including a vast run-up in debt. After the fall of the Tweed Ring, reformers wanted a new charter. Since the city's poor financial condition was a result of unchecked departmental spending, the reformers proposed to reestablish the council's financial powers as a check against the departments. The city council would be reformed in order to provide the proper degree of restraint. Under the reformers' proposed charter, the comptroller and four other commissioners of the treasury were to prepare the budget; the aldermen were to appropriate funds, but could only decrease and not increase the estimates of the finance commission, "a provision apparently copied from European parliamentary customs" (Durand 1898, 157). This reform proposal was vetoed by the governor.

A reform Democratic mayor elected with the support of Republicans made the next set of suggestions. He emphasized the need for more mayoral power (presumably to control the departments) and favored the retention of the Board of Estimate and Apportionment, but with aldermanic substitutes for the heads of the Public Works and Parks departments. Slightly modified, the bill was passed, and it became the basis of budgeting in New York City in 1873. In some form, the Board of Estimate lasted until 1989.

The charter reforms of 1873 did not increase the power of the mayor over the departments, nor did they strengthen the council's power over the budget or the departments.

> It was undoubtedly intended in many respects to be a real reform measure, and was quite generally so considered by the public, but it was after all essentially a jumble. It was a compromise, not between government by the council and government by the mayor—which

indeed are far from being inconsistent with one another—but between the indefensible system of irresponsible executive departments which the Tweed charter had established, and the system of subordination of the departments to the council, proposed by the Seventy [the reformers' group]. (Durand 1898, 163)

Since the council and the mayor remained relatively powerless, the only control over the departments was the Board of Estimate and Apportionment, "that anomalous body which has come to be the main governing power in the metropolis" (Durand 1898, 163).

Because of the large amount of debt and the financial chaos the Tweed Ring had created and the deep recession that began in 1873, the emphasis of the Board of Estimate was on keeping expenditures down. Distrusting lump-sum appropriations, the Board of Estimate required detailed estimates from the departments, listing employees and their salaries and the purpose of each expenditure. The Board of Estimate drew up the budget proposal based on this information and submitted it to the council, which responded with the changes they wanted. The budget went back to the Board of Estimate for final vote. The Board of Estimate could accept or reject the aldermen's requests (Schiesl 1977).

The Board of Aldermen tried to add to the amounts recommended by the Board of Estimate and Apportionment. From 1873 to 1888 they added on average about $500,000 annually. "Responding to consistent pressure for economy in government, particularly from middle-class groups experiencing the brunt of taxation, the Board of Estimate ignored the proposed increases of the council and continued to reduce the level of public expenditures" (Schiesl 1977, 91). Discouraged, the aldermen added less over time.

By 1898 the charter granted the council some formal budget authority, but only to decrease the estimates. There was to be no reconsideration by the Board of Estimate after council action to reduce the proposal submitted by the Board.

The intent of these reforms was to strengthen the ability to reduce the budget, rather than to centralize power and responsibility or spend money more efficiently. Pressure to give additional power to the mayor gradually increased, but it was not until 1893 that a fifth member, the corporation counsel, was included in the Board of Estimate and Apportionment. Since corporation counsel was an appointee of the mayor, the mayor gained majority control of the Board of Estimate. Nevertheless, both the president of the Board of Taxes and Assessments and the corporation counsel had terms that exceeded the mayor's, which made the mayor's power less than absolute. The need for efficiency and accountability encouraged the city to give the mayor more centralized power, but the reformers' fears of a powerful mayor remained. The legacy of the Tweed Ring was a fear of the executive as a potential source of corruption.

Although the creation of the New York Board of Estimate and Apportionment suggests something other than systematic reform, because it was associated with holding down expenditures after the recession of 1873, the budget process of the city appeared attractive to reformers in other cities. But as the desire for more public projects began to vie with the desire to keep costs down, the appeal of a more centralized structure increased. The later, more centralized form of the Board of Estimate, the version that gave some control to the mayor, appealed to reformers in Baltimore.

Baltimore: A Board of Estimate
for Budget Balance and Growth

Baltimore created a Board of Estimate and Apportionment in its 1898 charter reform. Baltimore's Board of Estimate was patterned on New York City's charter of 1893, by which time New York had granted the mayor some control over the Board of Estimate. In Baltimore, the mayor controlled the board from the outset. The Board of Estimate was authorized to draft the annual budget. The powers of the city council to appropriate public money, set the tax rate, and grant public franchises were transferred to the Board of Estimate. The mayor's dominance of the Board of Estimate gave him considerable power over budgeting and finance at the same time that the council was stripped of financial power.

The board was composed of five members: the mayor and two of his appointees (the city solicitor and the comptroller), the president of the upper house of the city council, and the president of the department of public improvements. "The intent of this arrangement was to centralize financial responsibility in the mayor" (Rea 1929, 15). Note the presence on the board of the president of the Board of Public Improvements, a feature of the Tweed Board of Estimate, which was intentionally discarded in New York in 1873 because it seemed inappropriate to have a major spending department judging its own budget.

The inclusion of this position in Baltimore's Board of Estimate probably reflects the desire of the reformers at the turn of the century to improve services and increase project spending, while the focus in New York in the 1870s was on cutting back on projects.

Besides creating the Board of Estimate, Baltimore substantially increased the powers of the mayor in 1898. The term of the mayor was extended from two to four years, and his salary was increased to $6,000. He was given veto power over all ordinances of the city council, which could be overridden only by a vote of three-fourths of all members of each branch (Hollander 1899).

The lower house of the council retained its structure of one member from each of the twenty-four wards in the city; but the size of election districts for the upper chamber was increased so that there were only four councilmanic districts. Councilmen from the upper chamber had their term of office increased from two to four years. The president of the upper chamber was made an independent official with the same requirement for property ownership as the mayor ($2,000). His salary was to be $3,000 per annum, and he was to be elected for a term of four years. The property ownership requirements of the councilmen remained unchanged at $300 for the lower house and $500 for the upper house, but these provisions were made effective by the stipulation that property taxes must have been paid for one and two years, respectively, prior to election.

These changes, when added to the shift of financial and budgetary powers to the Board of Estimate, appear to be a belt-and-suspenders approach to making sure that the propertied and taxpaying classes increased their power at city hall. Both the mayor and the president of the upper house had extensive property ownership requirements for office. The council was basically disempowered from making financial decisions, but even so, the size of election districts for upper house members was increased, making narrow ethnic and neighborhood appeals more difficult and the election of members of minority groups more unlikely. In addition, council members' terms of office were lengthened, which gave them less incentive to immediately respond to neighborhood demands. The property-owning requirement was retained and made more effective for council members of both chambers. All this was in a city that had had political machines but had not suffered any major political or financial scandal.

The reasons for the charter reform in Baltimore that introduced the Board of Estimate and Apportionment were varied. One reason was that reformers opposed machine Democrats. The reformers began with the belief that the machine distorted people's real preferences. The machine could be cut off at the knees if electoral fraud and corruption could be controlled so that the real will of the people could dominate. Charles J. Bonaparte, the leader of the reformers, expressed this idea in a speech:

> If any man helps in, or works at or covers over any kind of cheating at the polls, that man is not a misinformed or misguided fellow citizen to be argued with or shown his error. He is a scoundrel, and he should be called a scoundrel and dealt with as a scoundrel by every honest man. A party which would gain or retain power through election frauds is not a party to which honest men can or will belong. It is not a party at all in any true or worthy sense of the word. It is a conspiracy against the most vital interests and against the most sacred rights of the people. (Crooks 1968, 45)

A number of reforms were passed, including direct primaries, Australian ballots, and laws against corrupt election judges and payments for votes. Underlying this model was a basic belief in democratic reforms and a belief that the citizens should be educated to carry out their responsibilities. The dominant force necessary to achieve good government was an "enlightened and organized public sentiment" (Crooks 1968, 85). Baltimore reformers supported citizen referendums and the right to recall elected officials. They believed that an educated citizenry should be able to control or bypass a potentially corrupt legislative body.

A second reason for the charter changes lay in widespread dissatisfaction with the level of public services. "The general feeling among reformers that city services were inadequate, particularly in the area of education, and that financial arrangements were out of control set the stage for the new charter movement" (Anderson 1977, 24).

Reformers such as Mayor Alcaeus Hooper were concerned about the lack of a city hospital for infectious diseases, the small size of the morgue (it could handle only eight bodies), and the overcrowded jail that mixed juveniles with hardened criminals. Building inspection, testing the water supply, and improved street cleaning were also on the agenda of services needing improvement. "Most of the departments combined inefficiency with politics and got mediocre results" (Crooks 1968, 94).

A third factor contributing to pressure for a new charter was the growth of floating (unfunded) debt. The problem of expanding floating debt resulted in part from the lack of a central agency with the authority and the responsibility for assuring good financial management (Anderson 1977). Council members' reelection depended more on the funds and favors obtained for the ward and for friends than it did on a well-planned budget. Revenues lagged behind population growth. The resulting increase in demand for services with limited revenues made good management more necessary.

While financial irresponsibility may have contributed to the floating debt, state laws controlling the city's indebtedness probably also did their part. The city had run up considerable debt after the Civil War, and poor financial management induced the Maryland constitutional convention of 1867 to restrict local borrowing power radically (Hollander 1899). The city was prohibited from creating any debt or giving or lending its credit for any purpose unless it was authorized by both a special act of the General Assembly and an ordinance of the city council that had been submitted to the legal voters of the city and approved by a majority of the votes cast. Exemptions were granted for temporary loans to meet any deficiency in the city treasury, to maintain the police, safety, and sanitary conditions of the city, and to provide for municipal indebtedness incurred before the adoption of the constitution. Because the restrictions exempted temporary loans to cover deficits, they probably contributed to the growth of unfunded debt.

The constitutional restrictions were not particularly effective, although they seemed draconian. Citizens continued to want and vote for large capital projects to make the city healthier and more livable. Council members responded to those demands, and the state legislature did not intervene.

The initiative with respect to any proposed municipal loan was taken by the City Council and an enabling ordinance passed on the eve of a session of the legislature. The General Assembly ordinarily viewed the proposal as entirely a matter of local concern and yielded to the preference of the city delegation.

To an electorate, of whom considerably less than fifty per cent were taxpayers, municipal borrowing was peculiarly "an agreeable process" and the referendum served as a potential rather than as an actual check. The natural predisposition of the general body of voters to ratify a long term funded loan for costly public improvements, offering large opportunities for local employment and expenditure, was strengthened after 1888 by the use of composite loans, wherein . . . several desirable items were able to carry through one or more unworthy ones. (Hollander 1899, 346)

This quotation suggests that property tax payers were burdened by projects approved by those who did not own property and hence presumably did not pay the property tax.

Besides the constitutional restrictions and the continuing demand for capital projects, a low tax rate contributed to an increase in floating debt. After the Civil War, a low tax rate became a central issue in municipal election campaigns. The tax levy was ordinarily determined less with reference to sound budgetary principles than to its probable effect on the voter. This was especially the case in election years. (This process is reminiscent of similar competition in San Francisco; see chapter 2). A low tax rate in the present with a possible floating debt in the future was more attractive than a higher tax rate and a balanced budget. A similar effect was achieved by overestimating revenues.

The increase in floating debt suggested that council members were too vulnerable to popular pressure and established the need to insulate the council from the public's demands. Demands for reform resurfaced when the city experienced another round of floating debts in 1894 through 1896. The cause was the same as in the 1870s, namely, a reduction in tax rates from $1.80 in 1889 and 1890, to $1.55 in 1891, 1892, and 1893. The mayor suggested tax increases to pay the accumulated unfunded debt, but the council chose to issue a bond. Thus the issue of floating debt was vividly in mind as the city drew up its new charter, and the council's role in choosing debt over a balanced budget was clear. It is not surprising in the light of these events that Baltimore chose to disempower the council in financial decisions, give the mayor more financial responsibility, and strengthen the requirements for budgetary balance.

The new budget process forbade the creation of floating debt. If revenues were insufficient to pay for obligations, then the budget would be cut across the board, except for those areas of spending required by law (Rea 1929). The city council was permitted to reduce any item, unless the amount was fixed by law, but it was forbidden to add new items, increase any item, or transfer funding to a new purpose. The council was required to set a tax rate sufficient to meet the difference between the expenditures provided for in the budget and the revenues from sources other than taxation. The mayor and the city council were both forbidden to reduce the tax rate below that necessary to produce the revenues required by the budget. The new budget process did help balance the budget. The new process also facilitated spending for major projects and helped the city adapt to increasing population while reducing waste and inefficiency.

In short, Baltimore borrowed the idea of a Board of Estimate from New York, but tailored the reform to its own concerns. Baltimore had little experience with outright corruption, especially of bosses who were also mayors, and hence probably was less skeptical of giving the mayor a major financial role to play. Boss Tweed's high spending levels and the recession of 1873 combined to create pressure in New York to hold down spending. Its Board of Estimate held down spending, as expected. By the turn of the century, Baltimore was more concerned with the improvement of mediocre services. Reformers were willing to spend money, but not waste it; they wanted projects that would give them clean water and sanitation, but they also wanted balanced budgets. Baltimore's charter reform of 1898 strengthened the requirement for balance while allowing spending to grow with the population.

The New York Bureau of Municipal Research: More Democracy and More Efficiency

Baltimore represented a mixture of themes on the issue of the relationship between democracy and budgeting. On the one hand, the reformers believed that machines distorted the public's view and that a properly educated public would not allow political machines. Thus they supported election reforms, including direct primaries and honest election judges. On the other hand, reformers were suspicious of the voters, many of whom did not own property (and hence were not believed to pay property taxes) and who therefore voted for public projects because they created employment and because someone else would pay for them. Belief in the vulnerability of the council to public pressure as a cause of financial mismanagement clearly colored the Baltimore reform agenda. That agenda included giving financial power to the mayor and the president of the upper chamber of the council, both positions that had major property-owning requirements for office.

In contrast, the New York Bureau of Municipal Research, and its predecessor, the Association for the Improvement of the Condition of the Poor (AICP), beginning about 1905 or 1906 (the bureau began its budget work in 1906, but the AICP had been engaged in reforms before that), espoused a more clearly democratic viewpoint. They agreed with the Baltimore reformers that machines distorted the public's view; they argued for more public education. The goal was to energize the public in its role as watchdog, to keep government honest. To do that, government had to improve its accounting and reporting mechanisms. This would allow the city to control its own finances because its officials would know its financial situation at all times, and it would allow citizens to know how their money had been spent. The bureau advocated budget hearings at every stage of the budget process so that public officials would know what the public wanted and could build those projects into the budget; officials would also know the citizens' preferences for taxation and hence the limits on spending.

The bureau was even more explicitly in favor of expanded public spending than the Baltimore reformers had been. Bureau staff added to the reform agenda by doing surveys to show the extent of public need for services and tried to get governments to carry the burden. Government, however, was only to undertake those services that it had been able to convince the public were important. Public officials should not tell the public what to do as much as listen to what the public wanted.

Because bureau staffers knew that expanded government would be expensive, they focused intensively on how to spend money more efficiently and, at the same time, democratically. Keep in mind that they were working in a city in which the Board of Estimate had taken virtually all budget power away from the council, had forbidden the council to raise the board's estimates, and had allowed the board to overturn any new items that the council might add. For years, the Board of Estimate functioned to keep spending down, regardless of need. Bureau members felt that the need for services and projects was overwhelming and that government had to be able to deal with these needs in an efficient yet democratic manner.

During the early years of the bureau, all three of the bureau's directors—William Allen, Henry Bruere, and Frederick Cleveland—supported the importance of budget hearings. By 1916, however, Frederick Cleveland had become disillusioned and sought other techniques to achieve accountability. Allen then engaged him in debate. Allen, whose role was as publicist and educator of the public, stated the argument in favor of hearings with passion:

> Frankly, I am among those who believe that the right of the taxpayer to be shown legislative proposals and to be heard regarding them is among the bedrocks of democracy's fundamentals. Taxpayers have a right to stay away from taxpayers' hearings. They have a right to be foolish and unreasonable at hearings. They also have the right to come before city and state and national appropriators of public money, armed with constitutional and statutory rights to be informed and to be heard before their money is spent. . . .

> For the same reason that Governor Hughes when removing Borough President Ahern said that "the majority, no matter how large, has no right to inflict upon the minority, no matter how small," an incompetent government, believers in taxpayers' hearings answer those who consider them unnecessary and fruitless: "The majority, no matter how large, has no right to take from a minority of even one, the right to be told what budget alternatives are and to be heard regarding them before it is too late." (Allen 1917, 488)

Allen went on to argue that even if only a few interested and informed people showed up at a hearing, the evidence provided could influence the outcome. Moreover, the opinions and evidence of the witnesses were often reported in the newspapers and repeated in clubs and people's forums. Thus the small number of participants should not be used as evidence of failure of the hearings.

A belief that the solution to inefficient or machine government was more democracy, rather than less, required a set of techniques to involve and educate the public. Budgeting had to be made interesting. Here again, the New York Bureau made a major contribution. To get publicity for the budget, and to get the public involved in issues of waste and mismanagement, the bureau set up a huge, fairlike display, with charts and graphs showing items that had been overcharged in the budget. The items, the price charged in the budget, and the price at the local hardware store were all displayed. Evidence of padded payrolls, unnecessary supplies, and misdirected appropriations were included (Allen 1908). The aims of the budget exhibit were to get the public to see and talk about the exhibits and to force the city to face the issues once the public knew about them. The budget exhibit combined public education and improved financial control. New York City adopted the budget exhibit as a publicity device, but it never became a permanent part of the budget process.

The idea that the public could be educated, that it was the responsibility of research bureaus and city governments to do so, and that the public's involvement was both a basic democratic right and a solution to fiscal mismanagement and political corruption, did not take deep root. Other, less directly democratic alternatives became more prevalent, such as increasing the budget power of the mayor.

Boston: The Evolution
of the Executive Budget

Boston was in some ways like Baltimore in that government was not corrupt, only inefficient, and hence expensive. With no history of a major political machine, Boston reformers had no particular reason to fear strengthening the mayor. Reformers in Boston (as in Baltimore) were often themselves mayors or former mayors. Understandably, they argued repeatedly for more authority for the mayor.

Boston entered the Progressive era early, expanding the number of projects and increasing spending before many other cities began to do so. But a lack of expertise resulted in inefficiency, which pushed up spending even higher. Boston found that its expenditures per capita were the highest in the country. In an effort to produce public projects more efficiently, beginning in 1885 and culminating in the charter reforms of 1909, Boston gave more and more budgeting and financial control to the mayor.

Boston's reforms, however, reflected not only the need for capacity and efficiency, but also the desires of the propertied class to take disproportionate control over taxing and spending decisions. One of Boston's key reformers, former mayor Nathan Matthews Jr., was wonderfully frank on the subject.

Matthews was a reform mayor in the 1890s. He later headed the commission that created charter reform in 1907 (effective in 1909), which finished concentrating power in the hands of the mayor by giving him the responsibility for budgeting. In his valedictory speech in 1895 summarizing his experiences as mayor, Matthews argued that the high costs of government in Boston made executive control through charter reform necessary. But he maintained that it was not simply the need for increased efficiency that justified increasing the power of the mayor and disempowering the council; politics was also involved. City councils could and did make complex decisions in Europe, but not in the United States. The reason was that the United States was more democratic, and the franchise was more widely distributed. There were more nonlandholders in the council, and collectively, council members held less of the city's wealth (Matthews 1895).

Matthews argued that in the United States more people would be comfortable with a government dominated by landowners who had a known interest in keeping tax rates down. One way of achieving more efficient and less expensive government would be to reverse or shrink the franchise so that only those with property could vote or run for office, but Matthews felt such a solution was both undemocratic and politically impractical. He wanted to achieve a similar goal without damaging democratic institutions. To do that, he felt that empowering the mayor (and disempowering the council) was the best idea.

Matthews argued that giving financial power to the mayor, rather than to council committees, was actually more democratic. The committees of the council, he argued, did not represent faithfully the desires of the citizens as a whole. Councils represent local and special interests, while mayors, who are elected at large, can represent the broader community. The mayor is nearest and most responsible to the people. "The mayor, unlike the members of the City Council, cannot shield himself behind a committee report or majority vote; he is less open to influence by the organized private and special interests of the city, because he is elected by the people as a whole and must account to them; and his control makes the government more truly democratic by bringing it closer to the people, and by making it more responsive to the popular will" (Matthews 1895, 172). This idea, that the mayor was more invulnerable to special interests, was a bit fanciful, as Boston found out when a nonreform candidate won the election after the executive budget reforms were implemented in 1909.

Matthews assumed that if the mayor was empowered and the council disempowered, the large property owners would be in control, and their interests were synonymous with those of the public in general. The real danger, as Matthews saw it, was

> the demand of individuals, interests, classes, sections, and sometimes of the whole community, for extravagant expenditure; and this difficulty is constantly increasing as the belief gains ground that the

community in its corporate capacity owes a liberal living to its individual members. A gradual change has come over the spirit of the people; and a large part of a population once the most independent and self reliant in the world is now clamoring for support, as individuals or in classes, from the governments of this country—federal, state and city. These symptoms ... constitute the chief danger of popular government, and a danger that will be greater before it is less; the demand for a systematic distribution of wealth by taxes. (Matthews 1895, 175)

In line with these beliefs, Matthews opposed any expansion of the franchise and opposed direct democracy expressed through referendums and recall. He did not want the members of the public to be in a position to vote themselves what they wanted at the expense of the wealthy.

Matthews described the decline in influence of wealthy property owners on the Boston City Council. The Board of Aldermen increased from eight to twelve from 1822 to 1895, and the common council increased from forty-eight to seventy-five. The proportion of aldermen owning property dropped over the same period from 100 percent to 75 percent, and from 93 percent to 21 percent for the common council: "... during the first fifty years of our municipal history from 85–90 percent of the representatives elected by the people to the city council were themselves owners of property, [but] the proportion today has fallen to less than 30 percent" (Matthews 1895, 171). He admitted that wealthy property owners were represented in proportion to their role in the population (they were only about 20 percent of the registered voters) but argued that proportional representation was not enough because with proportional representation the council was still too sensitive to public demands for projects and the demands of land speculators for city improvements.

While Matthews explained the emerging strong mayor and executive budgeting reforms in terms of politics and the propertied classes' fears of confiscatory taxes, he also made clear that part of the pressure for change was the inadequacy of the charters the city had been living under. Financial control was too widely diffused and the mayor had too little power.

The 1854 charter gave the mayor a qualified veto over the action of the city council. This veto power did not include the right to disapprove separate items in an appropriation order or a loan bill. Bigger changes occurred in 1885, when a few amendments transferred all the executive powers formerly exercised by the mayor and council to the mayor exclusively, to be exercised through the officers and boards of the city, under the mayor's supervision. These powers were defined as supervising contracts; purchasing material; hiring labor; constructing, repairing, and managing public works, buildings, institutions, and other city property; and directing and controlling the administrative business of the city.

With respect to financial and budgetary controls, the amendments required the mayor's approval on all contracts over $2,000 and prohibited the departments from overspending their appropriations. They gave the mayor the right to veto every order passed by either branch of the council and to disapprove separate items in loan bills and appropriation orders, subject to a possible override by a two-thirds vote.

The 1885 charter also provided that heads of departments and all other officers and boards having authority to spend money had to submit annual estimates of their requirements to the mayor. The mayor was to examine those estimates and submit them with his recommendations to the city council. The council had to approve or disapprove the budget (Boston Municipal Research Bureau 1939).

Other legislation in 1885 limited the rate of taxation for municipal purposes and the amount of debt. Civil service rules also went into effect that year (Matthews 1895). The goal was to keep expenditures down through the elimination of patronage hiring, control of contract awards, and scrutiny of departmental requests. The city would then be able to afford important and necessary expenditures.

The tax limit held down taxes for a while, but after 1895 expenditures began to grow rapidly. From 1885 to 1895, spending rose only a little faster than population, 30 percent compared to 27 percent; but from 1895 to 1905, it rose twice as fast, 55 percent compared to 22 percent. "There seemed no easy way to stop the acceleration" (Burns 1984, 136). Municipal debt also increased rapidly, more than doubling from 1894 to 1907. Per capita debt rose from about $63 to about $110. One-quarter of the tax levy in 1907 was taken for interest and sinking fund requirements (Van De Woestyne 1935, 120–21).

The legitimate needs of the city were expanding, but observers charged that the increase also resulted from extravagance and waste. Reportedly, patronage hiring was common and money was spent in response to demands of constituents more than for the needs of the city as a whole (Van De Woestyne 1935). Part of the city's financial problems stemmed from overly tight controls since 1885. Boston was subject to both a tax limit and a debt limit during these years. In the face of so many demands, staying within these limits proved impossible. Borrowing outside the debt limit, under special authority of the legislature, became common.

The reformers focused on their role as outsiders, looking for evidence of corruption (Burns 1984). A group of Progressive activists from the city's business community formed the Good Government Association (GGA). They imitated colleagues in other cities where real corruption had been revealed, but they could find little, and their campaign failed. A number of businesses dropped out of the GGA, leaving in the association a small, specialized group of businessmen, the downtown landowners and their lawyers, and bankers, who defined reform narrowly as reduced taxation.

These reformers proposed a new charter to remove local influence and partisan politics from city government. "The new politics would be dominated by a powerful mayor, checked only by a weak council and a permanent Finance Commission" (Burns 1984, 151). The council would be small, and elected at large. "The mayor would have near-absolute power over the budget and over appointments" (Burns 1984, 151). Locked out of party politics by the narrowness of their support base, the reformers sought to reduce the power of parties in government and to institutionalize their role as finance commission watchdogs. They also sought to reduce or eliminate the power of local neighborhoods and ethnic groups through elections at large.

The reformers were willing to have the Republican legislature pass their proposed charter binding the Democratic city, without the city's consent. The key parts, the mayor's control over the budget and a new Finance Committee, never went to election, but were mandated by the state. Boston still has a mandatory Finance Commission. Changes in the composition of the council did go to referendum and won narrowly.

The 1909 charter added to and clarified the mayor's budget powers (Boston Municipal Research Bureau 1939). Among other provisions strengthening the mayor's hand was the budget section stating that all operating budget requests were to originate with the mayor, that the council could reduce or delete but not increase mayoral recommendations or add new items, and that the mayor's veto of council action in fiscal matters was to be final. Either the council or the mayor could propose borrowing, but the mayor could veto a council request for borrowing in whole or in part, and could also reduce any item proposed for borrowing (Van De Woestyne 1935). Thus the council, which had had the power of final approval of the budget under the 1885 charter, was disempowered in 1909; it could do little other than reduce the mayor's requests and propose loans, and if the mayor vetoed the council's changes, the mayor's action was final.

Although the 1885 amendments tried to separate the executive and legislative functions and keep the legislature out of financial and employment decisions, it did not provide any penalties if the council did interfere with executive branch activities. The council continued to get involved in the employment of city labor, awarding of contracts, purchasing, and public works. In the 1909 charter, a penalty was imposed for council interference with executive business (Koren 1923). The mayor was given absolute veto power over all acts of the city council, extending to any item in a bill requiring the expenditure of money and to any part of such an item. The mayor's term of office was extended from two to four years, and the council was reorganized. The two-house structure of the council was eliminated. A new council was created with nine members, each elected at large for a term of three years, only three being elected each year. A permanent finance committee was written into the charter, its members to be selected by the governor, with the idea that a body independent of the municipal government would be able to serve as a check on waste and corruption.

The reformers assumed that whoever became mayor would have reform leanings, but there was little reason why this should be the case. During the campaign for the charter, machine supporters endorsed the change because the new power of the mayor would help any mayor, reformer or not. The reform candidate for the 1910 election, the crucial one to implement the new charter, failed in his election bid.

The reformers in Boston were unable to make much of a case for public support. They mostly imagined corruption, and their failure to demonstrate their claims weakened their case. The narrowness of their concern to keep the tax rate down, in the face of overwhelming demand for services, cut off their support. Their willingness to use the state to force the city to their will without popular approval further narrowed their base of support. In other cities during this time period, reformers often framed a much broader list of goals that included not only municipal improvements but also services that would help the poor as well as those that would help the rich. Boston reformers did not do this and, as a result, though they won the charter reform and strong mayoral powers, they lost control of the mayoralty to popularly elected machine politicians.

Mayor Matthews of Boston had argued in his valedictory speech in 1895 that a city was not a business and should not be run like a business; it was political. Because it was political and because its purpose was not to make a profit, it should be governed by a political form that gave major power to a strong mayor. Matthews was arguing against a strong current among reformers who insisted that cities should be run like businesses. Those who sought to eliminate party and machine politics and run government like a business often preferred the commission form of government. Rather than the Boston approach, which worked on separating politics and administration and putting administration under the supervision of the mayor, the commission form blurred the distinction between legislative and administrative. The commissioners were in charge of a department and served as legislators. Houston created an unusual combination of the strong-mayor and the commission form.

Houston: The Commission Form of Government Combined with the Strong Mayor and Executive Budget

Houston was the first city to adopt the commission form of government in the absence of a major disaster, such as a flood or hurricane. The adoption of the commission form in 1905 was part of an effort to restore the dominance of the business-commercial elite and to restore the city's emphasis on growth and services to and for the elites. The business elite took over in 1902 from Samuel Brashear, who had emphasized the needs of neighborhoods, supported labor, opposed the utilities, favored municipal ownership, and reflected a general sense of social justice. The business elite, in contrast, opposed labor, wanted reconciliation with the utilities, and wanted to limit spending to projects from which they would benefit directly, especially the improvement of roads. They did not want to pay for routine services to be spread to every neighborhood in the city (Platt 1983).

Houston reformers followed a strategy of limiting the franchise.

On top of that, business leaders created the commission form with its small council elected at-large. They added to the commission form the strong mayor that Boston had developed and that had been endorsed by the National Municipal League in 1898.

The Brashear administration spread services widely throughout the city, but it had not been able to control the costs of service expansion. Under Brashear, the bureaucracy seemed to become an engine for further service growth. After 1902, when the business elite replaced Brashear in power, one of the first steps of the new administration was to try to rein in the bureaucracy by imposing centralized fiscal controls. The new mayor, Oran T. Holt, hired the accounting firm of Haskins and Sells to help set up such a system. This was the nationally famous accounting firm that helped set up Chicago's accounting system at about the same time; it was also the accounting firm that Frederick Cleveland, who was later to be a director of the New York Bureau of Municipal Research, worked for. In short, the new administration brought in major outside professional help.

Despite the financial reforms and despite some charter reforms in 1903 aimed at curtailing neighborhood influence, ward politics "continued to subvert efficient public administration" (Platt 1983, 192). The reformers had made efforts beginning in 1898 to disenfranchise black people. The Democrats had prohibited black participation in primaries. Well-organized groups continued to agitate for maintaining neighborhood services, so the businessmen reformers who wanted metropolitan growth at the expense of neighborhood services excluded blacks from city services. "Throughout the New South, the disfranchisement of blacks went hand-in-hand with the enactment of Jim Crow laws excluding this group from the benefits of public services" (Platt 1983, 182). In 1903 a state poll tax drastically reduced the number of poor who could register to vote.

When excluding blacks and the poor failed to produce a balanced budget, the growth-oriented business elites turned to charter reform as a solution. They endorsed and forced through a commission charter, then added a strong mayor to the commission form of government. The new form provided for a board (or commission) with five full-time aldermen, elected at large, and four departments. The aldermen served as council and as departmental managers. The mayor chose which aldermen to assign to manage which departments (Clute 1920).

Houston's budget process was unusual among commission governments because the city combined the executive budget with the commission form. Estimates from departments, which were basically previous years' actuals, were submitted to the mayor, who could add to them or deduct from them as he chose. The mayor's proposals would then be submitted to the commission for approval; if the commission did something the mayor did not like with his budget proposal, he could veto their action. The mayor was so much in charge of the budget process that the commissioners did not scrutinize the budget requests, merely discussed them with the mayor (Bruere 1912).

Mayor H. Baldwin Rice, who was a successful businessman and part of the businessmen's movement to introduce the commission/strong-mayor form, delivered a speech in 1910 before the Chicago Commercial Club (Carroll 1912) summarizing the form and its accomplishments.

He included under the benefits of the new system a better quality of elected official. "Under the old system of government, by which twelve aldermen were elected from as many different precincts of the city, it frequently happened that unfit men came to represent certain wards in the city council. Now, [because of the at-large elections] unless a man has sufficient standing and reputation throughout the body of the city as a fit man for the office of alderman, he will not be elected" (Carroll 1912, 99).

Rice also argued that the new system eliminated the logrolling that characterized the larger, district-based council. "Under the old system," he argued, "the conduct of public business was continually obstructed by a system of petty logrolling going on among and between the representatives of the numerous subdivisions of the city" (Carroll 1912, 99).

Another benefit Rice listed was the ease and speed of coming to decisions with a small group of aldermen. He argued that with executive sessions before the council meeting and the small number of aldermen, it was possible to administer the affairs of the city in a prompt and businesslike way.

It is interesting to see what aspects of the old system aggravated the mayor, and what he meant by businesslike government, since Rice felt that its businesslike nature was one of the strongest arguments in the favor of the commission form.

> With a majority of the aldermen always in session, public business can be, and is, promptly attended to. It is no longer necessary to go before the city council with petitions to have something done. Any

citizen who desires to have a street paved, taxes adjusted, a nuisance abated, or anything else, has only to call at the mayor's office and have the matter promptly adjusted.

After a hearing, the matter is decided by the council in the presence of the applicant. To illustrate the great difference between this method and the old one the following comparison is made. By the old method a petition was addressed to the council. This was referred to a committee, which acted when convenient. Then a report to the council was made by the committee. After the action of the council it went to the mayor and from him to someone else for execution. The people do not pay their taxes for such treatment. They want their business attended to promptly and that is what is being done under the commission. (Carroll 1912, 99)

Rice asserted that the power conferred on the mayor was one of the most striking features of the new charter and one of the most sharply criticized, but he maintained that it had turned out to be one of the best features of the charter (Carroll 1912, 100).

The mayor had the power to hire and fire department heads and control the other commissioners. Rice declared, "The mayor is practically an autocrat. The commissioners are largely secretaries in charge of their functions. In one case a commissioner who displeased the mayor was deprived of all participation in the city government during the remainder of his term." Rice also observed with satisfaction that "not a speech has ever been made in the city council under the commission form of government" (Carroll 1912, 105).

Because the mayor could fire staff, he could bring some discipline to city departments. As a result,

the city attorney does not refuse to collect taxes and say to the city government that he was elected by the people and is responsible to them; and that he does not favor collecting taxes. Because of it, the chief of police does not refuse to enforce the criminal ordinances of the city and give the same excuse for declining to do so. Because of it, the tax collector can not arbitrarily select what persons he is to exempt from the payment of taxes, and inform the government that the people elected him and that he is responsible to the people. The mayor under the charter is the responsible head of the government. If things are permitted to go wrong, it is his fault, and if any officer of the city refuses to enforce the law, the mayor can remove him in five minutes time. Of course it is necessary for the people to select a man of good sense and character to be mayor, but when they have done so, they will know that he will not be, as under the old system, a dummy and figure head and a helpless spectator to wanton disregard of law and mal-administration. This so-called, "one-man" feature of the commission embodies its whole aim and intention—a responsible head to the city government, chosen by the people themselves. (Carroll 1912, 100–101)

Rice's emphasis on the democratic element of the election seems a bit exaggerated, given the city's history of disfranchisement of blacks, its laws denying blacks municipal services, and the state's disfranchisement of the poor through the poll tax. "The people" who were to choose the mayor were to be white middle- and upper-class residents. Nevertheless, his speech captures the advantages of the commission/strong-mayor system for its advocates.

From the businessmen-reformers' perspective, the commission/strong-mayor system was successful over the next few years. The city government contributed to the weakening of organized labor as an interest group in the city, helped reduce utility prices, and improved the city's finances. The price of gas, which was in private hands, was brought down from $1.50 to $1.00 per gallon; the cost of electric light was reduced; and the city cut water rates from 50 cents for 1,000 gallons to 15 cents. Some offices were eliminated, while others were consolidated. Suits were filed against delinquent taxpayers, resulting in the collection of almost $100,000 in eight months. Over the next few years, the floating debt of $400,000 was wiped out, and a number of improvements made, including an auditorium, water mains, and school buildings. These projects totaled $1.8 million paid out of current revenues. The tax rate was reduced 30 cents to $1.70 per $100 assessed.

What made the Houston form work, however, was not the commission form so much as the strong-mayor form with which it was linked. Without the addition of a strong central administrator, the commission system worked poorly. The council-manager form, however, corrected these weaknesses but retained for the council much more authority than under the strong-mayor system. As in the commission form, the council was to be small and elected at large to reduce the influence of the neighborhoods and political machines.

The next two cases, Berkeley, California, and Rochester, New York, reflect the transition to council-manager government and the accompanying changes in financial and budgeting practices. Like the commission form, council-manager governments were intended to be run like businesses. A professional city manager would be responsible for the business of the city. This new manager would be accountable to the council, who could fire the manager at will if council policies were not being carried out. Council-manager governments were activist in intent, but in practice they tried to hold down tax increases by increasing efficiency. Council-manager government was more centralized than the commission form, providing more accountability and more financial control over the departments.

Berkeley, California: The Transition from Commission Government to Council-Manager Government

Berkeley adopted the commission form of government in 1909, modeled after the commission form adopted in Des Moines, Iowa. The Des Moines plan was a compromise between the Galveston commission form and the Houston form. That is, it used the whole commission to run the city, not the mayor alone, as in Galveston, but, as in Houston, the commission members were actual heads of departments, not merely policy setters (see Clute 1920, 1:180).

Weaknesses in the form gradually became apparent: the lack of a unified executive authority and a legislative body entrusted with administrative functions. None of the elected officials worked full-time. "During the years immediately preceding the adoption of the manager plan, there was also considerable dissatisfaction with the financial condition of the city, since the fiscal years ending June 30, 1922, and June 30, 1923, showed real deficits" (Rocca 1935, 8).

Those who favored the manager plan argued that it would provide more unification in government and would establish sound financial procedure, especially a rigid budget system. The governmental form would operate economically, making tax increases unnecessary. The skeleton of the new budget system, reacting against the failures of the commission form, required that "the expenses of each department will be determined in advance and limited by the passage and publication of an ordinance" (Rocca 1935, 10). A proposal to adopt the council-manager plan was approved by the voters in 1923, by 5,226 votes to 3,076.

The budget system promised in the charter amendment campaign was actually implemented. Under the new process, the heads of departments were required to send to the city manager careful, written estimates of their departmental needs for the ensuing fiscal year. The manager then submitted a tentative budget to the council containing an estimate of probable expenditures for the following year, the amount necessary for each fund and department, and an estimate of the amounts and sources of city income. The council, after considering the tentative budget, made a final budget and passed the annual appropriation ordinance.

A key element in this procedure was that the manager controlled the process of departmental estimates. The manager insisted that department chiefs "distinguish between wants and needs." The manager accompanied his request for estimates with a statement of what he regarded as the tentative minimum allotment for the department, that is, his estimate of what they needed. In more prosperous times, department heads were asked to list on a separate sheet and in order of importance those items that they regarded as desirable but not absolutely essential, that is, their wants. The practice of listing wanted items was discontinued when the Great Depression caused such strain in resources that additions above the absolute minimum were not possible. The manager also sent a budget bulletin to all department heads, giving pertinent advice for making budget requests.

The manager and the budget officer spent a large amount of time each year working over the departmental estimates, revising them, and preparing the tentative budget. Department requests were not approved as submitted, although the manager kept pretty close to their requests. For example, the original departmental budget requests for the year 1934–35 amounted to $1,022,065.87, but the adopted budget allowed only $990,797.24 in expenditures.

Once the budget was presented to the council, it was discussed in a committee of the whole. Only a few major items were thoroughly investigated. The tentative budget submitted by the manager was accepted by the council with only slight modifications. The council then held a public hearing on the budget, although few citizens attended.

After the appropriation was passed by the council, each department head was asked to divide his appropriations into monthly allotments, showing objects of expenditures and totals. The monthly sums were intended to reflect the flow of work and were not required to be equal from month to month. The budget officer planned the cash flow accordingly. Department heads learned to keep their monthly requests within their totals for the month because they had to make up any overdraws later (Jamison 1928).

The system of financial control was devised to hold departments to their appropriations but at the same time to be flexible enough to meet unforeseen circumstances. The allotment system linked a work plan for the year with the cash budget. More construction in warmer months could be offset by less construction in colder months. The manager maintained an emergency fund for the departments and could make transfers between line items if they had been misestimated. The budget office monitored revenues on a monthly basis so that cuts in spending could occur in a timely way if revenues did not materialize as predicted. During the first five years of the council-manager government, the city ran cash surpluses ranging from $20,000 to $106,000, of which the budget director was clearly proud.

The city had been experiencing financial difficulties before the adoption of the council-manager government, caused by a 1 percent tax limit as well as salary and pension fund increases for police and firefighters. Salary increases occurred across many cities at this time because of rapid post–World War I inflation. Berkeley had outstanding debts for water supplies but had drawn down its required cash reserves and was unable to replenish them without creating deficits. Because tax increases were ruled out, improving the quality of financial management seemed the only alternative for the city (Rocca 1935). The city manager did not consider the option of cutting back services; instead, he argued that the city should not build up large surpluses but should use them for the expansion of services and capital projects.

The financial condition of the city improved during the first few years of the city manager system. The city adopted an economical budget, and stuck to it, without hampering or cutting essential municipal services. Service was extended in street maintenance, sanitation, and health. Taxes were not increased and, during the depression years, actually decreased.

The Berkeley case was one in which leading citizens wanted to maintain services levels and balance the budget without raising taxes. Post–World War I inflation helped push up costs, and tax limits constrained revenues, which helped create deficits. The inefficiency of the commission form was blamed in part, so the option that seemed best was to centralize the government, separate executive and legislative responsibilities, and require improved financial management. Berkeley was not reacting to a machine government or to overspending by a publicly elected district-based council, only to the need for improved financial management. Under its first city manager, Berkeley was one of the first to work out efficient and flexible budgetary controls over the departments, including what is now called target-based budgeting. The focus was not opposition to the council so much as control of the departmental requests.

Rochester, New York: From Board of Estimate to City Manager

In the late 1800s, city government in Rochester was characterized by increasing use of citizen commissions and ex-officio boards to administer particular governmental functions. These boards and commissions reflected general mistrust of public officials and a feeling that government should be slowed down, if not rendered incapable of action. Practically all the city's functions were entrusted to some variety of plural body (Mosher 1940). This widespread use of boards limited the power of both the mayor and the council. The large number of independently elected officials encouraged jealousy between officials, contributed to duplication of effort, and sometimes led to open conflict.

The charter was gradually amended to strengthen the mayor and weaken the council. Suspicion of the legislative body, combined with increasing demands for administrative services, led to amendments that gradually transformed a legislative government into a strong-mayor structure. The trend toward a strong mayor was climaxed and that toward boards and commissions was abruptly checked by state law in 1900. This law, applying to all second-class cities in the state, established a strong executive for the first time. Most of the boards and commissions were replaced by departments with one administrative head responsible to the mayor. Only two important ex officio boards remained, one on purchasing and one on budgeting, and these were controlled by the mayor and his appointees.

One of the two remaining boards was the Board of Estimate and Apportionment. Through its control of the budget, the Board of Estimate was the most powerful executive agency in finance. In line with earlier efforts to disempower the city council, the council was allowed to reduce the Board of Estimate's budget proposals; it had no power to increase them. Since the Board of Estimate was dominated by the mayor and his appointees, a degree of central control and coordination was assured, but there were still many opportunities for conflict, duplication of work, and accumulation of red tape in the operations of the various agencies. Both the comptroller and the treasurer had to keep accounts for all departments, the purchasing procedure was complicated, and control over expenditures was scattered and ineffective. During 1926 and 1927, the mayor and the comptroller, representing different political factions, did not communicate with each other often, and when they did, they frequently clashed.

The increased centralization in the hands of the mayor was intended to create accountability and control spending, but it did not prevent the city from being controlled by a political machine. For about twenty-five years, until his death in 1922, Republican "Boss" Aldridge managed the city. His administration was not flagrantly corrupt. He backed able administrators, and he vied with reformers to spend money to educate the new immigrants to the city (McKelvey 1973). He did not support council-manager government, however, so it was not until after his death that proponents of the form were successful.

Two key elements in the introduction of the council-manager form in Rochester were the creation of the Rochester Bureau of Municipal Research by wealthy industrialist George Eastman and financial problems that resulted from increased spending.

The Rochester Bureau of Municipal Research was set up in 1915 and was financed by Eastman until his death in 1932. Eastman appointed ten prominent men interested in civic affairs to form the board of trustees. The Rochester Bureau was an offspring of the New York Bureau and inherited its ideals, purposes, and methods. Eastman knew Frederick Cleveland, then director of the New York group. The first director of the Rochester Bureau came from the New York Bureau. The Rochester Bureau was a source of factual information and was especially important in bringing the council-manager form to Rochester (Mosher 1940).

The staff of the bureau assembled data to help promote efficiency. They did one study to improve city contracting procedures and another to help the city improve garbage pickup. They made suggestions for repairing streets and plowing snow. The bureau attributed the financial problems of the city to expanded functions, rather than corruption, adding pressure to look for a more efficient form of government (McKelvey 1973).

The bureau operated in a low-key and nonmilitant manner, offering both sides of issues, generally working through those in power. Its success depended on the cooperation of city hall. Sometimes that cooperation was not forthcoming, which also encouraged efforts to change the form of government (Mosher 1940).

The Rochester Bureau of Municipal Research did a study of twenty-four cities with a variety of forms of government and recommended the council-manager form because it offered greater efficiency. The Bureau got support from Eastman for this recommendation. Eastman's support was critical, because he commanded enormous respect among Rochester's business and social circles.

Supporters of the council-manager plan criticized the budget procedure and the ongoing borrowing to cover deficits. A manager would lower the cost of government and drive out the spoils-oriented politicians. Supporters argued that the council-manager form operated like a corporation and that Rochester needed professional administration.

The city's finances directly contributed to the pressure to adopt the council-manager form. City expenses exceeded the state's constitutional 2 percent tax limit, forcing the city to borrow short term to finance current operations. The short-term borrowing was then rolled over into long-term debt, the repayment of which was exempt from the 2 percent limit. Borrowing to cover annual deficits increased each year until it reached a peak in 1927 of almost $3 million a year, more than one-quarter of the city's operating budget. "The Republican administrations were budgeting only the amounts they were expecting from current taxes and then, when funds ran low, borrowing whatever more they needed to complete the year" (Mosher 1940, 33). Backers of the manager plan confidently expected that the plan itself would almost automatically reduce costs of government and eliminate this borrowing.

The source of Rochester's fiscal problems is important in judging the appropriateness of the council-manager form as a solution. When mismanagement, departmental overspending, or council addbacks are the problem, the reorganization of the form of government may well resolve the problems. When the financial problems are caused by population growth, postwar inflation, and state-mandated taxing limits, it is more difficult to see how the manager system can resolve the difficulties. Improved financial management can save only so much money if poor management is not the initial problem.

Expenditures had increased 242 percent between 1910 and 1922.

This increase reflected added functions, expanded functions, and the post–World War I inflation. Much of the cost increase resulted from the schools, which were the financial responsibility of the city, but which were not under its financial and administrative control (Rochester Bureau 1923). The Rochester Bureau of Municipal Research argued that wartime inflation hit expenditures hard in Rochester, but also argued that the scope of government was increasing. Efficiency would not solve the problem, the bureau predicted, because it would lower unit costs but not total costs. So the issue was how to finance the increased scope, especially in the light of revenue limitations imposed by state law.

The addition of new services, while real, was a relatively minor contributor to the increase in expenditures. Most of the new services were only modestly funded and some appeared in the budget for only a few years. Rochester made a small contribution to the Society for the Prevention of Cruelty to Children of $720 every year from 1910 to 1922; the city had a Bureau of Health, which included a hospital, but it was never a big budget item; the city had a milk investigation program in 1917, 1918, and 1919, and the costs peaked at about $16,000. The city funded an art commission beginning in 1915, but with few dollars. A Bureau of Fire and Police Telegraph was added in 1916; a public library, which later included a Bureau of History, was budgeted for $9,399; a municipal museum, begun in 1916, was also funded very modestly. The city also maintained a Department of Charities, a GAR relief commission, a city garage, a bureau of weights and measures, a public market, a city engineer's office, and a bureau of planning. Most of these functions, too, were only moderately funded. General debt service, education, and education debt service were the big items. Their rapid expansion accounted for much of the increase (from Rochester budgets, various years).

From 1910 to 1922, while expenditures increased rapidly, assessed valuation grew much more slowly. The tax rate had to increase. The state limited cities over 100,000 population to 2 percent of the assessed valuation, excluding taxation for debt service. The city reached very close to its legal limit by 1923. Rochester tried to get around the rules by defining spending as not for city purposes, but was defeated by the courts (Rochester Bureau 1923, 43). Thereafter the city went beyond the limit by borrowing for current needs. Total bonded indebtedness in 1922 was $35.7 million, with an additional $5.9 million in temporary notes.

The new council-manager system was intended to allow major city projects by providing more efficient and businesslike government. The first manager, Steve Story, was inaugurated in 1928. He laid out an ambitious plan with fifteen objectives, including capital projects for the city's utilities, elimination of current expense borrowing and deficits in sinking funds, adjustment of the pension funds, classification of positions and standardization of salaries, and installation of a scientific property tax assessment system (Mosher 1940). Story proposed the enlargement and improvement of the municipal airport and the lake port; the construction of a port terminal, a civic center, and a new water supply system; and many street and bridge improvements. The capital improvements proposed and undertaken by Story illustrate that Rochester was still in an expansionist, "Greater Rochester" mode.

The financial system was reorganized in accordance with a plan previously prepared by the Bureau of Municipal Research. A central purchasing system was established, and a municipal warehouse was put in place. Services were improved: the police department was modernized, and a training school was added. The fire prevention division was reorganized. But Story was unable to eliminate current expense borrowing because of the 2 percent tax limit that remained in place. A full modernization of the assessment practices might have captured inflation increases in assessed valuation and solved the problem, but Story was unable to implement this reform because of fear of public reaction to increased assessments.

In addition to the increased capital projects, Story started an unemployment work relief project in 1931, financed by the city. The city's expenditures increased greatly during the early years of the Great Depression as a result of the unemployment burden and the ambitious capital improvement program. The year 1931 was the most expensive in the city's history up to that time. This embarrassed the administration's supporters because they had promised economy. Republicans could point to a greatly increased debt, a failure to balance the budget, and an increased total tax payment, telling arguments during the depression. The Republicans won the election, and Story was out. A former city engineer under the old Republican administration was chosen to be the manager, under the assumption that the mayor would manage the city and the manager would be office boy (Mosher 1940.)

The new council repealed the nonpartisan provision in the charter and the features that prohibited political activity and the collection or contribution of funds for political purposes by city employees. The administrative branch of the government returned to partisan practices. While department heads changed, bureau heads were protected by the state civil service. To make the bureau heads more subject to party control, the charter was modified to change the bureaus into divisions. The former bureau heads, now division heads, could be removed without a hearing. The machine's power was complete, and its methods were the same as those before 1925. The group supporting the council-manager form saw much of its earlier work destroyed.

Financial problems endured as the depression continued. The city had to make drastic cuts to pay the bills. Capital improvements were abandoned, and employees were asked to accept salary reductions. The offices of personnel director and director of police were abolished. The Parks Department was cut about 22 percent, the library about 30 percent, and the museum about 70 percent. In 1932 the administration appointed a Financial Advisory Board to help restore the city's finances. This board, composed of all business and professional men, recommended sharp cuts in costs, especially welfare payments. The mayor and council ignored the recommendations.

At this point, the banking and business community demanded a change. As in many other cities during the Great Depression, the bankers controlled the flow of credit to the city and so had irresistible control over the city's policies on spending and borrowing. The business community demanded a city manager and a mayor of their own selection and insisted on a continuing voice in the financial affairs of the city. The business community put together an advisory staff, picked a businessman with little government experience to be manager, and approached the city's problems as if they were business problems. This administration was in office only a few months, during which time it restored the city's financial solvency. Costs were held down, and many of the services that had been cut back were restored.

Under the council-manager system in Rochester, financial management and control was improved and the executive budget process was streamlined and made workable. Before the adoption of the council-manager form in 1928, the mayor controlled general policies, purchasing, and salary rates through the Board of Estimate and the Board of Contract. The Board of Estimate was responsible for the revision and presentation of the budget to the council, the establishment of salary rates, and supplementary appropriations; the Board of Contract and Supply was responsible for city contracts and purchasing. After 1928 all financial management functions were performed in the Department of Finance, under the comptroller, an appointee of the manager.

Under the council-manager system, the city manager was responsible for the revision of budget estimates, the submission of the budget to the council, and development of financial policy. The comptroller was responsible for the administrative supervision of the finance department, preparation of the budget and financial reports, the administration of debt, selection of depositories, advice to line departments, and control of expenditures. The comptroller helped the manager formulate financial policy. The manager controlled the departments through the budget. Many improvements were made in financial management, and although the budget could have been better, it was an improvement on the old one.

To summarize, the highly fragmented, decentralized, quarrelsome boards and commissions gradually gave way in Rochester to a mayorally dominated model, as they did in New York. Then the strong-mayor position was taken over by a machine politician. Political party was the dominating influence in administration. Continuing financial problems helped focus attention on the council-manager reform, which was adopted with an explicit goal of improving financial management. Budgeting and financial management did improve, but the council-manager system had a rocky beginning. Activist management to solve problems during the depression ran into the alternative model requiring lower costs. Government shifted to a restored machine model and was then subjected to a takeover by the bankers and the business community.

Conclusions

Beginning in 1873, during a period of sharp economic downturn, a system of boards and committees developed to handle budgeting. This clumsy system was designed to hold down expenditures and often represented a fear of machine government as well as the executive and legislative branches. This highly decentralized form of budgeting gradually gave way to more mayoral dominance, especially as the Progressive period approached and municipal goals shifted from keeping costs down to building major projects and taking on new functions and performing them efficiently.

Taxpaying elites reacted strongly to the new, poorer voters in the cities and in the councils. In some parts of the country, this reaction led to disfranchisement of the poor and blacks and a politics of exclusion from city services. In strong-mayor cities, it led to a drastic reduction in the budgetary power of city councils, which were seen as the seat of neighborhood, ethnic, and machine influence. Another response was to reorganize the councils, in some cases requiring or enforcing property ownership as a requirement for holding office, and in other cases eliminating neighborhood representation by substituting at-large elections. Smaller councils elected at large were typical of both commission and council-manager forms. From the reformers' perspective, once the council had been reorganized and could be trusted to represent the property owners and taxpayers, rather than the consumers of city services more broadly, the councils could play a larger role in budgeting.

The major enemy, the target of the reforms, changed from time to time. Sometimes the council was seen as the enemy; sometimes political parties or strong mayors; and sometimes the department heads themselves. As the diagnosis shifted to the departments as generators of expenditures (perhaps a natural fallout of the commission form, where the department heads and the commissioners are the same people), the solution shifted to stronger executive control, whether by mayor or manager.

There was a great deal of imitation from one city to another, even when the problems were quite different. New York City generated the Board of Estimate and Apportionment; the resulting structure was widely adopted by other cities because it held down expenditures successfully. Many cities set up research bureaus patterned along the lines of the New York Bureau of Municipal Research. These bureaus did studies and made recommendations for reforms.

But, more peculiar, those who supported various reforms attacked political machines and corruption even when machines were weak and corruption was undocumented. They had seen or heard of dishonesty in other city governments and used the charge of corruption as a way to force a change in their own communities. As a result, these reformers sometimes created solutions that did not work in their own cities. Boston, for example, created a strong-mayor form and disempowered the city council in order to fight corruption, although the reformers were never able to demonstrate that there was much of a problem. Rochester created a council-manager government to solve the city's financial problems, but the problems were not primarily efficiency or corruption based. Problems included a 2 percent tax limit, poor assessment practices that the manager was unable to change, and unemployment due to the depression. Hence deficits did not go away.

The historical pattern was marked by initiation of a structure in one or several cities that was soon widely imitated by other cities. The resulting structures often lasted for many years, well past the initial problems they had been designed to address. St. Louis, for example, maintained a Board of Estimate into the present period. Boston maintained its Financial Commission from the early 1900s until the present. These enduring structures constitute only one part of the story. The other part is the evolution of budgeting patterns and forms of government, from the boards of estimates into the strong-mayor form; from the commission into the council-manager form. These changes reflected the changed needs and demands of the period and the apparent weaknesses of earlier forms.

5

Boards of Estimate and Council-Manager Cities: Current Cases

ITIES EXPERIENCED major upheavals from the 1930s to the 1960s, including the Great Depression, World War II, and the postwar boom. The boom was accompanied by rapid suburbanization. Cities expanded their boundaries to include the new, wealthier suburbs whenever possible, but for the older cities with fixed boundaries, migration to the suburbs left a concentration of poor people in the inner cities. Some businesses followed customers and labor forces to the suburbs, and others moved south for cheaper and more docile labor markets or left the country completely. The result was a gradual and continuing economic base erosion and continuing fiscal stress.

Blacks, who had been disenfranchised in the South and whose political participation was curtailed by political reforms in the North, rebelled in the most dramatic and successful grassroots movement of the century, the civil rights movement. Blacks and other ethnic groups helped restructure city councils for greater neighborhood participation at city hall. Major spending for downtown urban renewal was gradually opposed by the poor, by organized neighborhood groups, and by ethnic groups, who, though they were now paying the taxes, were not enjoying much trickle-down benefit. Deep and long recessions added pressure to pass and enforce tax limits so that taxes would not grow faster than people's incomes. In expanding cities, tensions grew between progrowth factions and those who wanted to maintain the quality of life of existing residents. The antigrowth faction not only opposed the costs of added development but were reluctant to fund more growth, which would generate more traffic, more apartment buildings, and more smog.

By the late 1960s, these trends began to affect municipal budgeting. The period from the late 1960s to the early 1990s was one of almost continual change and reform in municipal budgeting. These reforms responded not only to problems inherited from earlier periods but also to the new financial problems resulting from tax-base erosion, more stringent tax limits, and acute economic recessions. Budgeting also responded to pressures from neighborhoods and from the formerly disenfranchised or disempowered. For some cities, getting more aid from state or federal sources seemed the only viable solution, making them more vulnerable to state and federal mandates.

Varying patterns of structural reform had left cities with different capacities to deal with financial problems and demands from the neighborhoods and ethnic groups. Cities with boards of estimate and those with commission and council-manager governments experienced one set of problems; strong-mayor cities experienced a different set.

The strong-mayor cities had problems demonstrating their efficiency, since they could easily (and often did) lapse into machine governments with highly decentralized management. Mayors in cities with the strong-mayor form often experienced tension between their roles as managers and as politicians. This tension sometimes arose as conflict between comprehensive or needs-based planning and strategic, partial, and often political, or interest-group-based, planning. Other times, it manifested itself in the extent of openness about fiscal stress. The managerial role suggested a quick acknowledgment and response to fiscal stress; the political role suggested a more strategic response, denying fiscal stress on the one hand and affirming it on the other, depending on the audience and likely consequences.

In strong-mayor communities accountability was highly dependent on the mayor. Election (and nonelection) was the major vehicle for expressing public will. With each new mayor came a new policy emphasis and often a new budgeting system. The more established and less partisan council-manager cities were better equipped to develop budgetary practices over time.

The strong mayors were adept at winning public support but not as good at dealing with many of the technical aspects of managing fiscal stress. In contrast, boards of estimate and commission and council-manager cities had problems gaining and keeping public support. One of the main themes of this chapter is that the boards of estimate and the commission and council-manager reforms often went too far in reaction to political machines and in the effort to keep decision-making power in the hands of a small number of elite taxpayers. They intentionally cut themselves off from the public in order to buffer themselves from expensive budgetary demands. Later, as homeownership became more widespread and as revenue sources were diverted from property taxes to sales taxes, the lack of broad public concurrence meant that the older elites had difficulty gaining enough support for their projects and policies. In earlier years, the taxpaying elites financed only the projects they preferred and justified not funding programs for the poor; in more recent years, the public at large has paid the taxes, and policies against spending for the public in general have become harder to justify. Those who pay the taxes want the benefits to flow to them, not just to an elite who will benefit from rapid growth or redevelopment projects.

By the 1960s, most political machines—and their ability to represent a wide set of constituencies—were gone. The governments designed to destroy them stood like the Great Wall against an imagined enemy. In cities where fear of the public, fear of executive dominance, and fear of corruption had resulted in disempowering citizens, it became difficult to gain sufficient support from the public to pass tax referendums. The necessity of regaining public support created pressures to change public budgeting.

This chapter demonstrates that attempts to regain public support resulted in a variety of efforts to change public budgeting. Additionally, cities had to cope with national trends in budgeting and with fiscal stress, and these factors resulted in relatively widespread changes in municipal budgeting that were not specific to the form of government or to the history of the communities involved.

This chapter describes recent trends in budgeting in St. Louis, Phoenix, and Dayton. These cities reorganized early in this century to buffer themselves from citizen and neighborhood pressures, St. Louis through its Board of Estimate, and Phoenix and Dayton through council-manager reforms. All three cities were experiencing substantial fiscal stress.

In St. Louis in recent years, tax and bond referendums failed continually, as the city pursued primarily a downtown development strategy that helped alienate neighborhoods whose support was essential.

In a historic reversal, the poor and minorities who felt they had been excluded from the benefits of public services and projects were unwilling to pay for the projects of corporate elites. They said no, and kept saying no. In Phoenix, voters rejected referendums, and the city learned to live within constrained revenue limits while expanding its area and watering down service levels to the neighborhoods. Pressure from the neighborhoods for services finally helped force a reorganization of the city council to be more representative of the neighborhoods. In Dayton, after citizens rejected a tax referendum, city officials found a way to improve public accountability and gain support from the broader public, including the business community and neighborhood groups, for spending and taxing programs. The procedure involved considerable neighborhood input, especially into capital projects.

With respect to fiscal stress, Dayton and St. Louis were experiencing tax-base erosion that cut into revenues. Phoenix was not hampered by tax-base erosion as much as by growth, tax limits, and recession. Dominated for years by a business class that favored low taxes and low services, Phoenix underfunded the costs of growth. Hampered by tax limits, each city wrestled with devising and implementing the budgetary tools to manage fiscal stress in a way that was simultaneously rational and politically acceptable.

St. Louis, Missouri

St. Louis is one of the few cities in the country that still has a Board of Estimate and Apportionment. The form of board that St. Louis adopted was like the one New York City used before it began to increase the power of the mayor. By adopting a form of government that reflected the fear of overspending that characterized 1873, St. Louis locked itself into a structure that disempowered the council in budgetary matters, circumscribed the powers of the mayor, and limited spending through tax limits and referendum requirements. Locking the council out of budgetary decision making was expected to lock out the spending demands of the poor. The curtailment of this source of popular support for taxation proved problematic because the city failed to come up with other mechanisms for gaining broad public approval.

How did St. Louis get into such a situation? The answer begins with the financial problems the city encountered during the recession that started in 1873. Landowners feared that if drastic changes were not made in finances, the property tax would rise in order to eliminate the deficit (Barclay 1943). In a story that should be familiar from previous chapters, the 1876 charter was designed to hold down expenses. "To get a higher class of people and to ensure that the interests of the propertied classes were represented, the upper house had a property [ownership] requirement for election, and the lower house had a tax-paying qualification" (Rubin and Stein 1990, 422). The salaries of members of both houses were small because it was assumed that those elected would be wealthy (Barclay 1962). The writers of the charter felt that property ownership would "prove a safeguard against extravagance and a protection to all property owners." The upper house was to be elected at large, to offset the narrow interests of ward politics (Barclay 1962, 25).

In 1914 St. Louis drew up a new charter, changing its structure from a bicameral legislature to a single house and a Board of Estimate and Apportionment. Under the new system, three public officials, each elected at large, were jointly responsible for proposing the budget. The new single-house legislature was granted virtually no budgetary power, and the aldermen were to be elected at large. They could reduce, but not increase, the budget proposed to them by the Board of Estimate.

Over the years, the budgetary power of the Board of Aldermen has further diminished, to the point where the aldermen cannot effectively change the budget proposed by the Board of Estimate. District elections were reinstituted in 1941, but since the aldermen had so little budgetary power, their increased representativeness made little difference.

The Board of Estimate and Apportionment did not grant major powers to the mayor either, but over the years some budgetary power has migrated informally to the mayor. Some aldermen see their disempowerment in terms of the mayor's power to overrule them, not in terms of the powers of the Board of Estimate and Apportionment.

Mary Ross, an alderman, described the limited role of the Board of Aldermen in budgeting as follows:

> The aldermen should have more power over the budget, but that would require a charter change. The mayor keeps a coalition in his back pocket for any action. We would have to go to the citizens. [Then if] he would decrease [the staff by] thirty people, we could put them back.

We made cuts this year that were absolutely necessary.... They were sent to the Board of Estimate and Apportionment. The mayor had the votes to keep them [restore the cuts]. Gerry [chair of Ways and Means Committee] can't get a second; her committee is stacked [in the mayor's favor]. If Gerry says she wants to cut peanuts, they will say no.

That is a lead-in to Gerry. I feel sorry for her. No one wants Ways and Means, that is, to chair it. It's a powerful committee, but when its stacked the way it is, you can't get anything done. Any extra staff we cut gets back in, but now Gerry can't even cut them in the first place. (Interview, January 1990)

Note that in this circumstance, it did not matter whether the mayor was making cuts the aldermen opposed, or the aldermen were making cuts the mayor opposed. The aldermen had no power in either case.

Alderman Ross also mentioned that the mayor controlled transfers between the line items. "What you want to grasp is that the budget is passed, we know the allocation, and it's not necessarily spent per allocation. They switch line items whenever he [the mayor] feels like it." Ross modified her estimate of mayoral power in this area. "Two-thirds of the wins go to the Board of Estimate and Apportionment."

Geraldine Osborne, chair of Ways and Means, in an interview in January 1990, reinforced the image of a Board of Aldermen with little budgetary clout. "We review the budget, and point out frivolous stuff, and once in a while we have an effect. We get viewed as negative because we can stop things, or nitpick. The bottom line is, you can try to redirect."

Another alderman, Fred Wessels, was a little more positive about the role of the aldermen in the budget process. It gave them some oversight capacity, allowed them to follow what programs were doing, and the Board of Estimate could, if it chose, honor specific spending requests of the aldermen.

Q. Does that happen often?

A. What? That they agree to our recommendations? The last couple of years we recommended nonmajor changes, minor things that one or another alderman thought important.... E and A [Estimate and Apportionment] feel these things are not important, but they argue, let them have them, it's a small amount and important to them. Some cuts we make they don't like, we may agree to support restoring those cuts when the vote gets to the full board [of aldermen] in return for the additional other add-on. (Interview, January 1990)

The Board of Estimate and Apportionment can restore aldermen's cuts by transfers, so making cuts that the mayor and the Board of Estimate would not like does not create much bargaining leverage for the aldermen.

The intentional and continuing disempowerment of the Board of Aldermen allowed the mayor and the Board of Estimate to ignore neighborhood needs if they chose to. Confronted with choices between economic development projects sponsored and supported by the city's business community and neighborhood demands for services, Mayor Vincent Schoemehl and the Board of Estimate chose the big economic development projects. Since revenues were highly constrained by economic base erosion and flight to the suburbs, service levels declined. Some citizens became highly skeptical of where additional funds would be spent and continually rejected tax referendums, adding to the city's financial problems.

The city's fiscal condition had been eroding since at least 1950. As Tom Villa, president of the Board of Aldermen, put it, "It is obvious what has happened to us. In 1950 we used to have 750,000 population; the estimate for 1990 is 406,000. There are fewer people paying taxes" (Rubin and Stein 1990, 421). Others have noted that "St. Louis has been the victim of disinvestment, deindustrialization and the consequent loss of economic activity. Total personal income and total income derived from industry have declined over the past twenty years" (Wendel and Cropf 1993, 17–18, citing Bernard 1990, 5).

Tom Villa explained the flight to the suburbs in terms of the search for better schools and the fear of crime. The response of many city officials was to try to enhance the tax base and motivate the middle class to stay in or return to the city. Those who wanted economic development to enhance business profits and those who wanted economic base regeneration to help provide services for the poor formed a loose coalition to reactivate city government, to create some momentum that could be carried on by the private sector. This strategy was pursued in a climate of decreasing revenues, resulting in marked decreases in service levels.

While struggling with economic base erosion, the city had to cope with tightening tax and debt limits. In 1981 the Hancock amendment to the state constitution required a referendum for property tax or fee increases. To make the financial situation worse, between 1978 and 1990 revenues from the federal government to St. Louis fell 71 percent, revenues from the state to the city fell 55 percent, and the city's own general revenues fell 22 percent (Wendel and Cropf 1993, table 7, taken from City Government Finances, U.S. Census series).

General expenditures fell by 19 percent over the same period. While much of this reduction was reportedly in savings that reflected privatization and cutbacks in the number of city staff, the reduced spending also reflected reduced services. Even expenditures touted as saving money through privatization were not necessarily viewed as such by citizens. Especially controversial was the shutting of Homer Phillips, a public hospital in an area of the city primarily populated by blacks. This hospital was a black cultural institution, not just a means of delivering health care. Its closing was treated not simply as a financial decision but as a blow to the black community.

Alderman Mary Ross explained the significance of the closing of Homer Phillips:

> The hospital was completed in 1936. It was the only hospital where black doctors could practice and it had a nursing school. It produced some of the greatest doctors. Phillips didn't see his dream. Each mayor has wanted to close it. In August of 1979, Jim Conway closed it. The two black aldermen on the board begged him not to close it, the neighborhood would die, and it's a symbol, it's our history. They said, "You do this, and you lose." He said, "You can't do it" [vote me out of office]. We marched every day for a year.... He lost [the election].

In 1979 blacks did not have enough power to force the mayor to keep the hospital open, but they were able to defeat the mayor's re-election bid. Vincent Schoemehl ran against Conway, arguing that he would reopen Phillips, and won with a substantial proportion of the black vote (Stein 1991). Schoemehl, however, was unable to reopen the hospital, and several years later, he ended up closing the remaining public hospital and helping the county finance a joint facility with privatized management. Within a short time, both public hospitals had been closed.

Services were also cut back in the police department, though less drastically than in other departments. Alderman Geraldine Osborne described the problem resulting from these cutbacks:

> Then there is the problem of the city and crime, in some places actual and in others perceived crime. There is a three-hour police response time for nonemergency calls. The police department does not have enough personnel: they were reduced from 1,700 in 1980 to 1,550 now. I am in the Third District; there are over 80,000 residents. There are seventeen officers on a shift. There are some shifts with no patrol officers, they have to be called from other districts. When I became an alderman, we had 259 officers—now it's 173, with more troubled neighborhoods.

In street maintenance and sanitation, the decreases in spending per capita were severe enough to be noticed by the public. The mayor borrowed against future Community Development Block Grant funds to do some repaving in response to public demands (Wendel and Cropf 1993). The situation remained problematic, however, with major overpasses deteriorating and no money for repairs.

Declining service levels and rejection of tax referendums were closely linked in the eyes of some city representatives. Geraldine Osborne argued that a tighter linkage between improved service levels and tax-increase proposals would have helped the referendum pass.

> Responsible folk want more police—Would they vote for more police? Of course. Last year the mayor said, on the half a percent tax increase proposal, the resulting funds would amount to one hundred officers. People said, where does it say that in writing? It did not say that. They did not believe it would go to the police. I think the people were right. It was rejected.... We need to say ... all revenue from this source will go into a fund for increases in the number of police and their salaries. The votes are there, but the city administration doesn't want to do that.

Alderman Mary Ross argued that it was not just a matter of money not going to services and staffing but also a lack of belief in the quality of financial management.

> The citizens know where the money should go, to citizen services, to staff salary. Agreements often unravel. The mayor funds studies to

design projects, but then provides no money for running operations [in mayoral programs like] Brightside, Conserve, anything.... The citizens are aware that the money isn't being spent on the best interests of the citizens, so when the mayor proposes a tax increase, it fails, because fiscal integrity doesn't exist.

Ross put the argument about lack of services and poor management in the context of the mayor's propensity for large economic development projects. Referring to a refurbished large boat that was to be a dockside entertainment center, she protested, "The city could sink $7 million into the *Admiral*, which doesn't float. After all that money, it's still closed; it's a white elephant." Ross noted that Union Station, which was a large, highly successful commercial redevelopment project, was funded with an Urban Development Action Grant. The project generated enough revenue to repay its original funding. Ross argued that the repaid money should have been utilized for housing or commercial development. Instead, it went to the *Admiral*, another downtown economic development project. She implied not only that there was no balance between the larger, flashy downtown projects and smaller, urgently needed neighborhood projects but also that some of the larger projects remained unviable, visible symbols of wasted money that should have been spent on the neighborhoods.

The tension between large economic development projects and basic neighborhood services was also underscored by Geraldine Osborne, chair of the Ways and Means Committee. She pointed out that several of the large downtown development projects did not go to public referendums and resulted in millions of dollars of debt. People were in essence ordered to pay for the projects, "then they get told we'll lay off service [delivery personnel] unless you pay more taxes. If we hadn't entered other agreements, we could have sufficient dollars for basic requirements."

Mayor Schoemehl had formed a close relationship with Civic Progress, a group of twenty-nine CEOs of St. Louis's largest companies. The kinds of projects he carried out were generally the ones they preferred, including the privatization of the city hospital. Nevertheless, their support was not sufficient to ensure the passage of tax referendums.

The citizens had limited influence over budget priorities through the council; they could only say no to new taxes, and they did, over and over. Finally, they ejected Schoemehl from the mayor's position and elected a black man instead. Schoemehl had miscalculated the increased voting power of nonelite citizens; when they rejected referendums, he turned to forms of financing, like lease purchase, that did not require referendums. When confronted with tax rejections, Schoemehl did not adjust his budget priorities enough to reach the broader public and get their approval. The citizens, presumably in an effort to change the city priorities, changed mayors, but since so many of the large projects Schoemehl supported were bond funded, and since the city's financial situation continued to be precarious, the new mayor did not have much flexibility to change priorities.

What changes were made in the budget process and format during the Schoemehl administration? During the late 1980s, there were four specific changes, but none of them was fully geared to winning widespread public support for the mayor's goals and for additional taxation. One change was the introduction of a program and performance budget. This helped enhance the mayor's policy control and create some flexibility within very tight budgets. A second change was the merging of the annual budget with a new strategic planning process. This new planning process could have been used to generate support for budget goals, but was only loosely linked to the budget. A third change was the creation of a new capital planning process and budget. The new capital process in St. Louis ratified and put in priority order the department heads' requests; it did not tap the neighborhoods for their priorities. The fourth change was an altered timetable for budget production that further shifted power from the aldermen to the Board of Estimate and Apportionment and the mayor. Just when a shift toward the aldermen's priorities might have helped balance spending on economic development projects with more neighborhood-oriented spending, the mayor further reduced the power of the Board of Aldermen.

Program and Performance Budgeting

One informant interviewed by the author described the situation before the introduction of the new budget format:

> In practice, we had always been budgeting suboptimally. Voting was line item by department, it did not even always jibe with service delivery. Formerly, deals were cut before they went to the Board of Estimate and Apportionment. The budget went to the aldermen, and they would say, "Oh, the office supplies are up $3,000; what is this

$3,000?" They never asked, "What is the department trying to do?
Are you more or less efficient?"

This informant implied that the new budget format could change
the basis of decision making in the Board of Aldermen, but since the
board played little role in the budget process, this outcome seemed unlikely. The aldermen were not consulted in the preparation of the new
format, nor were they formally notified of the changes after they were
in place. Those few who did know about the changed format were
suspicious of it, coming as it did without warning and in the context
of prior budget manipulations to keep the aldermen's influence minimal.

If the purpose was not to improve the aldermen's decision making, what was it? Most likely it was to increase the control of the
mayor over the departments and to increase the amount of flexibility
in the budget to respond to mayoral priorities. The decline in revenues
as a result of decreases in federal and state assistance and the city's
own economic base decline was exacerbated by the city's policy of
contracting hundreds of millions of dollars in debt for economic
development. The flexibility in the budget was minimal. This lack of
flexibility curtailed the mayor when he wanted to engage in some program or project. The program and performance budget allowed programs to be compared and their costs known, so the budget office and
the mayor could make tradeoffs between programs.

Within the executive branch, as a result of the program and performance budget there has been much more emphasis on explicit
tradeoffs between programs and between portions of programs during
the formulation of the budget. The budget office presents policy
choices and the mayor picks the ones he wants to guide the budget.
The mayor can pick not only between programs but also between levels of programs. "We can talk about how many immunizations versus
how many trees." The budget office frames the choices and the mayor
makes them, which greatly increases his policy control.

Strategic Planning

Beginning in 1987, the city also tried to implement a strategic planning process with direct links to the budget in order to provide a focus
on outputs. According to a city budget document, the planning process was instituted to improve allocations by continually evaluating
the needs of the community, focusing government efforts, and evaluat-

ing the effectiveness of programs. This process produced a list of needs that was used to develop policies for allocating discretionary revenues not already committed. These policies provided fairly concrete guidance for allocations. Some examples from the fiscal 1989 budget included: a city commitment to replace or repair its infrastructure and equipment; a decision not to provide services that someone else could or did provide as well as, or better than, the city; control of pension costs; and a possible realignment of departments to improve service delivery (City of St. Louis 1988, 14). While the process produced fairly concrete planning goals, the loose linkage to the budget made it difficult to judge whether a goal had been achieved. If the aim was to demonstrate to the public that the goals they expressed were being accomplished and that revenues were being allocated to those goals, the linkage with the budget was too weak to fulfill the purpose.

Capital Budgeting Process

The capital budgeting process involved all the city departments and agencies and a capital committee. This committee was chaired by the budget director. The other members included an alderman, the administrative assistant to the president of the Board of Aldermen, an administrative assistant to the mayor, the president of the Board of Public Service, two representatives from the comptroller's office, and the director of the Community Development Agency. The city departments prepared lists of capital needs over the next five years and prioritized them; the lists were submitted to the budget office. The capital committee reviewed the list and developed a five-year needs assessment list. It also prepared the capital portion of the annual budget. Fred Wessels, the alderman on the capital committee, spoke enthusiastically about how well it was working.

> It works better than ever. We are reviewing capital needs with more objectivity and more thoroughness because we have a capital committee. The idea that we have a separate capital budget brings more emphasis on capital spending and highlights the inadequacy of spending on infrastructural maintenance and improvements. (Interview, January 1990)

The lack of money hampered the process in one sense but made it easier in another. With only $12 million in the capital budget, $8 million of that was committed to long-term leases. That left only $3 million to $4 million of discretionary capital spending. Despite the limited amount of money, however, the committee established criteria for ranking projects, such as safety concerns, return on investment, and federal mandates. Once the mandated activities and the high-priority safety issues were handled, there was not much left. There was so little money that the city made only minimal progress on the five-year list of projects.

In January 1990 the capital committee had not yet convened to draw up the capital budget for the next year. One likely reason for the late start was that the amount of capital budget would remain unknown until the cuts for the following year were known, cuts made necessary by the lapse of a sales tax with sunset provisions and several unsuccessful attempts to get the voters to extend the tax and make it permanent. As one informant put it, "We now have priorities, with no money to fund them."

This new procedure for deciding on capital projects was a marked improvement over earlier methods, but there was little about it to suggest outreach to the public. Yet one informant described the changes in the capital budget as intentionally copying Dayton's model. Dayton had created local priority boards with major input into how the capital budget would be allocated. This program was adopted as part of a response to a rejected tax referendum. The only part of the St. Louis capital program that resembled Dayton's capital program was the mayor's housing stabilization project, called Conserve. If St. Louis intended to copy Dayton's process for gaining public support for taxation, however, it was wide of the mark.

Depending on to whom one talked, the mayor set aside anywhere between $600,000 and $2 million for Conserve. The mayor asked the neighborhoods to form housing corporations, to incorporate as not-for-profits, to hire consultants and draw up plans for housing rehabilitation, and thereafter, presumably, he would give them money from program funds to carry out projects that would help stabilize neighborhoods and stop the outward flow of population. It was never clear to many aldermen where the money was supposed to come from, that is, what would be cut from general revenues to fund the program. Also, Conserve was narrower in scope than the Dayton program, which allowed the priorities to be set by the neighborhoods, not by the mayor. Third, the mayor wanted to appoint the community boards; in the Dayton model, neighborhood leaders are picked by their neighborhoods and receive some training from the city. Fourth, the mayor said that a city attorney would file the papers to make the housing groups eligible for nonprofit status, but the attorney had not done so. More than a year and a half after the program was announced, with several housing corporations ready to run, no program money had been dispensed.

Charter Change to Eliminate Delays
Alterations were made to the timing of the budgetary decision process and the beginning of the fiscal year. This change was included in the charter. A long-time city employee described the background:

> We used to have a terrible time passing the budget. By the time the Board of Estimate and Apportionment approved and passed the budget over to Ways and Means, all this controversy would start. One year we were eight months into the fiscal year without a budget. It hurt the bond rating. We were operating out of a resolution of the Board of Aldermen, under the comptroller's emergency powers.

The chair of the Ways and Means Committee admitted that her committee delayed the budget, partly in response to the powerlessness of the committee and the Board of Aldermen.

The budget office suggested, and the mayor agreed, that a charter change would force each budget actor to get the budget out in a limited time period, or the budget from the previous stage would become law. Such a change would encourage all the actors to make decisions in a timely way or forfeit their input completely. This eliminated one of the few powers remaining to the Board of Aldermen, delaying the budget to embarrass the mayor and hence pressure him to include their preferences in the budget.

To summarize, St. Louis suffered major economic base erosion, population loss, and revenue declines. Faced with these problems, Mayor Schoemehl allied with large business executives and followed their agenda for economic development, with major emphasis on projects associated with the downtown, commercial redevelopment, and boosterism, such as sports and convention facilities. To fund such projects in straitened circumstances required an aggressive policy of reducing city staff, privatizing, and cutting back services. In a city deeply divided between black and white, where personal income was falling, the neighborhoods often felt left out; they were called on to pay more taxes, without sufficient assurance that the additional taxes would go to services. The mayor's allies in Civic Progress were not the key taxpayers of the late 1800s who paid for their own projects with their own taxes; the newer projects had to be paid for by the public at large, often without its consent. Voters responded by continually saying no on the tax and bond referendums that did come to them and, finally, by saying no to the mayor himself.

The city needed desperately to find a way to gain public support for taxation, but changes in budgeting that could have helped achieve that end did not go far enough to accomplish much in the way of building public support. When the public rejected referendums, city officials found ways of funding projects without public approval, rather than make the changes necessary to get the approval they needed and possibly drop some projects that did not have popular support. When the mayor adopted a neighborhood housing improvement program, he tried to appoint the local boards himself. He failed to understand the need to listen to neighborhoods; instead, he wanted the neighborhoods to do it his way.

Phoenix, Arizona

Phoenix is an intermediate case. Like St. Louis, Phoenix had adopted a political form intentionally to disempower the public and the neighborhoods. Under the influence of the business community, the city expanded its boundaries enormously, growing rapidly in population, but it systematically underfunded growth. Recessions and fiscal problems were met with additional service cuts, often focusing on the poorer or more dependent population groups. Citizens became dissatisfied and demanded more services. The result was a change in the structure of the council and a number of budgeting modifications. While some of these changes led to greater openness, the level of responsiveness to the public was only moderate. The degree of openness has oscillated, according to one seasoned observer.

Phoenix grew rapidly during the first decade of the century. There was little graft or corruption compared to other major cities at the time, but businessmen-reformers wanted the city to look progressive (Luckingham 1989). The charter they proposed called for four commissioners, a mayor, and a city manager. The charter also included at-large elections. It was approved by the voters in 1913, effective 1914.

Advocates knew that by eliminating the ward system, they eliminated the political power of the less affluent, less numerous part of the population residing in south Phoenix. Under the old structure, the city was divided into four wards.... As R.L. Dyer, secretary of the Good Government League, put it at a meeting of that charter reform organization in early February 1914, "the third and fourth wards are composed of a class of people who do not meet with the high ideals of those here present." Under the new charter, elected at-large officials for the north side would replace those who had represented the less affluent, less numerous residents of the south side wards in the past. As a result, it was felt by dominant interests, the government of Phoenix would be in the hands of the "right people." (Luckingham 1989, 67)

The business leaders who pushed for the charter reform in 1913 were more interested in the appearance of being progressive than the reality of reform. The city manager they chose proved too reformed for their taste because he attacked patronage positions, introduced competitive bidding, encouraged municipal ownership, and collected business license fees. He was fired and the powers of the city manager were curtailed, to prevent the same thing from happening again.

The quality of government after the weakening of the manager's powers was described as at best mediocre and at worst corrupt, excessively political, patronage oriented, and somewhat inept. After World War II, when the city boosters wanted to push again for rapid growth, the low esteem in which their government was held seemed like an obstacle. They agitated for and successfully passed a charter reform to strengthen the manager's powers and assure the manager's independence of the council. The reformers wanted to prevent the council from manipulating the manager and dominating the departments, as they had been doing.

They found that reform was not enough, however, when the council and manager did not enforce the changed charter. A group of businessmen and professionals formed the Charter Government Committee to help elect candidates who would uphold the reforms. They successfully elected their slates and introduced a "businesslike approach to government" (Luckingham 1989, 150). They provided competent, honest, and growth-oriented government.

The Charter Government Committee dominated Phoenix government for more than twenty-five years. Though it offered competent government, it had some drawbacks. One drawback was that it was not representative of the general population; its members were largely white, middle or upper class, and business oriented. A second drawback was that the committee generated little interest among the broader voting population: "The normally difficult task of creating citizen interest in local government and politics has been compounded in Phoenix by elitist nomination and election procedures, an increasingly powerful administration, and increasing ambivalence over the Charter Committee's objectives" (Hall 1982, 55). The citizens' lack of interest was shown in the low turnouts for city elections; only 14 percent of those registered actually voted in 1973.

Ambivalence about the Charter Government Committee's goals became more marked during the financial problems of the early 1970s. The former budget director, Charles Hill, described it as follows: "We went through the oil embargo and recession of 1973 and 1974. It was a difficult time. In city services, the only tools [we had for dealing with this situation] were [financial] control [tools], balancing the budget through city vacant positions without regard to the consequences, such as the effect on the fleet" (Interview, December 1990). Cutting services, and not necessarily in a thoughtful way, was the only response the reform group could generate.

The dominance of the Charter Committee began to wane in the mid-1970s. Protests against the committee coalesced into a rival slating body, the Citizens for an Independent Council, which was successful in electing its candidates in 1975. After the recession and poorly managed cutbacks, and with the new composition of the council, priorities changed to include some increases in revenue.

The council passed the increases, but the chamber of commerce organized a referendum against it and successfully blocked the increases. The result was a sudden need for a rational tool for cutback. According to Charles Hill,

> The voters eliminated it in February 1977. We were in the middle of the fiscal year, and we were short $10 million. We needed a way to set new priorities. I educated myself to ZBB [zero-based budgeting]. I had positive communication with all the parties involved, department heads, the council, the public, and the media, so everyone could understand the priorities. It was put into effect in 1977. Interesting, to put ZBB into effect, we had to define the consequences of a reduction in output measure terms.

We had begun to develop that capacity under PPB [Planning Programming Budgeting] systems. In the late 1970s we switched from input to output budgeting, [and we got it] pretty well polished; we could define the service-level impact of revenue shortfalls. (Interview, December 1990)

Because citizens rejected tax increases in 1977, there was still no money to expand or improve services. Minority leaders and others still felt left out of municipal spending. They began to push for a larger council and district elections to increase their influence over spending decisions. It took them a number of years, but they were successful by the early 1980s.

Mayor Margaret T. Hance, who represented the Charter Committee point of view, was reelected in 1981, running on her record of supporting anticrime programs, water projects, better transportation, downtown redevelopment, and clean industry. The mayor and council emphasized provision of basic services during the economic downturn of the early 1980s; social services suffered (Luckingham 1989).

The early 1980s were marked by President Reagan's reductions in federal program spending and a deep recession. Moreover, more restrictive tax and expenditure limits were put in place in 1980 in Arizona. The state government, responding to taxpayer pressure, eliminated the sales tax on food and indexed the state's income tax so that the state's revenues would not grow more quickly than inflation. As a result, the state's ability to bail out the city was reduced.

The city's revenue sources were generally highly elastic with respect to the economy, growing well during periods of boom, but growing slowly during recessions. The sales tax in particular grew much more slowly than projections during the recession years of 1981 and 1982. Until then, elastic revenues had kept city income up, and continuous growth had expanded the tax base. Phoenix had managed with low property taxes by underfunding service extension into the newly annexed areas and by allowing the federal government to pick up the costs of whatever social programs the city provided, while the city continued to focus on the provision of such basic services as police and fire protection (Hall 1986).

Confronted with lagging sales taxes and declining federal grants, staff emphasized possible budget gaps and tried to get action on tax increases or service cuts. In particular, staff threatened that the swimming pools would have to be closed without some additional budget balancing action. Given the summer heat in Phoenix, the threat of closing public swimming pools became a symbol of the policy of cutting services to the poor and the elderly.

The combination of particular programs cut and long-simmering feelings that services were not evenly distributed throughout the city fed into the movement to expand the council and elect council members from districts. Charles Hill commented: "In my opinion the way the at-large council informed cutback approaches led to the district system. Because the at-large council was interested solely in the long range, it ignored barking dogs and traffic signals. The district system promised an open forum to people" (Interview, December 1990).

In December 1982 the public approved a change from six council members elected at large to eight members elected by district. This modification was not as radical as it seemed; the mayor continued to be elected at large, elections were still nonpartisan, and the council-manager system was retained. The increase in council membership was small. Nevertheless, for Phoenix, the change was important.

Some people at city hall argued that the chamber of commerce inadvertently contributed to the movement for district elections, despite its continuing support for the at-large system. The chamber had led the successful revolt against the tax increase in 1976. By keeping taxes down, the chamber exacerbated the problem of providing service delivery to the periphery. Thus the chamber aggravated those who were not getting their share of services from the city and fed the movement for district elections.

Supporters of the change to district elections complained that the council members elected at large had too little concern about neighborhoods. "Minority leaders in south Phoenix believed specifically that inadequate representation helped explain the lack of adequate services in that part of the city" (Luckingham 1989, 222).

Terry Goddard led the Committee for District Representation, to make the city council more responsive to citizens' needs. Goddard argued that the district system would "help break up the elite hierarchy of businessmen and other special interests who enjoyed unlimited access to city hall, and usher in a new era of representative government to the benefit of all the people" (Luckingham 1989, 224).

In addition to attacking the class basis of the government and its responsiveness to builders and bankers, Goddard appealed to citizens who felt shut out of city hall, neighborhood groups that saw their interests ignored, and virtually the entire minority community. Minorities felt totally neglected; as Alfredo Gutierrez put it regarding members of the power structure in Phoenix: "Hispanics have been totally out—when they do talk to us, it's like they're addressing ambassadors from a foreign country." (Luckingham 1989, 225)

Voters in Phoenix had turned down similar proposals for district elections in 1967 and 1975, but in 1982 they accepted them. Charter strongholds in north Phoenix opposed the plan, but the district system was approved by most voters in all other areas of the city. Goddard won the mayoralty and took office with a new district-based council in 1984. The change to district elections had a number of impacts on the budget process, some indirect and some direct.

One informant thought that the adoption of a strategic planning process for the city might have been a response of staff to the change to district elections. To quote Charles Hill:

About 1983–84, we switched to district elections; that might have brought this [planning] on. When we went to the district elections, there were eight councilmen interested in their geographic areas. Only the mayor [elected at large] and manager were interested in the whole. Long-range planning devolved to them. Prior to that, we had business-oriented councils that were more long-range oriented, not as interested in districts. I don't know if I would attribute the strategic planning to that; it may just have been good management. (Interview, December 1990)

City Manager Frank Fairbanks had a slightly different view of the adoption of the strategic plan. He emphasized the growth of the city, the complexity of functions performed, and the possibility of getting lost in the details of management and not having a sense of direction. He also noted that "politicians admit that social services are important, that housing is related to crime, our problems are much more sophisticated. They needed to be coordinated." These are precisely the policy areas that were emphasized when the new district council was elected. According to Fairbanks's argument, it was this new recognition of the complexity of the problems addressed and the range of services required to address them that required more planning, more focus on the goals and direction.

Goddard and the newly elected council made some changes that affected the budget more directly. In an effort to increase openness, the new mayor and council agreed to hold council sessions at times convenient for the public, to establish offices and hold forums in each district, and to assign staff assistants to handle the anticipated flood of complaints and requests from district residents (Luckingham 1989). The mayor used the new citizen forums to present the budget in the districts and sought council member input on the budget.

The public information office worked up a sound-and-slide show in order to present the budget in a popular way. The mayor, the district council member, and the budget director would attend meetings in the districts. The mayor and council member were there to hear public comments; however, there was not necessarily a budget meeting in every district every year.

In an interview in December 1990, Andrea Tevlin, the former budget and research director, described these district hearings as effective. "They provide valuable citizen input. The council members present the manager's proposed budget to the neighborhoods. Input from these hearings serves as the basis of the council's changes to the manager's budget. It is positive citizen input that the council takes very seriously."

Mayor Terry Goddard solicited suggestions from the council members about how to change the city manager's proposed budget. The council members used the input they gathered from the district forums to help formulate a list of changes, including additions to requested spending.

The council members' list of proposed changes was only one of several ways of getting council priorities in the budget. As Tevlin, the former budget and research director, described it in 1990:

We work closely with the mayor and council throughout the budget process. We present budget reports to the council at least once a month before any budget proposals are floated. The council is closely involved through a very effective council ratings process. This process provides an opportunity for the council to rate a wide range of budget expenditure and revenue issues, which provides valuable input to the city manager.

Even though there were other techniques for gathering council input, the process of council add-ons was an important part of the impact of the district elections. According to Charles Hill,

> 1984–85 was the first [year with a] district budget. We saw that impact, more geographical neighborhood things. Neighborhood coalitions became more powerful and affected budgeting. Capital budget on construction, we began to produce reports on each district. We informally set aside a sum for council add-ons, recreation, school officers, etc. That is the way the council adapted their budgets, add-ons after the manager's budget. With the manager's full understanding that that was the way it would work. It grew each year until last year; [there were] $2 million add-ons for various programs. [Author's note: the add-ons were eliminated the following year.]

Although there was concern among staff that the council would be too exclusively neighborhood oriented, that apparently did not happen. Council add-ons were not strictly for neighborhood projects and services but also for citywide expenditures. As Tevlin explained, the council also maintained a balance in capital projects for the districts and for the city as a whole. What is perhaps most interesting is that the council add-ons were used to extend service to the newly annexed northwest territory. In the 1988–89 budget, there were over $5 million in add-ons; of that, over $2.6 million was spent on service extension. These recommendations were additions to the manager's budget proposal, but spending did not increase without additional revenues, since the new territory was expected to generate enough taxes to cover the service extension. The council add-ons did represent, however, a change in priorities for how new revenues would be spent.

The council add-ons adhered to a policy of extending services into any newly annexed areas. Council members generally did not request small projects to be distributed to each district. The district council also restored items that were cut back during the recession of 1980 and 1981. The public demanded good-quality services, even if some business groups, such as the chamber of commerce, did not want to pay additional taxes. To quote Charles Hill once again:

> The previous cutbacks in 1981–82—library, swimming pools, senior citizen services—they were all restored by the district council. Like a frog climbing out of the well, halving the distance each time, but the long-term trend is toward public expectations for good quality [services]. We went through a contracting-out phase, but there have been

more cases where the city took over private services, such as the private ambulances. The bus system became public. There are more public goods, not the other way around.

Granting the new district council more influence over priorities was one way of improving responsiveness to the public, but it was not the only way that Phoenix tried to involve the public and increase support. There was some decentralization from city hall to the neighborhoods. The cost of staffing this effort was substantial. In 1988 the manager listed among the issues the manager and council would have to deal with over the next few years, "rapidly emerging neighborhood involvement requiring more staff time" (from Phoenix 1988 budget). To ensure citizen involvement in decision making about the level of taxation, the city council appointed the Citizens' Tax Fairness Commission (Luckingham 1989). Then, in 1988, in order to assure sufficient support for a bond issue, the city put together a new capital budget process with major citizen input. In 1990 Tevlin, the former budget and research director, spoke about this process:

> More than 200 citizens served on our citizens bond committee. This committee was appointed by the mayor and the council and was charged with identifying capital needs throughout the city, including police, fire, parks, libraries, streets, aviation, water, wastewater, arts, and culture. The committee then made recommendations to the council on the size of the bond program that should be presented to the voters. The results of this effort was voter approval of $1.1 billion in bonds—the largest municipal bond program in the history of the country. This success can be attributed largely to the significant involvement of the community in developing the bond proposal.

The bonds did get popular support and were approved by referendum.

In short, pressures from citizens and from the district-based council members were a major source of budgeting changes in in Phoenix. As City Manager Frank Fairbanks put it in December 1990:

> Neighborhood involvement trends are reflected in budget pressures. As community needs have arisen, and as trust ebbs and flows between the community and the city, [we] try to make the process more open and give the council more input [when trust is low]. When there is more trust, we shortcut the process.... Pressure from the

community or council to respond to community needs is an important factor explaining why budgeting changes.

Fairbanks also emphasized the role of national trends and self-evaluation and improvement as influencing budgeting practices. When asked whether fiscal stress influenced budgeting, he responded that fiscal stress did not influence the budget process as much as the other factors, but he did note that staff members were always trying to figure out better ways to cut the budget.

During an interview in December 1990, Pat Manion, deputy city manager (now deceased), summarized the changes in budget process in chronological order. In his overview, one can see all four factors at work: responsiveness to citizens, national trends, self-evaluation and improvement, and fiscal stress.

The first major change of the period occurred in 1970 when an engineering, operations analysis focus was added to the traditional budgetary analysis in order to boost productivity. The emphasis was on reducing the cost of inputs. This industrial engineering program reflected a budget crunch that hit in the late 1960s. Private-sector people on the council said they handled problems like that with industrial engineering, so the city adopted the industrial engineering approach.

As city staff [members] implemented the new approach, they realized they needed to look at effectiveness, not just efficiency. PPBS was the fashion in the late 1960s, so the city picked it up. The adoption of PPBS reflected at least in part the growth of the city and its hopefulness, as well as a tendency to adopt national budgeting trends. Phoenix was not one of the original cities to experiment with PPBS, but it adopted PPBS anyway, and has maintained something of the planning focus since then.

By 1971 and 1972, the emphasis on productivity had merged with PPBS, combining engineering analysis with effectiveness studies of major programs. PPBS included an extensive planning effort to coordinate service delivery, based on a needs assessment by census tract. Work standards from the productivity and effectiveness orientation became entwined in the budget, but engineering analysis went to the auditor's office instead of staying in the budget office.

By the late 1970s, the city added a serious zero-based budgeting component to help deal with cutbacks. This approach was modified to a target-based budget, and more recently, [the city] returned to a full zero-based approach.

The goal-setting aspect of PPBS evolved into two parts. One part was called performance achievement, implemented through a management-by-objectives system. The other part was the long-range strategic plan, [which] stated general goals and included detailed action plans. Then, in the late 1980s, an additional planning element was added, a citizen-based Futures Forum. This process taps citizens' goals and objectives. Many of these goals and objectives are outside the mission of city hall, but city hall operates loosely as a facilitator of the process and, when appropriate, as a facilitator of the achievement of the goals. Thus, what started as PPBS emerged eventually as the corporate or strategic plan with a community planning component.

The Futures Forum, the citizen component, was council driven and reflected the impact of the new district elections and the effort to enable the public to influence spending priorities. The plans resulting from the Futures Forum were only loosely integrated into the city's own plans, but the city had much more information available about citizen priorities as a result of this planning exercise than it would have had otherwise. The process of planning had changed from the time when planners did needs assessments by census tract.

The operations analysis, engineering orientation changed gradually to be more behavior oriented. Productivity was defined more in terms of employee development and less in terms of engineering. The city developed and implemented quality circles. These efforts became decentralized with the implementation of target-based budgets, in which the departments assumed responsibility for their own operations.

Budgeting changes have continued into the 1990s. In a letter to the author dated 15 April 1998, Budget and Research Director Cecile Pettle outlined some additional improvements.

Phoenix's budget process now includes numerous public hearings throughout the community well in advance of the city manager proposing his budget; significant advertising in English and Spanish, including a home-delivered newspaper insert explaining the proposed budget; and an opportunity for council members to submit proposed budget items. Closely related is a biannual citizens' attitude survey, and we are currently in the midst of an effort to involve the community in setting performance measures for city services.

To summarize, Phoenix's budget history since the end of World War II has been marked by major changes, beginning with the shift in

1948 from a poorly managed commission-manager system to a council-manager form with considerable discretion granted to the manager. This change was associated with the takeover of city politics by a business-led elite that controlled nomination and election to office for some twenty-five years. The agenda of this group included city expansion but generally underfunded the expansion and ignored neighborhood needs. Social services, to the extent that they were funded, were paid for by federal funds. The need for distributing services more equally throughout the city gradually generated pressure for change on the council and helped forge a different philosophy—of higher taxation and a more equitable distribution of services. A broader base of citizens was paying taxes, and they wanted the services they were paying for.

Even so, for many years, the steps taken to open the city were limited and controlled, mediated by a strong professionalism among the staff. The much-feared breakdown into district-based demands did not occur. Centrifugal forces were moderate and controlled. The mayor took the manager's recommended budget to the citizens in community forums and asked for comments, but the citizens had no mechanism to come up with requests of their own. The budget did not routinely go to each district every year: it went to each district only if a difficult budget year was upcoming, and popular support was expected to be difficult to obtain.

Phoenix made a number of changes in the budget process. Especially noticeable were the adoption of a planning orientation with PPBS and the gradual evolution of PPBS into management-by-objective and strategic planning. Also noteworthy was the adoption of zero-based budgeting and its cousin, target-based budgeting, to handle the continuing need for prioritization and cutback. The change in the election of the council from at-large to district based, while itself not a change in budgeting, reflected more interest in bringing the public into budgeting. This trend continued into the 1990s, when further efforts were taken to obtain public opinion and allow input from council members. These measures opened the budget process to the public.

Dayton, Ohio

The city of Dayton, Ohio, adopted the council-manager form of government in 1913 after almost twenty years of business agitation led by John Patterson, president of National Cash Register. Patterson wanted parks, better health care, libraries, and improved free education. The schools would teach business skills and manual skills in addition to traditional subjects. The expansion of services would be paid for through the increased efficiency resulting from adopting business methods in city government. The charter commission, dominated by businessmen (Sealander 1988), chose the council-manager form. The voters approved the new charter by a two-thirds majority.

Patterson was motivated in part by frustration with the city for not providing his business with the decisions and services he required. The city had forbidden railroad access rights at ground level, which made shipping difficult and expensive for National Cash Register. Patterson complained that inefficient streetcar service interfered with the punctuality of the labor force. He also wanted the city to build a bridge over the Miami River to open up areas for his workers to live near the factory. Patterson argued that better recreational opportunities would help him attract skilled labor, and he wanted better schools to help prepare that labor force (Sealander 1988).

Patterson's vision was not limited to benefits for his own company. The council-manager form in Dayton provided improved services to the whole community and accommodated a rapidly growing population despite the constraints of the Smith One Percent Law (see chapter 2). But even though many people benefited from clean water, improved health services, and better social services, council-manager government in Dayton was still a government of businessmen and primarily for businessmen.

One of the goals of Dayton's council-manager government was to run the city like a business. In order to do so, the city government had to insulate itself from the demands of the public. The new charter provided for a small council, elected at large, making it difficult for socialists, laborers, or representatives from neighborhoods to compete for office. Although the charter included provisions for referendum and recall, Patterson and his coalition made the referendum difficult for citizens to use if the council opposed the citizens' point of view.

Having successfully insulated local government from the populace, the reformers put considerable policymaking responsibility in the council. The charter shifted responsibility for drawing up the budget from the council to the city manager, but it gave the council responsibility for considering the manager's budget proposal. Initially, the council deferred to the manager, but gradually the council began to assert itself and make policy decisions apart from the manager's recommendations (Rightor et al. 1919). In this way, Dayton began a tradition of bureaucratic accountability to the council, if not directly to the public.

The council provided citizens access through budget hearings and citizen advisory committees. The budget hearings were well attended by the public for the first few years, but citizen attendance dropped sharply thereafter. An observer of Dayton's early council-manager system argued: "as a means of exercising administrative control over expenditures, the budget has proven to be a very effective instrument, but as a means of educating and interesting the public in civic matters, the public hearing on the budget leaves much to be desired" (Rightor et al. 1919, 172). The legal requirement for a hearing on the budget was in place, but the intent of interesting the public and getting people to participate was absent.

Although the new council-manager government did not stimulate citizen participation in government or actively solicit and respond to citizen demands, it did try to get public support for its programs.

> This policy [of getting public support] is based upon the theory that only by having the confidence of the public can a continuous program be successfully consummated. Every effort is made to secure an expression of opinion on important matters from neighborhood improvement associations, the labor unions and the central labor council, private (nonpolitical) clubs and the commercial organization known as the Greater Dayton Association. Publicity in the daily newspapers is courted, and the editorial and correspondence columns have more than once thrown the balance for or against action on proposed legislation. (Rightor et al. 1919, 42)

The council took public opinion seriously. When the city proposed a bond referendum to handle the irritating problem of multiple at-grade railroad crossings, many citizens objected because they did not wish to pay for crossing improvements in some other area of the city. The council backed off from the plan, awaiting a more positive consensus. "The commission is a unit in desiring to proceed, but must await the development of a popular sentiment to remedy the evil" (Rightor et al. 1919, 35–36).

Citizen commissions were also emphasized. The commissions were reportedly a way of getting citizen expertise free, while reaching a broader public concerning proposed policies. These commissions investigated and reported and then were disbanded. This technique represents an element of "government by the people," but the commissions did not consist of a very broad range of the citizenry and were hand-picked by the businessmen who controlled the government. For example, the three-man planning commission appointed in 1914 consisted of a manufacturer, a businessman, and an architect.

In short, while the council-manager government intentionally reduced the possibility of the election of a socialist or laborer through at-large elections, the new government was more open than the previous one and established a pattern of accountability to the council and solicitation of public opinion. This pattern was important in shaping its later responses to public rejection of tax increases.

Council-manager government improved services, but it reduced partisanship and discouraged citizens from running for office. Although expert citizens were consulted on commissions, most citizens had little or no direct role in government. As promised, issues tended to be defined more technically and less politically. In this sense, the council-manager system in Dayton insulated government from popular control. "And perhaps as a form of response, percentages of registered voters participating in municipal elections dropped" (Sealander 1988, 127).

By the middle of the 1970s, Dayton's economic situation had changed. Dayton, like St. Louis, had experienced considerable economic base erosion. In October 1989 the former budget director, Paul Woodie, said in an interview:

> The city was in fiscal stress. NCR [Patterson's company] alone had lost 20,000 jobs. Major employers were reducing staff. Technology had changed, and we were not prepared. We were in a bind, and the people got mad at us as we cut back. The more things got cut, the more they would not support a tax increase, and the more we had to cut. It was getting worse and worse.

Dayton's standard response to financial issues, to propose a program and get public backing for it, was not working. There was no money to create new programs. Instead, programs were being cut. Threatened with unemployment, people were saying no to taxes. But the city, continuing on a downward spiral, could neither accept the no, nor force taxation on the public. The city government needed to forge a new level of public support at the same time that services were being cut.

The first step was to improve the articulation of citizen goals for the budget early in the budget process. This idea had been endorsed by William Allen of the New York Bureau of Municipal Research many years earlier. Allen had consulted on the establishment of the Dayton Bureau of Municipal Research. His goals were achieved some fifty-five years later.

The Dayton system involved the establishment of community priority boards whose members plan a portion of the budget and for whom a certain portion of the budget is set aside. The former budget director, Paul Woodie, described this system:

> There are seven priority boards. There are sixty-five neighborhood groups; they are forced into coalitions. The priority boards are staffed with four people from the Office of Neighborhoods. The city creates a list of possible staff and the boards pick from the list. They write their own constitutions, but there are usually twenty-five to thirty-five members. They are elected by the citizens by mail ballot, and each neighborhood council has representation, too. They review everything the city does. They do a needs statement before the manager's budget message. They conduct neighborhood hearings . . . , the neighborhood prepares its needs, including its capital needs. There isn't enough playground equipment? They [the neighborhoods] submit [the request], the priority boards screen them, but don't rank-order them, and prepare a needs statement.

The council received this neighborhood needs survey, along with a statement of neighborhood conditions prepared by the staff and opinion data collected by the staff. The departments had to respond to every issue raised, whether by the council or by the neighborhoods. If department heads said no to a neighborhood request, they had to explain why and argue with the city manager.

The citizens also reviewed the capital budget. Projects were evaluated in terms of their impact on the economy, on costs, and on the poor. Paul Woodie described the process: "The professionals make the first pass judgment, then the citizens go over it. There is a group of sixteen that goes over it, change each other's rankings. Then it's resolved. The projects are ranked by the cumulative votes of the actors."

The citizen priority boards began in 1970. By 1974, a second round of changes took place. According to Woodie,

> I think it was sometime in August, I am not sure of the month, but it

was 1974. Taxes were put in the budget office. I said, we will spell out what service we will provide, and spell out a levy to provide those services for five years. If we fail, we will lose. The tax increase will die in 1979. It's a plan. There was a vote on the plan. After the vote, the clock began, and we had to implement it. By 1979, if we had failed to implement it, they could throw us out of office or not vote for the increase again.

The city added a system of evaluation to the budget and circulated it to the public and the press so that citizens could see if the city was achieving the goals it had promised to achieve when it asked for the temporary tax increase. The now enforceable contract with the public to provide a particular level and combination of services with the temporary tax money radically changed the roles of city hall and the citizens. The citizens were telling the city what it should do, what it would have to do, to get and keep their support for taxes. This plan was extremely successful. The temporary tax was extended again and again, supported in referendums by wide margins.

In evaluating progress toward these promised service delivery goals, the budget office initially selected from the departmental measures of performance those that were most important to circulate outside the departments. Woodie observed:

> That worked for a while. Then I began to ask, how did I know what was important? The city council needs to set objectives over five years that comply with the five-year plan. The city commission [council] should set the policy goals. We restructured the program budget based on their goals ... the council could then see it [the budget] in terms of their policies, and the manager could see if the objectives were met, not met, partially met, or exceeded. The extent to which the targets were met is reported in the budget.

Then the budget director focused on trying to relink the council and the citizens so there would be a direct flow of opinion and evaluation. The council was supposed to consider citizen input in policy-making. Under the initial council-manager plan, when the council decided on a policy, it then sought public support for that policy by consulting known interest groups. The budget director set up a system in which all the citizens fed the council opinions on services regularly, not just when the council had an issue on which it wanted support.

The assumption is often made that the council knows what goes on, and they don't. Council members get elected on advocacy of some issue, maybe housing or crime. Then we give them a line-item budget. They want to discuss the environment; we don't let them do that with the line-item budget. But they need information to be able to discuss the issues. So we put in a condition statement, a picture of Dayton neighborhoods. The description has to be both statistical and perceptual. From the politicians' perspective if you don't provide perceptual data you have missed it. It's not just actual crime rates that are important but how safe people feel. Perception is probably the more important of the two. . . . We began to measure public opinion in the early 1970s; now we do it every year. Each neighborhood has a perception of street cleaning that goes up or down over fifteen years.

The former budget director summarized the intent of the changes he made in 1975:

If you want citizen involvement, and I wanted real public input—we needed to pass the tax—we were going to become responsive. That means citizen input before bureaucrats' [input]; the public hearing means nothing. I kept saying, "We want substantive democracy, not procedural democracy."

The formal hearing at which no one shows up and at which no further decisions are made was not enough. That was merely pretending to listen to citizens, not actually listening to them. Dayton's system required public officials to listen to citizens and take their views seriously. But professional staff members were often skeptical of ordinary citizens making decisions. Said Woodie:

Some people say, but we can't trust them [the implication here is that they are ill informed]. Okay, then train neighborhood leaders. The city selects potential neighborhood leaders and takes them through six months of work programs and educates them. Many then run for city priority board. Then we do explicit training for the priority board. People gravitate from one level to another. Even if you don't like them, they aren't dummies.

There were other problems with the new system. Each neighborhood had difficulty working with other neighborhoods, and poor people and rich people had trouble working together. These problems were dealt with and generally overcome. The city was divided into seven pie-shaped wedges, with the inner part of each wedge likely to be poorer and have more rundown neighborhoods than the outer portions. Woodie related the workings of the system:

> These people had to sit together on boards. It wasn't easy at first, but it gradually became "our side of town" [rather than "our neighborhood"]. The more articulate people from the outside of the wedges began to articulate for the other, less articulate folks. People at the top of the hill talked to the people at the bottom.
>
> There were conflicts. The meaning of equity had to be worked out. If all the money was community development block grants, it all had to be used on the poor and middle-income people. Instead, you have to mix the goodies so that everyone can get something.
>
> Those on the outside of the wedge could help save a nearby neighborhood, but they could also gain something for themselves. Everyone has a combination of motivations, both altruistic and self-oriented. The big bucks go in to the center, but there are other things, like cul de sacs, for the outer ring. You can live in the central city and still have niceties you would get in suburbia. Many central cities threaten the middle class. We give them petunias. We don't say, petunias are not government block-grant funded.

In addition to the priority boards, which made specific recommendations for spending, the city drew citizens into planning and goals formulation for the six-year plan called Dayton Tomorrow. This planning function gathered opinion on where the city should be going, what it should be focusing on, and what economizing measures should be taken. Opinions were gathered systematically, from the whole city. Staff members received some 10,000 suggestions, which they winnowed down to about 70 workable goals and targets. According to Ted Bucaro, a Dayton budget analyst interviewed in July 1991, the goals were general: "like increase control of drugs, increase negotiations with other governmental units to improve sanitation, facilitate good relations between ethnic groups."

Despite popular support for tax increases, economic base erosion and recession-related financial problems led to fiscal stress in Dayton. The city adopted a form of target-based budgeting to help it get through the toughest years. In target-based budgeting, dollar limits are set to the departments' requests. They may not ask for more than a certain amount, but in turn they are given more autonomy over how the money will be spent in order to get the maximum out of every dollar. Target-based budgeting is a way of prioritizing expenditures at the margins.

Target-based budgeting had a second impact. The budgeting system changed the traditional roles of the legislative body and the executive. One consequence was a shift from legislative control of line items to control of totals. Such a shift reflected not only increased trust by councils of their professional staff and a reluctance to micromanage the departments but also trust by the department heads of the council that a bargain struck will be a bargain adhered to, that the departments will deliver an agreed-upon level of service for an agreed-upon sum and that politicians will not continually try to lower the sum and raise the expectations of service delivery. The budgeting system continued to change into the 1990s. More financial problems have resulted from a weak economic base, but citizen input remains strong. The focus for problem-solving has shifted away from tax increases and toward limiting the size and scope of government by prioritizing services.

Conclusions

The three cities whose budget processes have been sketched in this chapter all ran into difficulties as the result of too narrow a support base. The exclusion of the poor, which was part of the earlier reforms, later become problematic. In each case, the city had to make cuts as the result of financial problems and, in doing so, cut services and alienated voters, creating a diminishing level of support and episodic and resounding votes of no on referendums. Each city responded differently to this shocking slap in the face.

St. Louis's business-dominated government kept doing its big redevelopment projects, tying up revenues over the long run in debt repayment and finding ways around citizen rejection of bond and tax referendums. The city did not change its form of budgeting or the nature of its large, district-based, but powerless Board of Aldermen. The only thing that voters could change was the mayor; they elected a black man to office, with the expectation that he would be more sympathetic to the concerns of the underserved and needy. But any successor to Mayor Schoemehl would probably have very few resources to work with.

In Phoenix, the business community strove for expansion and

growth and simultaneously insisted on low taxes. As a result, they systematically underfunded the necessary service expansion to new areas of the city and did not support services for the elderly or poor. As the social problems of the city, including crime, became more acute, and as minorities gained more political voice, the dominant coalition of the city broadened, ultimately forcing open the council and the budget process to broader, but carefully controlled, participation.

Dayton changed its way of budgeting considerably, to create a much more council-dominated and citizen-dominated budget process. Although staff members could exercise a veto for cause, the presumption was that citizen preferences in budgets drawn up with money designated for this purpose would be accepted as part of the budget. The city set up a contract with citizens, with a five-year plan embodying citizen goals; if the city did not achieve the goals, the citizens could choose not to renew a temporary tax. More recently, the city adopted a new five-year plan and increased citizen involvement in prioritizing services. Dayton redefined professionalism in this new context.

While Dayton kept its political structure intact and changed its budget process, Phoenix changed its political structure to be more representative. Phoenix had been more clearly dominated by a narrow business elite. Citizens were willing to pay for services, if only they could get them. Phoenix has increased its outreach to citizens, and its staff is more sensitive to council demands and requirements. The city has begun to accommodate to big-city problems, like housing and crime, but it has not followed Dayton's example of building citizens into the budget process.

6

Strong-Mayor Cities and Budgeting:

Current Cases

ROCHESTER, NEW YORK; Tampa, Florida; and Boston, Massachusetts—all share a form of government dominated by the mayor. Rochester had a council-manager government but dropped it in favor of a strong-mayor system in 1986. Tampa and Boston have had strong-mayor governments for many years. In each of these cities, the council was basically disempowered with respect to the budget. The mayor was simultaneously responsible for accountability, leadership, responsiveness, and budgetary balance. He or she had to satisfy claimants on the budget and balance income with outgo. Claimants' demands were often contradictory, so the mayor somehow had to allow for downtown redevelopment and neighborhood renewal as well as basic and social services. And all this had to be done with an eye on the next election. Accountability to the public was defined as pleasing a majority of voters.

Strong-mayor cities have had some budgeting characteristics in common. First, budget reform in strong-mayor cities has been characterized by a start-and-stop pattern exaggerated by bouts of fiscal stress. Second, mayor-dominated cities often have tried to resolve their financial difficulties by getting more assistance from other levels of government. Third, the appearance of the city's financial state has sometimes been as important as, or more important than, the reality. The mayor has had too many conflicting roles. One way conflicts have been resolved has been to deal with symbolization and reality separately. Fourth, because of the likelihood of a rival on the council, strong mayors sometimes have sought to keep budgetary information from the council and hence from the public. Fifth, the mayors have sought policy control over what were often highly decentralized and independent departments. Mayors have needed to find a way to carry out election promises. One approach has been to impose mayoral appointees over the departments; another, to use target-based budgeting and performance measurement to assure that the mayor's priorities have been adequately funded.

Rochester, New York

In the late 1980s Rochester had not been a strong-mayor city for long, and so it was still in transition from a council-manager government. Rochester was an intermediate case also in the sense that when it had council-manager government, the reforms were neither complete nor extreme. For years, the city retained political parties and active caucuses in the council. While reformers bemoaned political machines, this party connection resulted in a less extreme isolation from the public than occurred in a number of other council-manager cities. Rochester's council was split between at-large and district seats—and was not extreme in either direction. And Rochester was characterized by strong and independent departments, even during its council-manager period, as many strong-mayor cities are. Rochester was more political under the council-manager system than were many other council-manager cities.

Rochester's budget changed in fits and starts. The city adopted a program budget in the late 1960s, but by 1970 line-item budgeting was restored. Budget reforms were not resumed until the mid-1970s. Then the staff worked on cost control, figuring out what cost groupings and centers were most appropriate. Once the cost centers were in place, attention shifted to the output side. In the late 1970s and early 1980s, staff members introduced performance statistics. This effort was interrupted by a service emergency, after which work on the budget was resumed. Then efforts to change the budget document tapered off. After the change to the strong-mayor form in 1986, the mayor made an effort to streamline the budget document, taking out redundant performance measures and those that were not used in decision making.

The restoration of line-item budgeting in 1970 resulted from a shift in the majority party in the council. From 1970 to 1974, the Republicans dominated. They were not very organized in the council, and there was a new city manager each year. There was no time for any manager to leave an imprint on the budget. During the four years of Republican dominance, little attention was given to financial control or budgeting. When the Democrats took back city hall in 1974, the city was in financial trouble, and budget and accounting data were so neglected and distorted that the source and severity of the problem were not immediately clear.

The Democrats found they had to raise taxes considerably to rebalance the budget. To help staff members figure out what had happened and how extensive the problem was, and to help explain the need for tax increases to council members, citizens, and other governmental agencies, staff members worked hard to improve the budget. They changed the budget format to include program descriptions, workload measures, and explanations of changes from the previous year. They cut staffing levels by attrition, engaged in productivity bargaining with the labor force, and revamped portions of service delivery mechanisms.

In 1978 the process of reforming the budget was brought to a standstill as a consequence of delayed maintenance and delayed capital outlays. Snow-plowing equipment was old; it had not been maintained or replaced; and it fell apart during a major snow emergency. Fiscal stress had contributed to the service deficit, which then took priority over improving the budget.

After the service problem was resolved, the city's fiscal stress escalated. Because the city at that time depended on property taxes, rather than sales taxes, it weathered the recession of the middle 1970s without too much trouble, but it was hard hit by the rapid inflation that affected expenditures more than revenues toward the end of the 1970s. In the spring of 1978 the New York State Court of Appeals ruled that Rochester had illegally excluded some expenditures from the property tax limit, forcing a last-minute change in the 1978–79 operating budget, which resulted in service and personnel cuts and increases in user charges, taxes, and special assessments (Rubin 1992).

Preparing for 1980, staff members found that the level of state aid was uncertain, wage levels depended on arbitration decisions not yet made, and the size of the tax refund the city would have to pay depended on a forthcoming court decision. The county would not create a refuse district to alleviate the city's burden, and assessed valuation began to decline. The manager wrote in his budget letter: "It was clear we had to prepare for a wide variety of alternatives and produce a budget that could be adjusted to reflect changes in the City's economic situation that were largely outside our direct control. Departments were, therefore, instructed to prepare basic budgets which would enable us to make further reductions if necessary or restore priority items if additional resources became available" (from Budget of the City of Rochester 1980, 2). By 1979–80, the city was overwhelmed with fiscal stress and began to rely on target-based budgeting as a way of handling uncertain levels of revenues while assuring that basic services were covered.

The fiscal crisis of the late 1970s and early 1980s was not resolved for several more years. The city was required under a court settlement to pay back somewhere between $20 million and $30 million that it had collected illegally, outside the tax limit—money the city did not have. Threatened with bankruptcy, the city borrowed money from the state; the loan eventually became permanent. The financial situation improved when an agreement was reached with the county in 1984 to share sales taxes. Bolstered by this new source of revenue, the city struggled to freeze and reduce the level of property taxes, which was undoubtedly a politically popular action.

The effort to gain the county's cooperation required convincing the county that the city really was in financial straits. That effort may have led to some distortion in revenue projections. After the financial problem was resolved, the city was able to concentrate on improving the quality of projections. In an interview in October 1989, Al Sette, the budget director, noted:

> The multiyear projection, let me put it tactfully. This is more straightforward than previously. There may have been a good reason, particularly in the early 1980s. The city was trying to get the county to recognize the financial problems of the city, the revision of the sales tax; we had to show how poor we were. Some gaps were overstated. I would ask, Is that the projection? Some said one thing, some said something else. It made me uncomfortable; it can come back to haunt you. Now, the projections hold up well.

Rochester began to use program budgets in the late 1960s, abandoned them in the early 1970s, resumed them in the mid-1970s, interrupted budgetary improvements in the late 1970s, and then maintained a relatively stable pattern, including the program format and target-based budgeting, throughout the 1980s. The creation of performance measures followed the general stop-and-start pattern, growing in the 1970s but stopping in the 1980s. Most of the work in the 1980s was focused on eliminating repetitious and unnecessary measures. By 1990 most departments listed only demand and workload measures, without efficiency or output measures. A few had one or two measures of output, but without any targets to compare actual with promised performance.

Several observers noted that more work needed to be done on the performance measures but that the process seemed to be stuck. One reason was that the traditional justification for keeping performance measures—to improve productivity—was seen as less relevant than responding to citizen requests and desires. Performance measures as conceived in Rochester did not satisfy this purpose. Budget director Sette described the shortcomings of the performance indicators:

> One [budget analyst] did a cost-benefit analysis of the mounted patrol, but that is like tar-feathering Mother Teresa. They shouldn't spend time on the mounted patrol; it's beloved. But performance indicators tell you very little. How many kids petted the horse, it isn't in there. If I knew how to do that I would, but I go with my gut instincts. [The mounted patrol] is venerated.

The outcome, as far as the budget director was concerned, was reelection, not more efficient pothole filling: "Reelection is the result; citizens showed that. For example, [you got] twenty-five calls for potholes, you filled them, used X tons of fill, each cost $100 dollars, but so what? You filled twenty-five potholes. That is what matters to citizens."

A second reason that the development of performance measures stopped was that research that would let the city evaluate the outcomes of services was expensive, and there was little support for it. The city was "not ready to share" the results of such studies if the reports suggested that some service was poorly performed. Presumably the mayor was concerned that measuring performance would make him vulnerable to criticism. When asked what he would improve about the budget, he did not include performance measures in the list, even when prompted by his budget director.

A third reason that progress on performance measures was stymied was that the departments often did not understand or accept what was required. Said Director Sette: "In the 1970s we wanted all types of indicators, demand, efficiency, results, but you would have repetition in all the categories." That is, the departments made no distinction between workload and the impact of their work. They used workload measures for everything. Departments sometimes feared evaluation and simply did not present meaningful numbers. The manager and budget office were unwilling to impose evaluation on reluctant departments (former budget director Robert Myers, interview with the author, October 1989).

Part of the impression of a relatively stable budget format and process throughout the 1980s was a result of the continuing use of the target-based budget process. With target-based budgets, departments were asked to prioritize their own expenditures and thus determine their own cuts. The process eased the relationship with the budget office during cutback. Said Director Sette: "When departments ask, why did you fund this as opposed to that, the priority setting by the departments helps a great deal."

The departments were supposed to make the priorities and live by them, but some departments refused to play by the rules. Sette argued:

> Some refuse [to make priorities]. They can't decide. They don't want to say, "Bureau X is number 1 and Bureau Z is number 3. They want to submit their requests by bureau [forcing the budget office to choose between their bureaus]. I won't let them.... [I tell them] You don't want us to do it. We get blamed anyway. They put in things they can't win and then blame the budget bureau. They want to be good bosses; they put it in because a subordinate wants it, but they know they won't get it. Most [departments] are reasonable in terms of requests. Some put the mayor's priority as number 30. But [if they do that] we won't fund the intermediate items. Sometimes they get by us, but only once.

Target-based budgeting was flexible in adapting to uncertainty and to richer and leaner times. It was also superbly adapted to a city with highly independent departments. It forced the departments to prioritize and thus helped tame the antagonistic relationship between the departments and the budget office. This feature of target-based budgeting was especially necessary during times of cutback because the departments were so strong with respect to the budget office.

Target-based budgeting had an additional advantage that became more important after the adoption of a strong-mayor government: it forced the departments to give higher priority to those projects and programs the mayor was emphasizing in public. If the departments did not accommodate the mayor's priorities, the budget office would deny any request the departments placed higher on the priority listing than the major's program or project. For all these reasons, once target-based budgeting was initiated, it stayed in place.

The budget director, Al Sette, described how the target-based process helped implement financial control and force the departments to live within assigned limits. This process helped centralize a crucial element of the budgetary system, giving the budget office better control of budgetary balance. The budget office took control of totals and delegated control of details. According to Sette,

> A frequent ploy is to ask for unanticipated expenses. "We had to plant two trees [so we need more money]." I say, there are unanticipated events on both sides, revenues and expenditures. I will take back what you did not spend [if you expect me to cover your increases in expenditures]. It's better if you just manage and stay in the black. And you won't hear from me.

In other words, the budget director forced a greater degree of responsibility on the departments. They could keep any money they saved or money that was unspent due to overestimates of costs, but they would get no additional money for emergencies. They were expected to reprogram their funds from the surplus to the deficit accounts or move money between line items. This lump-sum allocation could not work if the departments could request and get additional funding. The total budget allocated to each department had to serve as the primary fiscal discipline, forcing efficiencies. Hence the city strengthened the requirement that each department balance its own budget. This requirement was enforced beginning in 1988.

Most of the changes in the budget process and format had occurred by the early 1980s and were relatively stable throughout the decade. In the mid 1980s, however, the city changed its government from a council-manager to a mayor-dominated form. The modification influenced budgeting in some ways.

One obvious change in budgeting was that the mayor, rather than the manager, became the key figure in examining the budget. How extensively the manager reviewed the budget when the city had the council-manager form depended on the personality and background of the manager. Those who had come up the finance route were more likely to put together their own budgets, scrutinizing each request in detail. Other city managers left more responsibility to the budget director. Mayor Ryan, the first mayor elected after the abandonment of the council-manager form, paid considerable attention to the budget, but the budget office carefully sifted issues and brought only a small number to the mayor for resolution. For that small number of cases, the mayor would review the entire matter. The budget office would resolve most of the problems directly with the departments. This winnowing process allowed the mayor to deal with matters that involved setting policy, but it also enhanced the power of the budget office. Thus some of the work that had been done by the city manager shifted to the budget office. Also, some of the policy setting that had been done by a majority in the council was now almost exclusively the responsibility of the mayor.

Though the council played a substantial role under the manager system, operating as a sort of board of directors, its role became more that of a watchdog, almost an adversary of the mayor, under the mayor system. In order to be an effective watchdog, a council must have good budget information, but early indicators suggested that the council's access to these data had deteriorated, the quality of its staff was inadequate to the need, and its understanding of the budget was limited. The tendency of the mayor's office to shift lines and programs from year to year further confused the council because it was nearly impossible to calculate the costs of programs through time.

Council members generally went along with the mayor's proposals, in part because they agreed with him and in part because they lacked information to do much else. When the press attacked the council as mindless sheep being guided by the mayor as shepherd, the mayor determined that the council would make minor changes in his budget to show that they were alive. The council's role, both direct and indirect, was limited to this symbolic show.

Direct public involvement in the budget process was very limited in Rochester. The budget document itself was the key instrument of financial accountability. Under council-manager government, the budget was a remarkably open document, including financial information that could potentially be embarrassing to politicians. The shift to a mayor-dominated form of government made staff fear that this openness might make the mayor feel vulnerable and that, as a consequence, he would keep particular bits of information out of the budget.

Budget Director Sette argued: "There are things in the budget that are unflattering, but whether that will continue, I don't know. If it is politicized—other than what the charter requires, we don't have to present it this way." In other words, if the content of the budget were to become political fodder, other than meeting the requirements in the charter, the city could change the format of the budget and obscure the offending material.

The mayor was sensitive to what his opponents conveyed to the press about his budget. He was not supportive of strengthening the performance measures in the budget, and he deemphasized the performance goals that a staff member had developed and put in the budget two years earlier. Reportedly, the mayor was not comfortable with such goals because they would make him look bad if they were not accomplished. A former staffer said, "The mayor doesn't want to do the goals statement again. He was persuaded at the last minute to include it in the 1990 budget because it would look funny to have it only for one year. But here it is September, October, and the process should have begun again, and it's not happening."

To summarize, fiscal stress and uncertainty had a clear impact on the budget process in Rochester. At the same time, pressure to increase openness to the public had less influence on the budget process than it did in council-manager cities. The abandonment of the council-manager form represented more a yearning for policy leadership than a demand for more responsive government.

Nevertheless, the adoption of a strong-mayor government had some effects on the budget. Key among them was that the mayor, who was now responsible for the budget, was also interested in reelection. Performance measurement needed to serve the goal of reelecting the mayor. The target-based budgeting system forced independent departments to include in the budget those things the mayor identified as important. Thus target-based budgeting, too, helped reelect the mayor. Disempowerment of the council accompanied the shift away from the council-manager system. The mayor may have viewed council members as possible rivals, from whom potentially damaging information should be kept. As a result, almost all public accountability depended on the person of the mayor and what he chose to report or not report. Staff were concerned that the mayor's focus on publicity and image would limit what he chose to report.

Rochester did not emphasize long-range financial planning. Instead, the city took one crisis at a time. Sometimes the courts intervened to precipitate a financial problem; sometimes the city was rescued by other governmental units through loans and shared revenues. Relations with the courts, the state government, and the county were crucial in Rochester as the city struggled with fiscal stress.

Tampa, Florida

As in Rochester, the mayor in Tampa, Florida, was the major means of assuring accountability to the public on budgeting issues. The role of the council in budgeting was limited. Because of the importance of the mayor in the budget, when there was a new mayor, the budget process and format often changed along with him. A long history of independent departments started to change with the introduction of target-based budgets, which forced the departments to implement overall targets and helped the mayor control policy.

The Budgetary Power of the Mayor and the Council

Tampa has a strong-mayor form of government, but the council has not been completely disempowered. The mayor and his staff draw up the budget proposal and present it to the council. The council has the option of making changes in the budget, but the mayor has a line-item veto and can reject any items that in his estimation threaten the integrity of the budget. Council changes in the executive's proposed budget are considered to demonstrate a failure of process; budget staff members monitor council sessions and council pronouncements and try to incorporate council members' reasonable requests in the budget proposal. Council members should have little reason to change the mayor's proposal, and if the council members make last-minute or unreasonable changes, they risk public rejection. Normally, such requests are derailed earlier in the process. Council budgetary power is real, but it is often informal and limited in comparison to that of the mayor.

The mayor reportedly used the veto power sparingly, but he did not hesitate to cut out additional staffing requests. In 1990 a former budget director, Al Desilet, described it this way:

> The council will say, I want to hire 150 firefighters, you did it for the police last year. But the fire loss did not increase. So how do you

counter that argument? You have to be smart, one-upsmanship. You have to deflect that group of councilmen who want to hire. If they authorize the funds, they will be impounded. They can't sustain an override, if they get that far. They do sometimes override, it depends on the issue. They could say, we add $100 million in revenues so we can hire more firefighters. The mayor and the budget officer say no, I won't do that.

At the same time that the mayor can exclude staffing requests from the council, he can require that staffing requests be accommodated in the budget. The mayor may say, I need twenty-five more policemen; find a way to do it. In this particular area, the mayor's powers clearly outstrip the council's. In addition, the mayor and his staff set the targets for the target-based budgets. Since so much of the discipline of the target-based system is based on treating the targets as firm, the council cannot alter them during the year.

Besides the formal powers of the mayor, including a line-item veto, the mayor controls the nature and timing of publicity over the budget proposal. Said Budget Director Jim Stefan in October 1990:

> Pictures and graphics are important.... [The budget presentation got] more advanced; [we progressed from] slides to video. The presentation has phrases, rolling words. It goes out over the cable system; it reaches the whole city and county over cable, at the same time that it goes to the council. It runs a half a dozen more times during the week following the presentation to the council, and we take the presentation to the public too. We use the legal forum of presenting it to the council, but also present it to the public.

The presentation is intended to convince the council and the public of what goals must be accomplished and how they should be achieved.

The council often plays the role of watchdog. This relationship runs reasonably smoothly if no one in the council is running for mayor, but if there are possible rivals to the mayor in the council, council members may use budgets and city performance reports to spot and press the mayor's political vulnerabilities. This relationship puts pressure on the mayor to close down the information flow to the council. In 1991 a city planner, Roger Wehling, explained:

> The city council is a springboard for mayoral candidates; they try to make the mayor look bad. When she [the mayor at the time of the in-

terview] was a council member, as chair of the council, she was the interim mayor, and then she ran for mayor. She took the service-level analysis system [SLA] and looked at the unmet needs, using them as if the budget should have corrected all of them. It was unfair. But she is so aware of this tactic, and it was used against her, so she wants to get rid of it [the service-level analysis].

The mayor sends policy preferences along with targets for total spending to the departments before the original budget submissions. In preparing their budget requests, the departments put their expenditures in two lists. The first list consists of the items that are most important to the running of their operation. This list is trimmed to fit within the spending targets. The second list is composed of items department heads think are important but do not fit into their targets. When the mayor reviews these lists of unfunded items, he may choose to add some of them back into the budget. A small amount of money is set aside for this purpose. The following is a portion of an interview with Jim Stefan in October 1990:

> *Stefan*: We leave a small amount of money available for the mayor to review these [unfunded items], so the mayor can give some. It's called the mayor's holdback account. Some money for necessary things.
> *Author*: How much money is that?
> *Stefan*: In good years, up to a million, in bad years, $250,000, on a $140 million departmental total. It's a very little amount of money. Sometimes it's spent, sometimes it's not.

Thus in Tampa, the holdback was to be spent by the mayor alone, in contrast to the holdback in Phoenix, which was to be spent by the mayor and the council together.

Budget Changes

Tampa's budgeting was characterized by two major and interrelated features: target-based budgeting and service-level analysis (SLA). These features were introduced, modified, terminated, or restarted by different mayors, each eager to put an imprint on the budget process. Bouts of fiscal stress also contributed to the shaping of the process.

Service-level analysis in Tampa was a system of performance standards. It began in 1972, when the city put together a planning staff to deal with the federal Model Cities program. At the request of the planners, this group of staff members was located in the finance office, not the planning and zoning office. The planners felt they should do a needs assessment before allocating funds. In the mid-1970s, using established planning approaches to the subject, they devised standards and goals for city services so that staff members could examine facilities and neighborhoods and know if they were above or below standard and by how much. The planners met with the mayor to discuss their estimates of unmet needs and to get the mayor's support for the resulting list of projects.

Mayor William Poe liked the process and expanded it from the grant program to the rest of the city departments, keeping service-level analysis under the planners' auspices. The planners emphasized outcome measures, such as clearance rates for the police and successful prosecutions. The police chief did not use such measures. In his budget presentations, he emphasized dangers and the crime rate in order to get bigger budgets. To the mayor, it must have seemed as if the more money he spent on police, the worse the situation became. Hence he preferred the more objective measures of the planners. Because the mayor sided with the planners on this issue, he aroused the resentment of the departments against the planners and their performance measures.

The next mayor, Bob Martinez, "was bombarded by the departments asking him to get planning out of that role. He abolished half the planning staff and took us [planning] out of the budget process" (Roger Wehling, interview with the author, January 1991). But Martinez found he needed more information than a straight line-item budget provided. "His first budget was line item, without the city needs assessment and condition analysis," but he found that "he could be finessed to think that something minor was major" (Wehling interview). Martinez reinstated the needs assessment. It gradually grew into a major performance standards system, with goals and targets and measurement toward the goals for every department. These service-level goals were tightly linked to the budget so that the departments made an implicit contract to provide so much service of such a quality for so many dollars.

To implement the system once the planners were out of the loop required the departments to learn how to set up their own targets and measurements. The service-level analysis emphasized putting management prerogatives in the departments. The departments could deliver on their promised level of services any way they chose. As Roger

Wehling described it, the service-level analysis made the department heads managers because they were evaluated on the basis of their results. Some of the departments resisted the system at first, or dragged their feet in putting together the new standards, but the ones that refused to cooperate got poor evaluations. Over time, they adjusted.

The orientation toward planning and needs-assessment that underlay the service-level analysis was antagonistic to the neighborhood and squeaky-wheel basis of district-based councils. A district orientation would have disrupted the SLAs, but that did not happen. As Wehling explained:

> We decided where the need was greatest and put it there. Single district keeps a ledger and wants proportionate amounts [in each district], not the next dollar, where the need is greatest. But we never ran into a ledger system. They [the council members] bought into this, and it helped when you went to the neighborhoods. We could say, "You had a need, and we will address it, but it may take five years, because these neighborhoods have higher needs." They bought into it readily.

Target-based budgeting was adopted at about the same time as Mayor Bob Martinez entered office, in 1979. Informants suggested several different reasons for the acceptance of TBB. One reason was that it reduced the tension between the budget office and the departments, especially when dealing with a cutback situation. Another reason was that the new mayor wanted a new budget system, one that he could put his name on.

Al Desilet, who was budget director when target-based budgeting was adopted, argued that the reason he adopted it was that he was tired of playing games with the departments and that it should not be his role to micromanage the departments.

> I had been there before, but did not like receiving ridiculous budget requests. I spent ten years receiving budget requests that were 30 to 40 percent too high. My job was to find what to cut. That is silly, for a budget officer to do that; they did not tell me what needed to be funded. . . . It was my opinion that a professional in charge of a public service would be capable of doing the best he could, given a level of funding. Only he and his staff can do that. No one else can do that. If the police chief says he needs $30 million, how do you ask him what to cut? He will say, I will take policemen off the streets in

the ghetto. That is a stupid answer. He won't say, "Soft crap." He won't tell you the soft, discretionary stuff.

A former staffer in the budget office pointed out that one reason target-based budgeting was adopted was that the budget office in the previous year had made midyear cuts that were arbitrary and they now felt guilty. So budget staff members went out of their way to devise a system that would look fair and appropriate to the departments. The apparent objectivity of the targets and all the considerations that went into setting them helped reassure the departments that the cuts were made on reasonable grounds.

The mayor supported the target-based budgeting system, even when employees, including political appointees, were forced onto the unfunded list. The department heads expected the mayor or the council to overturn their recommendations to release employees, but the mayor backed the budget office and the target-based system. If the departments put staff members on the unfunded list, they were out.

In 1990 the former budget director, Al Desilet, argued that one of the reasons the mayor supported the target-based system was that it was different and could be used as a mark of his administration.

> *Desilet*: All new mayors want to be identified with new ways, even if it's program budgeting or target budgeting. . . .
> *Author*: Did Martinez want to get control over the departments?
> *Desilet*: Yes, of course, but primarily he wanted to differentiate himself from his predecessors, like all politicians. . . . If the previous administration was Democratic, then we do something different.

While the basic elements of the budget process in Tampa have been in place for many years, the budget system has changed somewhat with each new administration. As Roger Wehling put it in 1991, "From an academic standpoint, you can hypothesize the best system, but it has to match the management style of the chief executive."

In October 1990 Budget Director Jim Stefan, who began to work for the city in the last year of Mayor William Poe's administration, described the key differences between Poe and his successor, Bob Martinez, with respect to the budget.

When Martinez came in, he had a different management style—a lot more finance, budget, and control—he was a numbers person. He was public with that information. The documents switched to narratives; [the budget became] a policy document for the city. We started to give them out to people. Those are the major changes. Before, Bill Poe went to the council and gave them a computer report that was bound.

The service-level analysis begun under Poe was interrupted, but it was later further developed under Martinez. It reportedly matched Martinez's personality but not that of Sandra Freedman, who succeeded Martinez as mayor. According to Roger Wehling,

He [Martinez] wanted to manage, right down to the number of computers. He knew the details, and wanted that level of detail. He was on top of everything. . . . I am surprised it [service-level analysis] has lasted four years [into Freedman's administration]. But now she wants to get rid of it, and try something of her own.

The "Superchief"[1] of Public Works, Mike Salmon, contrasted Sandra Freedman's style with that of Bob Martinez.

I like the SLA process. I don't like the mayor's direction on that. She is not a detail person, she doesn't value the SLA system . . . this mayor won't know much about widgets.

Another thing that I like with this mayor—this I like—is her expansion of public participation. Everyone loves democratic process, but it can become elitist. Politicians like her allow enormous participation from citizens, which also serves her from an election perspective. It makes it hard for us to be unresponsive. This can be a problem if you are trying to do something for the overall good of the city that some people object to, like transportation . . . the upshot of her effort to get more input (this is a nationwide trend) into public policy development is extraordinarily positive and beneficial. As mayor, she isn't interested in the details of service delivery, how many times the streets are swept and the cost. She leaves herself vulnerable. The last mayor did hear these things, he was interested in details. But she brings the public into it, a phenomenal benefit.

---

1. Superchiefs supervise several departments and, along with the mayoral staff, are considered part of upper administration.

The Superchief of Public Works noted the tension between citywide needs assessment based on planning and citizen demands funneled through the mayor. He argued for the legitimacy of both. He also noted that although Sandra Freedman's requests were legitimate because they came from the citizens and kept the bureaucracy accountable, they created problems for the bureaucracy because they violated the kind of contract for service that underlay the service-level analysis and the target-based budget. That contract required the departments not only to stay within the targets for spending but also to provide a promised level of service for the money. Freedman was more likely to try to increase the service level in some area without increasing the spending target. In this sense, public (and political) accountability through the mayor was not necessarily financially accountable.

This tension between efforts to satisfy public demands and realistic demands on departments for a given level of revenue is inherent in the mayor's role in the strong-mayor form. As Mike Salmon described it: "We wrestle with service delivery and her less than rational priorities. She says, I want the streets swept twice a week all over town, and cut the budget. It's difficult to rectify. [It's] our challenge, but she reflects public interest, what the public wants, and I believe in that as much as in management."

Although Martinez's goals were concrete and achievable in the short term, such as reducing costs for grant administration from 17 percent to less than 4 percent, Sandra Freedman was more interested in goals that could be stated as a continuum, such as working on intergovernmental cooperation or emphasizing crime prevention. These goals are legitimate and popularly based, but difficult to measure. When goals are vaguely stated, it is difficult to show any kind of failure, but success of any sort can be claimed as progress. From a public relations perspective, vague goals are less dangerous. As Roger Wehling described it:

They [broader goals] match her personality; she is very people oriented. She won by a large margin. She could talk in these terms to the public. She won't go out and say, "A building inspector is doing 1,950 inspections instead of 1,900." Martinez could do that. But she can say, "I got the private sector involved and got people involved in designing [policy]." Martinez never met with neighborhood groups; she does. They get immediate, near-term results.

Sandra Freedman's approach was more like strategic planning, which dealt with only a few issues, while service-level analysis was more like comprehensive planning and dealt with everything, every detail of service delivery. The newer model is less oriented to measuring performance and more oriented to stimulating and responding to citizen demands.

While some observers saw the adaptation of the service-level analysis as a necessary antidote to the elitism of the comprehensive planning approach done *for* the community rather than *with* or *by* the community, others expressed skepticism of the newer system and viewed it as a triumph of politics. One source, who wished to remain anonymous, said:

> She is politically ambitious. She needs to look good; the city only has to run well for 3 or 4 years. She can emphasize clichés. Over the long term she will reinstitute the squeaky wheel; the phone will ring off the hook when people learn that's how it's done. But if it's at the tail end of an administration, it can be the best way, a quick allocation with quick political payoff.

Freedman's request for changes in the budget process were not exclusively the product of her personality or values, they also reflected the public's demands for accountability and responsiveness. In January 1991 the city clerk, Frances Henriquez, described how citizen participation had increased over the past decade, and how that participation reflected increased demands on city hall and increased public frustration.

> [Some groups are motivated by] self-interest ... [they have] their own agendas. There are lots of environmental groups, gay rights groups have an agenda; we see more of this. There are more housing and civic groups that want their neighborhoods cleaned; they are better organized and more vocal. They want something done. They are frustrated.

The budgeters in Tampa were mildly frustrated over the loss of service-level analysis because it had served the city so well and it was so difficult to find a suitable substitute, but the budget director clearly understood that some changes in the direction of increased public outreach and participation were going to be necessary and that the budget process would have to adapt to survive.

The Martinez administration was focused on downtown redevelopment and on reducing the property tax. Presumably Freedman's advocacy for the neighborhoods was to some extent a reaction against that approach. As Jim Stefan noted,

> You can't just do the downtown either; the neighborhoods need some, too. This mayor is interested in neighborhoods, to restore the old neighborhoods. She goes out to talk to people, and brings the senior staff. Like a little city hall. She says, "I will tell you a few things, but then you tell us what your problems are and what needs to be done. We are here to address your concerns." Part is equity, part is a vision of what the community needs.

Tampa was struggling toward a model that would collect input from the community and balance downtown renewal and neighborhood claims for housing and commercial development. At the same time, anticipated fiscal stress and possible tax increases created additional pressure to develop a budget process that would explain programs and costs and describe the city's efficiency.

Budget Director Stefan argued that financial stress was going to require city hall to communicate better with the public and that communication was going to have to be two-way.

> There are a couple of hard years coming up, financially hard times. Cities are concerned about taxation. Communication and linkages have to be stronger; people have to understand what government is doing for them. The budget process has to be results-oriented as well as getting inputs from people, what they want. You need both.
>
> We need to communicate how costly services are. We have to have rapport and communication—we need to get that out, disseminate it. [We need to focus on] how to formalize the process. There is a lot of citizen input, by neighborhood boards and the like. How should we make people aware of how to do that, how can they get involved? We have to create that partnership between the community and the government. That changes the format. I don't believe in change for its own sake, but our times have changed and we have to adapt. This, too, will adapt. Just a little slow in government.

The early 1990s saw economic contraction, especially in real estate. The assessed valuation was unlikely to continue growing, and the tax rate could not be indefinitely reduced. The need to anticipate possible tax increases was part of what was driving the budget process changes. As in Dayton, more democracy in the budget process seemed to be the antidote to a possible citizen rejection of tax increases.

To summarize, budgeting in Tampa had to adapt to changing conditions, including more activated citizens and interest groups. But in the strong-mayor system, the only built-in way for the public to bring about changes was to elect a new mayor. The importance of the mayor and the desire of each mayor to put a personal imprint on the budget process contributed to start-and-stop budget reforms.

The political ambitions of the mayors were relevant to the budget process. Martinez used target-based budgeting to hold down departmental outlays so he could reduce property taxes, presumably because he was eager to run for governor. Sandra Freedman used her ability to direct budget priorities to get results for neighborhood groups and other special-interest groups. The result in the Martinez administration was "creative financing" and high user fees; the result in the Freedman administration was an attempt to get something for nothing by increasing service-level targets to meet political promises without increasing budget targets to pay for expanded services. Both strategies have costs in financial management and both illustrate the tension created by having the mayor play the dual role of financial manager and politician. It is tempting for the political role—gaining votes—to dominate.

Boston, Massachusetts

Beginning as early as 1885, Boston took budget power away from the council and gave it to the mayor. Executive budgeting was formally strengthened in 1909. To this day, financial decisions, including the budget format and process, depend on the mayor. The mayor's personality determines the emphasis on managerial control versus machine politics. The mayor's choices determine to whom city hall is accountable and to whom it responds.

Shortly after the strengthening of the executive budget in 1909, the mayor's position was successfully claimed by an Irish machine politician. Machine politicians often showed more interest in spending money and creating positions at city hall than in tight fiscal control. When combined with externally caused financial problems, the result was repeated municipal fiscal crises punctuated by state intervention.

The machine politicians also left a legacy of highly decentralized departments, with patronage appointments at the top to ensure policy control.

In the 1950s and 1960s, Boston's mayors were deeply interested in downtown renewal and defined neighborhood renewal as tearing down neighborhoods and putting up luxury apartment complexes. These policies earned the anger of the neighborhoods. The best way to make policy change in Boston was to elect a new mayor. Kevin White, who represented an anti-redevelopment pro-neighborhood platform, became the mayor, followed by Raymond Flynn (in office from 1984 to 1993), who had to try to hold together this multineighborhood, black and white coalition with a pro-neighborhood agenda. To keep this constituency together, it was essential that Flynn come through on his campaign promises.

In order to carry out his campaign pledges, Flynn needed a mechanism that would enable him to take policy control of the highly decentralized departments. At the same time, he needed to make some overtures to a business community threatened by his requirement that downtown development be linked to development of the neighborhoods. Mayoral appointees forged a new budget process that would simultaneously appeal to the business community by improving financial management and allow the mayor's priorities to be included in the budget. The reform included a program and performance budget and a centralized capital budget process. Several years later, the budget office added target-based budgeting to reduce competition between departments during cutback and help ensure that the mayor's priorities were not cut by the departments. This change increased central control over departmental spending totals while leaving many details of management to the departments.

History of Repeated Financial Crises
Boston has experienced a great deal of fiscal stress over the years. This stress has had a variety of impacts on budgeting. When stress was severe, it captured administrators' attention and interrupted budget reforms. It also forced the city to look to the state for assistance. This assistance was often forthcoming, but with a variety of strings attached that affected budgeting and financial management. Severe and continuous underfunding of capital projects resulted in court orders against the city to fix or rebuild physical plants, eventuating in a new office of capital budgeting. And in recent years fiscal stress has led to

target-based budgeting as a way of preserving the mayor's priorities during a period of cutback.

Boston has had its share of externally caused fiscal stress, including economic changes that robbed the city of its economic vitality, declines in population, school desegregation crises, statewide tax limits, and declining assessed valuations. The city has often added to the financial problems by doing things like adding staff and reducing property taxes before elections, overestimating revenues, and maintaining poor assessment practices that were continually challenged by nonresidential property owners.

These bouts of fiscal stress have put pressure on the city to appear well managed to the state and the financial community. The widespread support for Proposition 2½, a stringent property tax limitation, brought pressure on the city to explain to the public how well the city's money was being spent. Presumably, if the public and the city council could be convinced, they would help convince the legislature to authorize additional revenue sources. The need to do this has influenced the budget format in recent years.

Focusing on the postwar period, between 1950 and 1985, the city had "12 years of appropriations [operating] deficits, 19 years of revenue deficits [deficits resulting from misestimates of revenue] and 28 years of overlay deficits [deficits resulting from underfunding claims made by real estate owners for overassessment].... Deficits became a way of life" (Slavet and Torto 1985, i).[2]

When Mayor John Hynes took office in 1950, he argued for improved financial management, but the city was soon mired in financial problems made worse by poor financial management. One of the problems was that the city overestimated assessments. When the assessments were challenged, the city normally had to abate the taxes, that is, give back the money it had collected. It seldom put aside enough money to cover these abatements. To make matters worse, the city did not reassess the property after the abatement, setting up a similar problem for the following year.

Another problem was the accumulation of floating debt. The city borrowed short-term against the next year's revenue, rolling over the debt from year to year. By 1957 Boston had $35 million of floating debt. The next step was rescue by the state government.

---

2. The material on the city's repeated bouts of fiscal stress comes primarily from Slavet and Torto 1985.

When crisis erupted in mid 1957, state intervention to ease Boston's finances became necessary. The city was authorized to fund its accumulated deficits over a period of years, as in funding loan acts of 1938, 1941, 1946 and 1950, but the legislature also included several safeguards in the funding loan legislation of 1957 to discourage fiscal mismanagement and to stabilize the city's finances. (Slavet and Torto 1985, 9)

These state-mandated improvements included a larger fund to be set aside to cover refunds for contested assessments, limits to the amount of short-term loans in anticipation of revenues that the city could have outstanding at the end of the year, a requirement that deficits resulting from overestimated revenues be offset in the next year's budget, and a limit on revenue estimates requiring that they not exceed the previous year's actuals.

When Mayor John Collins took office in 1960, he took an aggressive stance in cutting costs and tried to get additional state help. He imposed spending controls and a staff reduction plan. He effected some departmental reorganization and tried to streamline operations for greater efficiency. He managed to get legislative approval for some new revenue sources for the city. He generally adhered to the state-imposed fiscal controls and curtailed poor long-term financial practices. "From 1960 to 1963, there was steady improvement in the city's finances" (Slavet and Torto 1985, 11–12).

From 1964 to 1967, however, the city's financial practices deteriorated, possibly because Mayor Collins ran for senator in 1966 and may have been trying to make the city look good by borrowing from the future to reduce taxes in the present. Most disturbing was the practice of taking the cash balance that funded the first three months of the next fiscal year to balance the present fiscal year. While legal, the practice created cash-flow problems and increased the costs of borrowing. By 1964, the operating deficit had reappeared, and in 1964 and 1965, tax rates had to jump to compensate for poor financial management.

The most serious problem from 1963 to 1967 lay in use of accumulated "free cash" both for tax rate reduction and to cover supplementary appropriations in the face of escalating welfare costs, increasing expenses for pensions and debt service, and higher re-

quirements for salaries and wages. In 1966 this was aggravated by a
shortfall in state aid of over $6.5 million due to state withholding of
school aid because of racial imbalances. The results were a revenue
deficit of $17.5 million and a net operating deficit of almost $17 million at the close of 1966. (Slavet and Torto 1985, 15)

By 1967, the city was in fairly severe fiscal stress, although it was
moderated by the state's granting the city a sales tax in 1966.

Mayor Kevin White took office in 1968 under reasonably favor-
able circumstances. The state lifted the embargo on school aid that it
had imposed because of the city's school desegregation problems and
picked up the local share of welfare, a major spending burden. "There
was relative stability from 1968 to 1970" (Slavet and Torto 1985, 17).
Spending expanded rapidly to fill the gap, however, especially for debt
service for bond issues funding economic development. Pensions increased and property tax collections declined. Operating deficits in
water and sewer funds aggravated the underlying problems. Short-
term borrowing escalated.

The financial problems got worse from 1971 to 1973. From 1973
to 1975, city officials tried to reduce staffing levels and improve financial management. Several outside factors helped control the situation.
In 1972 the Federal Revenue Sharing program began to deliver revenue; assessed values increased, and the state absorbed part of the mass
transit deficit. It also lowered Boston's share of the mass transit system's operating costs. The reduction in staffing levels helped, too, but
many underlying problems remained. The sewer and water fund kept
generating deficits that were covered by general revenues. And the city
began to build a new floating debt. The sewer and water deficit problem was resolved with the establishment of an independent sewer and
water commission in 1978, which ushered in several years of relative
stability. In fiscal 1979 the state increased the local aid formula to help
hold down property taxes in the state, but Boston did not succeed in
holding its tax rate down, which may have contributed to the passage
of Proposition 2½, a statewide referendum limiting property taxes.

Passed in 1980, Proposition 2½ shocked Boston's finances again.
At the same time, Boston was wrestling with paying off a court suit
(called the *Tregor* decision) resulting from assessment practices. From
1981 to 1982, the city was forced to reduce its budget by $75 million
and to lay off about 2,700 employees and more than 700 tenured
teachers. The cuts included major reductions in police and fire protec-

tion, public works, the mayoral agencies, and most deeply, in parks and recreation. Citizens were upset by the cuts and protested.

Boston was vulnerable to expensive lawsuits because of its assessment practices. The city had a history of low assessment-to-sales ratios for property taxes and of not updating assessments, and an informal system of differential assessments by class of property. In 1961, when the state courts mandated reassessments at 100 percent of sales value, Massachusetts cities that had an informal differential assessment by class of property were reluctant to conform, because such a change would shift the burden of taxation considerably. Cities that had assessed businesses higher than residences would now have to tax them both equally, which would undoubtedly raise the tax bills for homeowners. In response, Boston pressed for and won a statewide referendum in 1978 legitimating differential assessment by class of property. Until revaluation could take place, however, cities were vulnerable to suits from citizens for overassessment.

To pay for the *Tregor* decision, the city had to sell its municipal auditorium, obtain state authorization to borrow money, and get state approval for new revenue sources to pay off the borrowing. The city and state worked out some new fiscal controls as guarantees of improved financial management, including a system of personnel allotments that was intended to enforce staffing limits. Also, the city was required to keep the lower assessments in cases where a taxpayer had successfully challenged the assessment. When combined with the new legal differential rates by class, these reforms helped eliminate a major source of deficits for Boston.

Deficits continued in 1984, however, resulting particularly from inadequately funded collective bargaining settlements. In 1985 Mayor Flynn had to find money to eliminate an outstanding deficit from the previous year. He did this with a number of one-time revenues, including the sale of parking garages. The Flynn administration kept the budget reasonably balanced for the next few years, but by 1989 city officials were concerned again about drops in revenues, especially from the state. Now more dependent on sales taxes, the city became more vulnerable to recessions.

Start-and-Stop Reforms

Fiscal stress affected the timing of budgetary changes in Boston and especially the start-and-stop pattern that characterized the reforms. Boston experimented with program budgeting in 1969 and 1970, at the beginning of Mayor White's administration, but then the budget returned to straight line items. The precise reasons for Boston's dropping the experiment are not clear, but growing fiscal stress and the lack of a federal requirement for program budgeting may have been factors.

The late 1960s were the early years of the nationally sponsored Five-Five-Five program, an experiment to improve state and local budgeting by introducing PPBS in five states, five counties, and five cities. Boston was not one of the five experimental cities, but like other cities not formally included in the experiment, Boston participated informally. The motivation for some cities was that they expected PPBS to be required for the receipt of federal grants (Mushkin 1969). That requirement did not materialize, and without strong continuing support from the mayor, the system disappeared in many cities.

By the mid-1970s, Boston was experiencing major financial difficulties that prevented any consideration of budget reforms. One informant, Robert Ciolek, in a 1989 interview speculated that because of the hunt for new revenue, the city was

> in a survival mode. It's hard to think of evaluating programs when you aren't fine tuning. They were making wholesale changes. That condition held from 1975 to 1984. There were sporadic efforts in between to improve the budget, but financial problems continued, especially after Proposition 2½ in 1980. We couldn't make budget changes until we stabilized the finances. We got the budget balanced in 1986, and it has been balanced since then. The relatively stable finances gave us the capacity to look at program budgeting. The budget was no longer acting as a triage system.

Capital planning was also characterized by a pattern of stop and go. The city had a capital plan from 1963 to 1975, but when the projects outlined in the plan were completed, no new plan was drawn up. According to Mary Nee, the director of capital budgeting, there was no money.

> Starting in the mid 1970s and early 1980s, there was not much impetus for capital planning. New York City was having its financial crisis and Boston was having its own minicrisis. The city was having difficulty issuing bonds. It recouped a bit in the late 1970s, but with Proposition 2½ [in 1980] the bond rating was suspended (virtually) for a year. It was a second crisis, and there were minimal projects.

When Mayor Flynn was elected, he established a transition team to deal with financial issues. The team gave a report in 1984 that included many recommendations on capital and debt management. According to Mary Nee, a second impetus toward renewed capital planning was a series of court mandates that covered the capital stock.

> There was a [school] desegregation case that had lasted eight years. A facility repair plan was involved; there was an injunction against school construction without a plan. The problems included the Charles Street jail, the Deer Island House of Corrections. Both ended up with new facilities. The superior court judges ordered repairs on county courthouses. So there were courts involved, a jail, a prison, and schools. And the others were in deplorable condition.

In addition, said Nee, the city had to comply with state mandates on open space. "The city was notified by the state that we needed to do open space . . . it fell to us. We hired a landscape architect, mapped 180 spaces, did a detailed condition assessment. I have a copy of that plan. The parks assessment helps us evaluate subsequent capital requests."

Some of these issues were resolved by other governmental units taking over responsibility for the construction or physical facilities, but others required planning to get out from under the court orders. When combined with the recommendations from the transition committee, these pressures resulted in a new, centralized office of capital budgeting and a new capital budget process, beginning in 1984.

Mayor Flynn paid particular attention to improving financial management as soon as he took office. Part of the reason was to convince the business community that he was a good manager. Barbara Gottschalk, the budget director, said in an interview in 1989:

> In response to the perception that he wouldn't be a good manager, and in response to a long string of deficits from 1976 to 1985, which were really affecting the city, due in part to Proposition 2½, Flynn convened a private-sector task force. That panel came up with recommendations, fiscal controls. We had no automated accounting system, no MIS; the budget provided no information on performance. It was line item. The mayor implemented the recommendations, by and large.

The second factor that contributed to the new drive toward improved budgeting was the court cases themselves. The court case that resulted in lawsuits from citizens claiming overassessment pressed the city to improve assessment practices and triggered the state to create new controls over the city's fiscal practices. The numerous court cases concerning the capital planning of the city certainly helped motivate the creation of the office of capital budgeting and the new capital plan.

The combination of the push from court cases, efforts to impress the state with the quality of financial management to get authorization for new revenue sources, and the election of a new mayor in 1984 were sufficient to motivate major changes in the budget process and format. Some of the changes dealt with the appearance and readability of the budget—to show that the city was improving. Some of the changes dealt with ways of improving departmental management and controlling the departments for the purposes of implementing the mayor's policies. Since the mayor's policies had to be implemented without substantially increasing costs, the result was a clash between the departments and the mayor over whose policies and priorities should be funded first.

In 1986 Boston began to use a program and performance budget (PPB), attributing costs to programs and using performance measures to describe what the program would try to achieve during the year. The actual achievements are reported outside the budget and are used to help improve management. In 1989, with the onset of a new round of fiscal stress, the budget office added target-based budgeting to the PPB.

The Mayor, the Council, and the Public

The program and performance budget system served a variety of functions, but one of the most important was that it helped the budget office accommodate the mayor's requests to satisfy public demands. For example, the mayor could set a goal for cleaner streets or more attractive thoroughfares. The departments would then set appropriate performance targets to achieve the mayor's goal. The budget office could allocate more money to the areas where the mayor put his emphasis. The target-based budget, in addition to restricting total spending by departments, helped assure that the departments were not cutting the mayor's high-priority projects and objectives to save their own departmental priorities.

The program and performance budget system was initially set up by Robert Ciolek, who came in with Flynn's transition team in 1984. Ciolek occupied the positions of budget director and head of the administrative division of the administrative services department. He tried to balance the recommendations in the private-sector report that the mayor had commissioned in 1984 and the mayor's personality. He reviewed the models of good budgeting that he knew, and chose St. Paul, Minnesota, as the general pattern, adapting it for Boston's use.

While Ciolek argued that the most important impact of the new budget system was helping the departments improve their management, that was not the reason for its adoption. The mayor was not as concerned at the time with getting more bang for the buck as with getting his priorities funded in the budget. The mayor's political advisers became his top-level staff and served as liaisons between the mayor and the departments. One of these political staff members created the budget process.

> *Ciolek*: The administrative services department was headed by Ray Dooley. Dooley was the mayor's campaign manager; he was the equal of the other advisers, maybe superior. He was a large pressure in the administration. Ray has the ability to be involved in the political and also support a better budget process. You can make better political decisions when you have good facts. It gives you effective controls over the bureaucracy. It informs and it controls. The budget office can respond to the mayor's direction.
>
> *Author*: Are you saying that the budget process makes the departments more responsive to the mayor?
>
> *Ciolek*: Yes, that was one of the major reasons why we did it. Sometimes we were disappointed. But it works better in 1989 than it did in 1984.

In addition to fulfilling performance measures, target-based budgeting was also expected to protect the priorities of the mayor, as Barbara Gottschalk explained:

> This year [1990] we will ask the departments to put down a maintenance [of effort] budget, and [we will give them] a target by department below which they will have to keep their requests. We will decide the target this weekend by departments.... Last year, there was [slugging] between departments as to who gets cut. The departments can also put in for more than maintenance [of effort], and they will have to explain how to get to the targets from the maintenance

budget. Then we will look at that. If they try to cut the mayor's priorities, we will catch it and tell them to take the cuts somewhere else.

This is standard procedure for a target-based budget. The budget
office asks the departments to draw up a maintenance-of-effort budget, figuring out how much it will cost next year to deliver this year's
level of service. Then the city allocates a target to each department,
and the departments must submit their requests at or under the target.
If the target is less than the maintenance-of-effort level, the department has to specify what it will cut, and with what impacts, to get
down to the target. The departments can also make requests for items
that do not fit into the target. By requiring departments to spell out
where they are taking cuts and with what anticipated impacts, the
budget office can review the proposed cuts and ensure that the departments are not cutting items that are high priority to the mayor.

While the mayor, the budget office, and the departments have
been deeply involved in the new system, in accordance with Boston's
long tradition of disempowering the council in budgetary matters, the
council has been almost completely powerless. Over time, the council
has alternated between at-large and district elections. It changed in
1983 to a thirteen-person council, with nine seats from districts and
four at-large. This change took place just at the end of Mayor White's
administration, after years of dominance by mayors who favored
downtown renewal. The change may have resulted from popular feeling that the neighborhoods needed better representation. Several years
later, the council created a Ways and Means Committee to review the
budget and to call executive branch officials to testify or explain to
them matters they disagreed with or found puzzling. This committee
was still struggling to find a role for itself in the early 1990s.

The council has reportedly been more active during years of budgetary cutback than years of growth. In 1989 the council successfully
opposed some of the mayor's cuts, rejecting them as too severe. The
council found enough money in the budget to cover the addbacks. Reportedly the mayor had overestimated the amount of money to be
spent on debt service. Said Robert Ciolek:

The relationship of the council and the executive branch is dependent
on the financial condition. The council gets involved in bad times,
not in good times. The chair of Ways and Means has done a good
job of learning about the budget and getting involved; he views him-

self as a potential candidate for mayor, and the position gives him some visibility, so there is some motivation to get involved. But the council does not have much real power. If the situation deteriorates, it will meddle more, but the relationship won't change fundamentally. The council has felt this [finance] office is straight and open, and has done a good job.

Despite this positive evaluation of the relationship between the council and the administrative services department, the budget office tended to think of the council's role as meddling in the budget. Former Budget Director Ciolek admitted that one of his major concerns was that council members were generally not interested in the financial impact of what they were requesting and that they put upward, rather than downward, pressure on the budget. The budget office tried to comply with council requests as long as the total amount involved was neither too expensive nor beyond the means of the city during that fiscal year.

We watch council preferences and try to accommodate them. They requested a supplemental for a crime watch; it was a good idea, so we did it. We attempt to be responsive. The legislative branch isn't initially interested in financial impact. Sometimes the money isn't there, and we'll tell them. A council member wanted a security system for low-income and elderly housing units. It's a good idea, but we can't afford it.

In addition to this role of making specific requests for new or expanded services, the council played a positive role in gathering and expressing public opinion and responding to complaints. According to Ciolek:

The council members have been pretty responsible. They make good, careful additional spending. We may have overcut. They are a real time check on the cuts we have made. They get complaints from constituents. It's not [a problem] as long as spending desires are reasonable. We have a $1.3 billion budget, so $1 million here or there should not be rejected out of hand.

Although it lacks much formal power, the council can delay the budget and thereby force changes in it. The mayor can get his budget even if the council disapproves, but the delay makes the budget late, and the mayor and finance office prefer the budget to be on time. As Ciolek remarked: "Sometimes they force restoration of cuts. It was the library budget last June. They vetoed the budget first and forced changes. We didn't worry too much about that, it's *de rigueur.* They do it every year. You do want the budget in place by July 1, so you accommodate to get it on time."

Ciolek felt that since the council was used to having a number of requests granted, when the budget got tighter and their requests were denied, they might be upset if they did not fully understand the extent of the financial constraints. It was therefore necessary for the Administrative Services Office (the finance department in Boston) to communicate openly and carefully with the council.

The formal involvement of the public in the budget process was limited, despite the neighborhood visits of Mayor Flynn. The capital budget promised community involvement but delivered on the promise in a limited fashion. Asked by the author if there was community input into the capital budget, or if that was an overstatement, Mary Nee said it was overstated: "The council holds hearings, but any projects—we get aware of those from the community and have an awareness of community demand. Then we involve the community in the design once the project is funded."

Most of the project selection is based on an awareness of community need and on a needs assessment derived from departmental requests, but it is not based on organized community input. Once the projects have been funded, however, they are taken to the communities for input on design. Mary Nee called this an occasion for credit claiming on the part of politicians.

> I stay in touch with the council. [They don't provide] a direct input, but I know what the council wants and what their constituents want. I brief them before it comes out, and I leave flexibility for small projects, to satisfy a few requests. I go through a political process. . . . We do design meetings. Some [council members] show up at the design meetings and take credit with the neighborhoods. Some state reps do, too. There have been so many projects, it's easy. They can take credit.

Thus the capital budget process is sensitive to community need and council members' requests, but citizen and council member input is not systematically sought. Because of Boston's history of years of neglect of the capital plan and multiple court orders to get the capital plan in shape, especially for jails and schools, the city was dealing primarily with emergencies for the first few years after the new capital budget planning process was installed in 1985. But more direct public input did not seem to be on the agenda once the emergency nature of the capital budget was resolved.

It is clear from this brief survey that mayors dominate the budget process in Boston. Mayors have generally been interested in reelection or election to higher office. As a result, they are sensitive about their image and the image of the city with the public and the press. This political atmosphere has had an impact on budgeting.

Budgeting in a Political Context

In a political context appearances are sometimes more important than reality. Information may be withheld or given limited circulation because it might not look good.

The budget document in Boston does not contain a long-term revenue and expenditure forecast. The city makes such projections but does not put them in the budget. Ciolek explained: "The business group that met in 1985 recommended that the budget office do a long-term financial plan. We have a contract with an econometric firm. We do multiyear budgeting and revenue analysis . . . but the decision was made not to include it in the text of the budget."

Ciolek argued that because the economy had been so unpredictable, putting a long-term estimate in the budget was likely to make the budget office look incompetent. He added: "And the numbers look scary. We were concerned about the message we would be giving about where the city would be, and it's pretty grim. . . . I do share the results with small groups of people who understand the limits of projection and discuss the city's future."

Part of the problem was that if the bond markets picked up a whiff of fiscal crisis, they would push up the price of bonds. And part of the problem was one of credibility. If the budget office was able to force action based on negative projections, then the predicted bad future would not occur, and the budget staff would be accused of exaggerating. Ciolek concluded that omitting the projection from the budget was the wisest decision.

This caution about what to show in the budget and how certain information might be abused was echoed in the limited circulation given to the performance reports. The budget reported the programs' targets for performance, but not what they had achieved. The city drew up the reports on actual performance to use for internal management but remained cautious about who could read and possibly misinterpret the results.

A second impact of budgeting in an overtly political environment is the rapid turnover of upper-level staff and the need to carry out quickly the tasks set by politicians because they have a limited time frame. The program and performance budget was set up very quickly; the bulk of it was up and running within a year. The result was that many of the performance measures were not useful. One informant described what it was like to engage in budget reform that was put together in such haste: "The mayor gets out a press release. You have to do it; you don't touch all the bases you need to, to make it work. Someone needs to take a longer look, but you can't do it. The real goals are all short term. It's a rare manager that has a three- or four-year time horizon. The city auditor used to have that kind of horizon." Thus it is difficult to plan with elected officials. Top appointees change regularly, and no one can imagine themselves in position long enough to implement a change.

Politicization shows up in other ways as well. Since the administration department is headed by one of the mayor's inner circle, and this office supervises the budget office, some of the departments don't trust the budget office to be neutral and managerially oriented. Because they don't trust the process, they just try to look good on the performance measures. One informant, a former city employee, remarked: "Sometimes the performance measures change; it's a political process. To make a program budget work, you have to assume a budget office would be disinterested, but that isn't the case, so it results in PR statements. It's a wonderfully bureaucratic process with no services added."

Barbara Gottschalk, the budget director, thought the departments saw the system as more political than it was. She struggled to teach the departments that the performance measures would not be interpreted politically and that the departments could set goals that they would have to reach for and possibly not make. The city could do this because the performance reports were not made public. The reports were primarily between the budget office and the departments.

While much of the evaluation of success or failure on performance measures was kept between the departments and the budget office, the mayor's staff did sometimes monitor performance indicators if they dealt with issues the mayor was concerned about. This monitoring probably reinforced the departments' view that the perform-ance evaluations had a political component.

The short-term nature of the elected officials' goals affected the implementation of the new budget process because short-term goals clashed with longer-term service goals of the departments. Presumably if the mayor's staff was monitoring performance, the departments had better show progress in the short term on those elements of the per-formance report—their own management goals would get lower pri-ority.

The departments did not initially buy into the system. From their point of view, the budget system took away time that could be better spent in direct service delivery. Nevertheless, the central budget office did not back off because of lack of departmental support. With the backing of the mayor, the budget director told the departments, you *have to* do the performance measurements and monitoring.

The budget office had the role of mediating between the depart-ments' expectations and the mayor's demands. The budget director felt that the mayor's goals should dominate if they clashed with de-partment goals. Said Barbara Gottschalk: "The budget analysts can recognize the departments' tendency to keep their priority programs, as opposed to the mayor's. Some of the mayor's priorities may not al-ways be logical, but it is the mayor's right to want it, and it's his choice."

Departments sometimes failed to comply with the mayor's initia-tives in a timely way. One illustration occurred when the mayor imple-mented a complaint hotline. Said Gottschalk:

> One special goal for the mayor is to be responsive to the neighbor-hoods. He set up a twenty-four-hour hotline in the Neighborhoods Office. They get all kinds of requests and complaints to the depart-ments. It's an automated system. Some complaints go to Public Works, some go to other departments. They are supposed to report back to us how fast the complaint was resolved. Now we put the time to respond in the performance measures. "Fix 95 percent of all complaints within so many hours." The recordkeeping isn't yet up with the system. But that is a quality measure.
>
> It's very nice in theory. In practice, it's three-quarters nice. This kind of quantified recordkeeping; the field operators know their dis-trict, they don't want to write it up. We are imposing discipline on them. They will adapt eventually.

While the departments sometimes lagged in responding to the mayor's requirements, they had powerful reasons to try to comply with the performance goals. One reason was that the budget office had power over them. One department that was delaying on the performance measures found that the budget office intentionally delayed that department's paperwork.

From the point of view of the Administrative Services Office, compliance was spotty in part because some departments were better managed than others. The better-managed offices were often better at budgeting and grasped more quickly how to use the system to their advantage. Some departments, for example, quickly created a kind of contract in which they promised to achieve a given level of performance if the budget office would guarantee a given level of budget support.

Another interpretation is that the budget changes were forced on the rather independent departments. The mayor insisted that they comply, rather than convince them that the system was useful. When a budget system comes in with a mayor, it may create this underlayer of reluctant compliance, of tension between routine departmental tasks and policy mandates that often interrupt routine tasks. Because of this top-down implementation, when the mayor leaves office, the budget system may go with him. In this case, the next administration, led by Mayor Thomas Menino, maintained the same basic budget system but allowed departments to help determine the performance measurements.

To summarize, mayors have been dominant over the budget process in Boston for many years. The council has been rendered nearly powerless in financial matters, and the public plays little direct role in the budget process. Mayors in Boston have reflected changing constituencies. The coalitions supporting the mayor have gotten broader and broader, both ethnically and across social classes. At the same time, especially as federal money for economic renewal diminished, the mayors have put less exclusive emphasis on downtown redevelopment and more emphasis on neighborhoods and on responsiveness to complaints and requests. Pressure for more representation of the neighborhoods has shown up in a changing composition of the council and in the mayor's and budget office's sensitivity to reasonable council demands. In an effort to be responsive to this broader constituency, Mayor Flynn used budget reform to make the decentralized bureaucracy more sensitive to his policy direction.

Both the performance measurement system and the target-based budget help make the departments responsive to the mayor's policy direction. The older system of appointing political associates to the top positions in each major department did help the mayor control the departments, but it had some drawbacks, including the cost and visibility of a large number of upper-level political appointees and the clumsiness of exerting control by firing appointees who did not work out. The budget is a much finer tool for controlling the departments' policy outputs.

The relative politicization of the budget had a number of consequences. One was that certain information necessary for improved financial management was kept internal to city hall in order to prevent the information from being used against the departments and against the mayor. Fear that the performance measures would be used against them led the departments to set low targets that they knew they could achieve. The budget office had to mediate the tension between the mayor's short-term policy goals and the departments' longer-term routine service goals. Moreover, the top-down imposition of the budget format resulted in hasty implementation and a lack of negotiated agreement with the departments beforehand. The overly hasty implementation led some to think that the performance measures were silly and wasteful of time; the lack of negotiated support from the departments made it questionable how much of the program and performance budget would survive a change in mayors.

Episodic bouts of fiscal stress, caused by both internal and external factors, have made the city dependent on the state's approval. At times, the city has had to accept improved financial management measures as a condition of state assistance; other times, the city has improved budgeting and financial management in order to appear well managed. Regardless of the goal of impressing the state and business community, however, the improved budget has been more than window dressing.

Conclusions

Budget reform in the strong-mayor cities had a start-and-stop quality. One reason was that each mayor needed a budget system to match his or her personality and political goals. Another reason was that fiscal stress and service emergencies interrupted budget reforms.

The short terms of office required budgeting systems to be implemented quickly, sometimes without touching base with all the relevant actors. Decentralized departments combined with quick and sometimes inadequately thought through systems that were mandated, rather than negotiated, resulted in some footdragging. Rochester's departments used workload measures in place of outcome measures; some of Boston's departments delayed their reporting on how long it took to resolve complaints.

While budgeting reform in the mayor-dominated cities was marked by interruptions, changes of course, and partial implementation, what remained constant was the need for the mayors to control the independence of the departments. The mayors had to create enough flexibility in tight budgets to accommodate political priorities and accomplish political promises. What also remained constant was the need to gain public support for tax increases. These cities relied not only on the budget document to explain city services and spending but also on the budget process itself. Mayors took the budget to the neighborhoods to explain it; the budget office spent time and creativity preparing videos to announce budget proposals.

There is less direct citizen participation in the budget process in these mayor cities than there was in Dayton, although Tampa seemed to be moving in Dayton's direction. The councils in the mayor cities were more likely to represent districts but had very little budgetary power, except to argue against service cuts to neighborhoods. Representation of the public remained largely a function of the ability of the mayor and his staff to read the desires of the council and the citizens and turn them into budget priorities.

Target-based budgeting was a feature of all three mayor cities. Target-based budgeting adjusts well to declines and increases in revenues and helps balance the budget by forcing limits on departments and making them manage within those limits. Target-based budgeting helps create the flexibility within constrained budgets, allowing the mayor to implement policy goals and providing a mechanism to assure that the departments do not substitute their own goals for the mayor's. While target-based budgeting takes the budget office out of micromanaging the departments, it puts the budget office in the position of assuring that the mayor's, rather than the department's, goals are accommodated when there is a conflict between the two.

Target-based budgeting makes some radical changes in traditional budgeting concepts. It substitutes control of the totals for control of the line items. A line-item structure allowed councils to control departments in spite of increasingly dominant executives, a way to by-pass the emerging executive budget reforms. In mayor-council cities, however, the council does not have this control. Target-based budgeting is primarily under the executive branch; the executive sets the targets and assures their implementation.

Lump-sum budgeting grants major discretion to departments, which could be a problem in cities with traditions of highly independent departments. If the departments stay within the targets, will they be well managed, and will the city get the best services it can for the money? It is the role of the executive, which sets the targets and oversees them, to ensure that the quality of management remains high. This is best done through some form of performance measurement and monitoring system. Such a system depends on high-quality, professional department heads; it also depends on mayors refraining from demanding the impossible, continually asking for more service for fewer dollars. The mayors have to abide by the implied service contract—so many dollars for so much service of such a quality. Because mayors are trying so hard to be accountable and responsive to the public, it is tempting for them to pass on to the city's bureaucracy the public's demands for more services at less cost. The mayors sometimes ask for something for nothing. Departments do what they can to comply, but such requests can create an irrational set of demands for departmental managers.

Since the major accountability in strong-mayor cities is electoral accountability, mayors tend to be highly sensitive to demands of the electorate and to competition from potential or actual mayoral candidates. As a result, mayors pay a lot of attention to appearances and sometimes use the budget to help create a positive image. Mayors are sensitive to the ways in which performance measurement may expose them to criticism. If they use performance measures internally to assure good, cost-effective management, they may not circulate the information widely.

The mayor form was intended as a way of providing activist government combined with good management and accountability. Accountability was to be achieved through frequent elections of the mayor. One person was to be responsible for all policy and financial outcomes. The model assumed that the mayor would have good control over the departments and would be oriented to fiscal conservatism, offering good value for tax dollars. The accompanying disempowerment of councils was supposed to protect against corruption and machine politics. Parts of this model have worked better than others.

The mayor did become virtually the sole focus of accountability. Mayors have often not been able to control highly independent departments. In recent years, however, program and performance budgets and target-based budgets have given mayors more policy control over the departments. A mayor who is interested in good management has the tools to achieve it. At times, the desire to respond to particular constituencies, whether the business community or neighborhoods or ethnic groups, has outstripped the commitment to budgetary balance. Factors outside the city's immediate control have also contributed to episodic fiscal crises.

The strong-mayor cities have often sought help from other levels of government and have oriented budgetary information to this end. Periodic fiscal stress and state or county rescue have had mixed effects. Mayor cities may adopt impressive budget and financial management tools to impress outsiders, but some of the information they put in the budget may be misleading. City officials may seek to make the emergency look more severe in order to get help, or they may seek to make their financial management look better than it is to impress the financial markets. Sometimes, as in Boston, the state may make improvements in financial management a condition of various kinds of bailouts.

7

The States and Local Budgeting:
The Formative Years

CITIES OFTEN depend on the state government for authorization to raise new taxes or to borrow to pay off loans. In Boston, the State of Massachusetts assumed a variety of functions to relieve Boston of financial responsibility but also set a series of requirements for the city. Sometimes the state set the maximum limit for taxation; other times, it set up minimums for contingency accounts or required the city to adjust its assessed valuation to a more reasonable level to avoid overspending its budget. Of all our case-study cities, the role of the state government was most clearly visible in Boston, but in fact, states have often played a major role in municipal budgeting and finance.

Municipal budgeting takes place in the context of state laws, many of which were designed during the early years of the twentieth century and later modified during the Great Depression. The states have a clear and comprehensive power to regulate municipal finance (including budgeting) and have used that power to varying degrees since the beginning of municipal budgeting. Some of the laws and institutions set up by the states in earlier years still exist and still frame the day-to-day routines of local budgeting. Others have been modified in recent years, but these modifications are understandable only in the context of the prior intent and structure of control.

The Importance of State Control and Supervision
As Frank Goodnow (1904), municipal reformer and legal scholar, ar-

gued: "the legislature ... has, under our system of government, the absolute legal right to regulate municipal affairs as it sees fit" (p. 73). States still have absolute legal rights to control local budgeting and finance:

> State governments supervise the financial activities of their municipalities. States determine where cities get their money, how cities borrow money, how cities spend money, and how cities manage their financial affairs. States have the legal power to regulate municipal finance by virtue of their superior constitutional position.... Because municipalities are legally "creatures of the state," state governments regulate their taxing, borrowing, spending, and financial administration. (MacManus 1983, 145)

Grants of home-rule powers to cities did not diminish the states' role in the control and supervision of local finance. On the contrary, as the states yielded more control and discretion to local governments, state officials became concerned about how that discretion was being used. In the modern period, when states granted more financial aid to local governments, state officials sought to ensure that the money they were granting the local governments was being spent responsibly.[1]

State supervision of municipal budgeting began more than 120 years ago. "The development of the modern budgetary movement has been coincident with the growth of state supervision. The budgetary technique employed in supervision, accordingly, is likely to reflect at any one time both the values and the defects of prevailing budget methods" (Kilpatrick 1936, 342). While the nature of supervision has changed somewhat over time, older forms of control and supervision sometimes survived into the present, and so "values and defects" of the past have gotten mixed up with values and defects of the present.

Sometimes the rules for state oversight were initially helpful, but when they persisted unchanged for eighty or ninety years, they began to hold back further development. Maricopa County in Arizona, the county in which Phoenix is located, ran into fiscal difficulties and became aware of how outdated the state laws were that controlled local

---

1. See, for example, Charles M. Johnson's discussion of the origins of North Carolina's system of budgetary supervision in 1919, in Betters 1932, 80. See also Carr 1937, 229, on state supervision in Oklahoma, in which he discusses the recent tendency to increase supervision as a result of increased grants.

budgeting and finance. These outmoded regulations held back improvements. The state law was passed in 1912 when Arizona became a state. The county found it could not legally pay bills by wire, even though that would help the cash flow, because warrants had to be approved individually by the board. Once the expenditures were determined for the year, the total could not be exceeded, even if more revenues were available during the year. And totals for departments could not legally be shifted around at the end of the year without declaring an emergency. The accounting system was required to be cash based, although exceptions were granted on an individual basis. The result was that staff had to fight the system continuously to do a good job of budgeting and financial management. According to Sandor Shuch, the deputy county attorney in 1995, the county planned to propose some changes in the state law.

Three broad questions inform this and the following chapter. First, what has been the effect of state control and supervision on municipal budgeting? Have the states set down a framework from which the cities could spring forward on their own, or have they held the cities back by contradictory, overly restrictive, and out-of-date requirements, as suggested by the Maricopa County example? Has state regulation of municipal finance been good or bad for cities?[2] Second, how have states varied from one another in their goals and techniques of regulation? Do states fall into clusters that have used similar means to achieve similar sets of goals? Third, how has state regulation of municipal budgeting changed over time? How responsive has state control been to changing problems at the local level? These questions are addressed by reporting how a number of states influenced local budgeting and finance during five key periods of economic, political, and financial change.

---

2. Judging the impact of state mandates and controls on cities has not been an easy task. Susan MacManus evaluated the impact of 88 state mandates on 243 central cities between 1974 and 1976. She found that states with restrictive property tax limits before 1974 had thereby forced revenue diversification in the cities, which enabled the cities to manage fiscal stress more effectively. More generally, personnel mandates, such as compulsory binding arbitration, disability regulations, and retirement provisions, worsened cities' financial conditions, while procedural and programmatic mandates, such as those that expanded local governments' financial management skills, improved financial conditions. See MacManus 1983, 174–76.

Periods of Major Change

State regulation of municipal budgeting and finance began virtually at the beginning of municipal budgeting, in the late 1860s and early 1870s. Early attempts at control were constitutional or legislative, rather than administrative, and tended to be rigid, across-the-board limitations or mandates. Many of these early efforts at control were stimulated by the growth of cities and the overexpansion of debt during the 1860s, followed by the deep recession that began in 1873.

The second period of development occurred during the Progressive era, from about 1895 to about 1910. With the beginnings of home rule around the turn of the century, states gradually granted local governments more discretion. States then increased the intensity of their monitoring of local governments' financial performance. The frequent failure of constitutional and statutory controls to implement themselves led states to set up administrative mechanisms of control (Goodnow 1904). In line with the Progressive era emphasis on accountability, states began to focus on reporting requirements and standardization of accounts. Once standardized, states began to scrutinize the accounts after the fact to ensure that they were balanced. In some states, if the accounts were not balanced, a state office or commission could take corrective action. The state structures developed for supervision of the tax system, especially the supervision of assessments, were sometimes adapted for examination of the proposed budget. The goal was to ensure that the tax rate was as low as it should be (Fairlie 1904).

The third period in the development of state supervision of municipal budgeting and finance occurred in reaction to the growth of expenditures in the Progressive era and the rapid inflation and delayed capital spending that resulted from World War I. This period witnessed the initiation of the Ohio county budget commissions and the Oklahoma county excise boards, both beginning in 1910, to review the local budgets. Massachusetts increased its financial control and mandated budgets for local governments in 1913. The New Jersey budget law began in 1917. The Indiana and Iowa systems began in 1919 and 1920; the centralized and integrated New Mexico system began in 1921.

The focus of this post-Progressive period was primarily on keeping taxes down and using budget examination and revision as a way of doing so. Efforts to improve local government finances also figured in some of the new systems; the Progressive era effort to control through after-the-fact accounting and examination was found inadequate, warranting the mandating of budgets and their uniformity.

The fourth major period for shaping state systems of regulation of municipal budgeting occurred during the Great Depression of the 1930s. The Great Depression was really characterized by two sets of changes in state supervision. The initial change was increased reliance on constitutional amendments and legislation limiting property taxes, a return to earlier, rigid, across-the-board formulations. The second response was heightened emphasis on centralized state budget supervision to prevent fiscal stress and excessive indebtedness.

In 1939 the secretary of the National Municipal League, Howard Jones, wrote about the transition from the first of these phases to the second:

> In the early period of the depression, efforts toward reduction of governmental cost bordered in some cases on hysteria. The period brought forth all sorts of unsound doctrines, such as overall tax limitation, whose ill effects are proving to be as serious as the evils it sought to cure.
>
> Leading thinkers today are instead directing their attention to the development of machinery which will keep the financial processes of government within the control of the citizen. Budget procedure which brings visibility and planning into the control process is among the most vital of these subjects, and one of its important aspects is state control and supervision of the local budget process. This is a phase that has been receiving much attention in the last few years. (quoted in Kilpatrick 1939, 3)

Jones was arguing that if municipal budgets could be made truly accountable to the public and if the public could control the budgets, there would be less pressure for across-the-board, rigid measures that starved cities of resources needed to accomplish basic services. But to get that kind of budgeting, he assumed that states would have to require it and monitor it.

The fifth period of concentrated change occurred in the 1970s and early 1980s. The period from 1940 to 1945, the war years, saw very little change in state and local budgeting. Wisconsin's law requiring local government budgets was passed in 1941, but in general, budgeting was put on hold. Capital spending at the local level was drastically reduced in an effort to free up capital for war industries.

Intergovernmental relations from the point of view of the cities was focused on how to deal with rapidly shifting populations and military impacts on local communities. Capital spending that had been delayed during the Great Depression, and again during the war, was finally released in the postwar years in a burst of expenditures similar to that after World War I.

By the 1970s, resistance to the growth of property taxes combined with a slowing economy to hasten statewide efforts to limit property taxation. California's Proposition 13 may be the best known of these actions, but it was not the first. There were nine levy limits and one tax-lid law in the early 1970s, and four states and the District of Columbia adopted full disclosure laws, requiring public hearings and notification to raise property taxes (Merriman 1987).

The property tax limitation movement intensified in the late 1970s. In November 1978, just five months after Proposition 13 was passed, voters in Alabama, Idaho, Michigan, Nevada, and Texas approved legislation or constitutional amendments that reduced the authority of local governments to raise taxes (Merriman 1987, appendix). Massachusetts's Proposition 2½, which was very severe, was passed in 1980. At the same time, voters in Missouri approved the Hancock amendment, which required that local citizens must approve any local tax, license, or fee increase (Merriman 1987, 28). Although new restrictions were passed in several states, the tax limitation movement seemed to be played out by the early 1980s.

In 1975 New York City experienced a highly publicized major fiscal crisis in which the lending markets closed on the city. The resulting brouhaha highlighted the fact that fiscal mismanagement contributed to the city's problems. Other states worried that such problems might have been widespread. The State of New York had a responsibility to help out the city—a responsibility it accepted only reluctantly—but also a responsibility to help prevent similar problems in other cities in the state. Other states saw the possibility of a fiscal meltdown in their own larger cities.

Partly in response to the New York City fiscal crisis and the impacts of tax limitations, the post-1975 period was one of renewed state mandates to local government in the area of budgeting and finance. But it was also a period of increased communication between state and local governments about what needed to be done. The states began to make efforts to monitor and control the number and cost of unfunded mandates in order to reduce the stress on local governments.

The most dramatic of these efforts was Florida's constitutional amendment to prevent unfunded mandates. The overall thrust in this period was for states to help prevent local fiscal stress, but unlike in earlier periods, the answers were not all top-down fiscal controls. States studied their own control and supervision patterns and found that while some of their rules were helpful, others actually made matters worse.

The first four periods are described in this chapter; the modern period, from 1970 onward, is described in the next chapter.

The First Period: After the Civil War

The post–Civil War period was marked by a rapid growth in taxing and debt and in state efforts to curtail both. It was also marked by early state efforts to require budgets or at least appropriation ordinances.

The relationship between Maryland and the City of Baltimore reflects the early state legislative responses to urban population growth, greater urban complexity, and increased municipal borrowing and spending. The early history of state and local relations in Massachusetts also reflects these trends. Note that, in both cases, the techniques of control were constitutional or statutory, not regulatory or administrative.

In Baltimore, the years from 1856 to 1868 were characterized by a rise in local government spending, the growth of floating debt, and an increase in funded debt. The funded debt was for water supply, defense, and bounties to volunteers during the Civil War, and for parks and city buildings. Indebtedness threatened to outrun municipal resources. Some of the debt contracted for internal improvements had probably been incurred unwisely, and debt was pushing up tax levies. In response, the constitutional convention of 1867 imposed a radical limit on corporate borrowing power (Hollander 1899).

The city was prohibited from creating any debt, or giving or lending its credit for any purpose, unless the debt or credit was authorized by a special act of the General Assembly and by an ordinance of the city council submitted to the legal voters of the city and approved by a majority of the votes cast. Exceptions included temporary loans to meet a cash shortage; to maintain the police, safety, and sanitary condition of the city; and to pay for debt incurred before the adoption of the constitution. The restrictive effect was probably less than the framers of the constitution expected because the legislature treated requests for borrowing as a local and routine matter, and the voting public generally approved bonding because it held down taxes and provided public works that created jobs.

While Maryland resorted to constitutional constraints, Massachusetts regulated cities and towns through legislation. While Maryland's controls were focused mostly on debt, Massachusetts focused initially on debt and then shifted to controlling taxes. Massachusetts's system of state control developed because the changes in economic and social conditions during the nineteenth century caused so many financial problems for cities that the state had to help solve them (Van De Woestyne 1935).

Following the Civil War, local officials were more interested in keeping down the tax rate than in sound financial policies. They borrowed, not only for permanent improvements but also for current expenses. Debt grew rapidly in the decade before 1875 but became especially burdensome after the recession that began in 1873. By 1875 popular complaint was so strong that the legislature passed an act to regulate and limit municipal debt. Limits were placed on the duration and amount of debt, and sinking funds were made obligatory. Debt was limited to 3 percent of assessed value. Debts for water and in aid of railroad corporations were exempt from the limits, but in 1876 the legislature also limited municipalities' investments in railroads (Van De Woestyne 1935). In 1885 the debt limit was lowered to 2.5 percent of assessment in cities other than Boston and to 2 percent in Boston.

By 1885 the focus of state regulation had begun to shift to curbing taxes. An act was passed to limit municipal tax levies in an effort to curb municipal spending, which had begun to increase. The limit for cities other than Boston was $12 per $1,000 of assessed value; for Boston, the limit was $9. Tax limits made the debt problems worse because, when cities could not raise taxes for legitimate expenditures, they often borrowed instead.

Growing populations and increased demands for services pressed against the tax and borrowing limits. Almost as soon as the legislation was passed, cities petitioned the legislature for exceptions. The legislature frequently granted exemptions from the limits. Some cities escaped tax limits completely, while others were permitted to exceed them. The legislature thus became the arbiter of many individual requests for spending.

More than 1,500 special exempting acts were passed between 1875 and 1911. By 1912, approximately $73 million in excess of the debt limit was outstanding as a result of this special legislation. In addition to petitioning the legislature, local governments evaded the rules by borrowing short-term and issuing demand notes (notes that were not paid until holders demanded payment). The issuance of demand notes was curtailed by the state in 1912 (Van De Woestyne 1935).

Overall, the limits on borrowing and spending through the early Progressive period in Massachusetts were not overwhelmingly successful. State laws could not stop the growth of population nor the resulting demands for services by the local population or the legislature. State laws did not succeed in curtailing borrowing for operating costs. What they did do was shift the burden for approval of projects to the state legislature on a case-by-case basis so that the legislature micromanaged the cities.

It was in this context of state efforts to prevent overborrowing and high property tax rates, such as those of Maryland and Massachusetts, that states began to regulate budgetary processes. Frederick Clow (1901) described some of the early efforts (pre-1900) of states to influence local budgeting. For example, Clow noted that the state governments often required local governments to levy taxes only for specific purposes—so much for schools, so much for parks, and so much for debt, and not a single aggregate sum. This provided the basic elements of a budget.

Clow noted that Illinois passed a law in 1872 requiring appropriation ordinances for all expenses and liabilities of local governments. The state took the main features of the pattern of budgeting from the city of Chicago and made them general. The appropriation ordinance was not to be changed during the year except by a majority of voters, either by petition or by election. If an accident required emergency action, however, the council could borrow to cover the cost if two-thirds of the council voted in favor. The debt so incurred had to be made up before the end of the next fiscal year. The intent was to ensure that the council did not pass a balanced budget at the beginning of the year and then unbalance it during the year.

Between 1873 and 1901, seven other states adopted laws like the one in Illinois requiring appropriation ordinances. Michigan passed such a law in 1873, Colorado in 1877, Wyoming in 1886, Nebraska in 1887, Dakota in 1887 (it had been a territory but became two states by 1901), and Montana in 1895. Michigan's law included all revenues and special assessments, loans, and expenditures, but it did not cover charter cities, which were the larger ones.

In 1894 Indiana imposed a form of executive budgeting on Indianapolis and four other cities with populations of more than 35,000. The departments were required to present their detailed estimates to the controller, who was to cut them back. The controller was to estimate the nondepartmental expenses. The mayor and the controller compiled the budget proposal and presented it to the council for approval. The council could reduce, but could not increase, the estimates. Any additional appropriations during the year could be made by a two-thirds vote of the council on recommendation of the comptroller. In addition to regulating budget processes, Indiana regulated the budget format of cities. The budget request was to be detailed and the appropriations broken into line items. The intent was to control expenditures.

The Second Period: The Progressive Era

A second wave of interest in state financial and budgetary control over local governments resulted from the expansion of municipal functions and increased spending of the Progressive era. This period was marked by a gradual transition from state control through across-the-board statutory and constitutional provisions to administrative supervision. Supervision began in the area of assessments and then was extended to accounting practices and budgeting (Fairlie 1904).

At the turn of the century, states collected property taxes from the local governments. These collections were based on the declared amount of assessed valuation. Consequently, state officials were intensely interested in local assessment practices. Most states set up state boards of equalization, "with power to change the aggregate valuation of counties so as to equalize the apportionment of the state tax" (Fairlie 1904, 3). These boards later provided a pattern when states made additional efforts to supervise local finance.

The states were less energetic in trying to supervise accounting methods than in controlling assessment practices, in part because the state's own accounting structures were poorly developed. As reformer and scholar John Fairlie (1904) put it, "indeed the imperfect and inadequate accounting methods of the larger cities have often been somewhat better than those of the states within which the cities are located" (p. 7). Nevertheless, some states did make an effort to improve local accounting.

Massachusetts had some supervision over accounting in counties by 1903 and was thinking about expanding it to the cities. Wyoming, in its constitution of 1890, adopted an office of state examiner. Legislation specified that this officer was to supervise every public officer in the state who handled public money. The state examiner was authorized to establish a uniform system of bookkeeping throughout the state and to examine the accounts of local officials. If he discovered serious problems, he was empowered to take further action. The examiner's function in Wyoming spilled over into budgeting. The examiner met with the boards that set the local tax levies, reviewing the expense budget and making reductions wherever possible.

Other states near Wyoming soon followed its example. Montana and North Dakota created offices of state examiner, with power to inspect books and prescribe accounting methods in counties. South Dakota and Nebraska appointed a state auditor, and Kansas appointed a state accountant. These laws did not provide thorough supervision. In 1903, however, Nevada established a more intensive system of control. A state Board of Revenue was required to approve the debts of local governments, prescribe the forms for financial reports to the state comptroller, and employ an examiner to scrutinize the accounts. Also in 1903, Florida created the office of state auditor, whose chief duty was to prescribe the form of county accounts and see that they were properly kept.

Until 1902, the movement toward state supervision of local accounts was confined to less important states and to partial measures in the larger states. But in 1902 Ohio provided for a uniform system of accounting, auditing, and reporting for every public office in the state, under the supervision of a new Bureau of Inspection in the office of the Auditor of State. The act also required separate accounts for every appropriation or fund and for every department, institution, and public improvement or public service industry. It required full financial reports to the state auditor and authorized annual examination of the finances of all public offices. The examiners had power to subpoena witnesses and interrogate them under oath.

Fairlie (1904) approved this developing state supervision over local government. It was particularly appropriate in the area of assessments because equalization required comparison across jurisdictions. A system of uniform accounting would allow a comparison of outlays with returns, he argued; moreover, if government was going to regulate the private sector, as in railroads and banks, it could certainly also regulate local governments' bookkeeping. Most important, he argued that these financial controls did not interfere with local choices of what to spend money on and how much to spend. He called for more supervision of local loans and debts because such supervision would be a more flexible and adaptable tool than constitutional and statutory limits on borrowing.

Later writers built on Fairlie's distinction between legislative mandate and administrative supervision. Legislative mandate was equated with determining local policies and usurping local priorities; administrative supervision was equated with setting up general rules and enforcing them. As it worked out, however, state administrative supervision sometimes lacked appropriate enforcement techniques; sometimes, too, administrative supervision exceeded its legislative policy goals. So the equation of legislative mandate with poor practice and administrative supervision with good practice was overdrawn. Fairlie's concern that statutory regulation might usurp local decision making was replaced with a concern that administrative practice might usurp local prerogatives. In some states, the concern was justified.

The Third Period: The Post-Progressive Era, 1910–28

As local government costs grew during the Progressive era and continued to grow after World War I, in part due to massive inflation and delayed capital costs, pressure also grew for the states to control and/or supervise local government finance and budgeting and to bring taxes down. Ohio passed the Smith one percent tax limitation law in 1910. County budget commissions were set up to ensure compliance with state budget procedures and tax limits. Massachusetts increased its financial regulation of local governments in 1913; Oklahoma began its highly controversial county excise boards to review the local budget process in 1910. In 1917 New Jersey codified and expanded its fiscal control over local governments with a detailed local government budget act. Indiana's widely touted state and county budgetary review boards began with a focus on assessment practices in 1919. In some states the review boards paid attention to budgeting, budget balance, and improved financial reporting; in others, the review boards emphasized keeping property taxes down, regardless of the impact on the quality of budgeting or financial management.

This section details the developing controls in Ohio, Indiana, Massachusetts, and New Jersey. Ohio emphasized tax reduction rather than improvement of city budgeting. Ohio set up county budget commissions composed of public officials to enforce tax limits. This enforcement process actually made budgeting worse and threatened home rule. Indiana also emphasized holding taxes down. In doing so, it empowered the State Board of Tax Commissioners to respond to citizen petitions. Any ten taxpayers could petition the tax commissioners on budgetary matters. The system was slanted to favor taxpayers who wanted lower taxes, even when the majority was willing to have higher taxes and more projects and services. In contrast, New Jersey and Massachusetts focused on improving the quality of financial management and budgeting, without paying much attention to lowering or enforcing tax limits.

The State of Ohio.—As detailed in chapter 2, Ohio passed a highly stringent tax limitation in 1910 in conjunction with efforts to improve assessment practices. The implementation of this tax limit was administrative and had a major impact on budgeting practices. Economy, rather than good budgeting and financial practice, was the effect of the Ohio law. The law not only contributed to poor budget practices but also to increased floating debt, delayed maintenance, and depleted sinking funds for the repayment of bonds.

The Ohio law limited property taxation to 10 mills, or 1 percent of assessed value, exclusive of interest, and 15 mills with interest and sinking funds included. These overall limits were subdivided by type of government so that cities had limits of 5 mills, or 0.5 percent of the assessed value (Wilcox 1922). County budget commissions, composed of the county auditor, the county treasurer, and the prosecuting attorney, all serving ex officio, were established to enforce the limits (Tharp 1933). They had very wide latitude to change local budgets if the proposals of any or all the local governments exceeded the property tax limits in the law.

If the total of taxation requested from all jurisdictions exceeded the limit, or if any jurisdiction exceeded its limit, the commission could reduce any item other than the contribution to sinking funds for debt repayment in order to make the budget and tax levy fit under the maximums. The commissions would typically negotiate such reductions with local officials. If the districts together exceeded the total state limit, the county budget commissions could apportion the reductions among the districts in any way they saw fit, cutting the county less and cities or school districts more, or the other way around. The commissions had no authority to make changes in the budgets if the requests were within the tax limits or to increase items other than necessary debt service or sinking fund payments. They could, and often did, reduce the school building levy to zero (Atkinson 1923).

Because apportionment among the local governments was left to the budget commissions if the total exceeded the state maximums, each taxing unit tried to present a convincing case to justify its budget requests. These sessions could become so competitive and stormy that the commission could not negotiate a solution. In such cases, the commission either imposed a judgment it thought suitable or came up with some kind of formula acceptable to the parties. Often the commission would just continue the apportionment from the previous year to avoid conflict. The authority of the commissions to reduce individual levies threatened home rule and went further than necessary to enforce the state laws (Atkinson 1923).

Each taxing district was required to submit a budget to the county budget commission each year. The budget was to include estimates of needs, balances brought forward from previous years, the probable income from other sources than property taxation, the amount spent from each fund in each of the five preceding fiscal years, and a detailed analysis of the public debt. But local jurisdictions often did not submit anything like a budget.

One observer reported the process in the following terms: Local officials tell the county auditor, who is a member of this budget commission, the total amount they will need in dollars. In rural districts, these estimates are rough and are not based on detailed estimates. The local officials estimate their needs high because any item can be cut, and they need to have enough to run their governments after their estimates are cut back (Wilcox 1922).

The budgets submitted to the county budget committees were so unreliable that they were almost worthless. Some of the budget proposals were just requests for the maximum rate under the law. Many other requests stated the total amount of revenue desired but provided no detailed justification for that amount (Atkinson 1923).

One reason for the poor quality of the budgets was that the commissions had to be done approximately eighteen months before the end of the fiscal year with which they were dealing; the officials of the various districts had to forecast their needs more than a year and a half in advance. In many cases they simply could not project expenditures that far ahead; in others, they tried, but their results were approximate at best. The task was complicated by the variation in fiscal calendars among local governments.

A second problem was that the budget form required for implementing tax limits differed from the standard budget form. In a normal budget for local use, expenditures would be classified according to objects of expenditures—what the money would be spent on in various departments. But the budget commissioners had to know whether the request was legal under the Smith law, so estimates for interest and debt retirement had to be split up to show what amount fell within the 10 mill limit and what amount was subject to the 15 mill restriction. Estimates for operating expenses also had to be classified according to the terms of the Smith law and its amendments. "This classification has been the despair of the local official," reported one observer (Atkinson 1923, 33).

Another reason for the poor quality of the budgets was that local officials used the budgets as backing for arguments before the commission, which undermined their accuracy. Local officials greatly exaggerated their needs in an effort to make their case and to assure that they would have enough revenue to carry on their responsibilities after the commission cut their estimates.

The impact of the Smith law, as implemented by the county budget commissions, was to hold down immediate outlays, delay the adoption of new services, and accelerate the amount of floating debt. Unwilling to reduce basic services and responding to public demands, the growing cities of Ohio ran deficits. The growth of floating debt may have been unavoidable, but the situation was made much worse by lax or nonexistent budgeting. Revenue estimates were not integrated into appropriation ordinances by city councils. Expenditures were frequently authorized in excess of revenues available. The inadequacy of revenues created a kind of despair about the possibility of balancing the budget, discouraging careful budgeting.

The Smith law did not encourage efficiency in government. Budgeting was not improved; purchasing procedures were not refined; and service delivery was not altered to get more from each dollar. Some services, such as street cleaning, health, and welfare, were cut back, and maintenance on public property was delayed. Sinking fund contributions were reduced, and deficits increased. The rise in taxation was temporarily checked at the same time that future costs were accumulating. The Ohio law was overly restrictive and its implementation overly enthusiastic, contributing to a worsening of both budgeting and financial management.

The State of Indiana.—The Indiana plan initially grew out of an assessment reform. In 1919 the legislature approved a requirement for assessment at full market value. To protect property taxpayers, the

law prohibited local governments from raising tax levies higher under
the new system than the old, without first getting the approval of the
State Board of Tax Commissioners (Tharp 1933).

More than two-thirds of the proposed increases at the local level
were disapproved by the state board that first year (Kilpatrick 1927).
When the local governments protested, the law was rescinded, and a
home-rule power of review was given to the local governments in
1920. That change was followed by a huge increase in local levies,
brought on in part by rapid inflation and delayed expenditures due to
World War I. The fear that such huge increases would continue resulted in a new law for state supervision (Tharp 1933). The new law
empowered the state tax commission to review any local budget or
bond issue upon petition of ten taxpayers. The tax commission was
then required to confirm the budget or bond issue, reject the budget or
bond issue, or reduce particular levies or bond issues. By ordering a
reduced levy, the board could force the spending of miscellaneous revenues and the reduction of fund balances (Kilpatrick 1927).

The Indiana tax commission was relatively useful when it faced
questions of budget quality and process. The board sometimes cut
padding from the budget, especially that resulting from faulty budget
making. The commission dealt with technical or procedural problems
such as a lack of adequate notice to taxpayers or failure to mention
the location of bridges to be repaired. Some appeals dealt with clerical
errors or miscalculation of assessed valuation. On the other hand, the
law and its implementation encouraged local officials to pad their estimates because they anticipated tax reductions and hoped for moderate
increases. If they asked for a lot, they might get some.

A state law passed in 1909 required the Indiana State Board of
Accounts to audit local accounts, but it was hampered by lack of adequate information from the local governments. It therefore experimented with different budget forms and by 1925 had installed a much
improved budget form in all the cities except Indianapolis. Nevertheless, there was no state requirement that the budget be filed prior to its
adoption. The auditors could examine the budget only after all the
money was spent. The only examination of the budget before implementation was performed by the tax commission in response to the
taxpayers' petition. So some budgets would be reviewed before the
start of the fiscal year, and others not. While the required budget
forms may have been the best available at the time, they still fell
far short of what good budgeting and analysis would require. Any

additions or explanations were up to the cities themselves and to non-profit research bureaus.

The Indiana system was highly controversial. It was revered by taxpayer associations as an example to be emulated by other states because it limited property taxes; it was criticized by other groups as an excessive and inappropriate use of state control over local budgeting and therefore a violation of home rule.[3] Critics also maintained that the state had little way of judging whether the proposed tax increases should be allowed because comparisons across governmental units and with past years were sometimes misleading, and it was nearly impossible to measure and therefore to mandate efficiency in government. A mistake was just as likely to be made by the state officials as by the local government, so why not let the local governments make their own mistakes? Other problems resulted from the strong focus on holding down property taxes, namely, an inability to raise taxes when needed to balance a fund or replenish sinking funds and a tendency to allow more borrowing to maintain the current levies.

Supporters and detractors quarreled about the advantages and disadvantages of the main feature of the system—that it was a review invoked on petition of ten or more property owners. This feature gave organized property taxpayers a convenient tool for negotiating tax reductions and budgetary improvements in their communities, whether or not a majority of citizens wanted tax (and service) reductions. Because of the petition-driven nature of the system, however, judgments applied only to the community making the petition, even if the problem discovered was more general. If the violated rule was one the state should be enforcing, it was difficult to see why the state should not enforce it in every jurisdiction, rather than just in the ones that happened to petition for redress.

Wylie Kilpatrick (1927), who was a well-known scholar of state and local relations, argued that the Indiana system was antidemocratic in its thrust. Three officials appointed by the governor and not responsible to the local governments made detailed decisions on taxing and bonding and could determine spending decisions in cases that could come from 6,000 districts. No matter what platform the gover-

---

3. Only Iowa adopted a system similar to Indiana's, which was based on the idea of taxpayer appeals. Unlike Indiana's system, however, Iowa delegated authority to make judgments on appeal to the state budget office. Iowa adopted this system in 1924.

nor was chosen on, he could not embody the desires of 6,000 districts; and if somehow he could, he could not implement 6,000 different sets of priorities. In any event, the tax commissioners did not represent the governor; he presumably chose them for their ability, not for their agreement with him. Finally, Kilpatrick argued, the courts were unwilling to review the decisions of the tax commission, denying citizens this democratic avenue of appeal. Kilpatrick's argument, in short, was that the system was indirect: there was no accountability to the governor, the courts, or to the public.

The emphasis on keeping property taxes down meant that there was a bias against even popular capital improvement projects. "Ambitious improvement programs, though backed by local opinion, are viewed askance by the Indiana board" (Kilpatrick 1927, 23). The state was considered to have the power to review cases independently of local public opinion. One of the tax commissioners in Indiana described his decision to ignore citizen support for spending. "They laid a petition on my table signed by 1,425 citizens asking that the bond issue be authorized. This was signed by lawyers, businessmen, and farmers. Everybody wanted the road. Along about eleven o'clock I said: 'Gentlemen, there isn't any use to proceed with this hearing because these bonds will not be authorized'" (Kilpatrick 1927, 31–32).

Disproportionate influence over budgetary matters was precisely what the organized taxpayers sought. The fact that they could bring a case before the tax commission gave them more power in local decision making. Claude Tharp (1933), the secretary of the Indiana tax association, described the influence of the county chapters in these terms:

> County associations have become so efficient that they consider and settle all of the perplexing questions arising from taxation matters, and the weight of their opinion has become so great in their respective communities that the elected officials abide by their decisions rather than attempt to fight the appeals, which they know will be taken if there is any hint of waste in the prepared budgets, or if the proposed levies are higher than necessity demands. (p. 16)

Tharp, speaking from the perspective of the taxpayers' associations, defended the appropriateness of a limited number of taxpayers preventing spending that was widely approved by others. Tharp argued that people who wanted more expenditures were wrongheaded and needed to be educated. They were viewing projects selfishly and not from the point of view of the collectivity.

> Strange as it may seem, the taxpayers' association must assume the task of educating the taxpayer against his own unwise acts. Substantial taxpayers are responsible in a large degree for the high cost of government, for they, as well as others, are often found among those who deluge public officials with demands for new government services. For example, they clamor for school buildings and other public structures which are beyond the ability of the community to finance; and others vote bond issues to be paid by future generations without realizing the unfairness of their acts. Again, taxpayers are often found in legislative halls lobbying for some pet project for their home town without perspective or balance with regard to the financial situation of the community. (Tharp 1933, 12)

This argument represents a radical departure from earlier arguments that divided the political world into tax spenders, including government officials and the poor who owned no property and therefore presumably paid no property taxes, and tax providers. In this argument, Tharp noted that the tax spenders were the same people as those who paid the taxes. But he claimed they should not have the right to make spending choices because their choices were uneducated; they were the wrong choices. Tharp equated control of debt with fairness to future generations, and he believed that refusal to build new schools was essential to staying within the community's capacity to pay. According to Tharp, he and his fellow antispending taxpayers represented the true community interest and hence had a legitimate right to overrule those who wanted more spending, even if those people also represented taxpayers.

The State of Massachusetts.—Massachusetts passed a law mandating budgeting for all its municipalities except Boston as part of a general overhaul of state supervision of local finance in 1913. The focus of the 1913 law was not to hold down property taxes; instead, the focus was to improve financial practices. The reforms were designed to eliminate borrowing for current purposes, excessive borrowing in anticipation of taxes, incurring liabilities by the use of demand notes without provision for their payment, diversion of trust funds, and the inefficient management of sinking funds. Sinking funds were abandoned and more fiscally conservative serial payments substituted. The legislature specified the purposes and the length of time for which debt could be incurred and prohibited borrowing for any other purpose (Van De Woestyne 1935).

As part of this overall effort to improve local financial management, municipal budgets were required, their content was mandated, and the budget process was specified. That process included a strong role for the executive in budget preparation and prohibited the council from increasing the executive's estimates. These reforms were designed to keep activist government efficient.

A second reason the state mandated budgets was the need for some objective means of judging municipalities' requests to borrow outside the state limit. If the state had a basis on which to judge both need and capacity of cities to pay for additional borrowing, it could possibly minimize borrowing outside the debt limit. Previously, only the self-interested testimony of local officials accompanied the petitions for special legislation and no one had responsibility to evaluate the information in the petitions. Under the new legislation, the director of the Bureau of Statistics had the duty of examining the petitions and reporting to the legislature an evaluation of the financial condition of the community making the petition. At the same time, the law increased the borrowing power of cities and towns, which was thought to reduce the number of petitions for special legislation that would be needed.

The budgetary provisions of the 1913 act required the mayor of every city, or the commissioner or director of finance in cities with the commission form of government, to submit to the city council an annual budget of current city expenses, consisting of an itemized and detailed statement of the money required. The city council could reduce or reject, but could not increase or add, any item without the approval of the mayor or commissioner or director of finance. Supplementary budgets were allowed (Van De Woestyne 1935).

The law did not check the growth of expenditures, at least in part because many of the provisions of the budget system were disregarded or circumvented. The cities and towns did adopt budgets, but they were not bound by them. Supplementary and emergency appropriations were frequently used or overused, and so the original estimates were not treated as limits. Transfers between funds were also common (Kilpatrick 1939). In Massachusetts, the rules generally made sense, but the level of enforcement was inadequate.

The State of New Jersey. — Like Massachusetts, New Jersey had a long tradition of supervising and regulating the financial practices of local governments that was mainly oriented to assuring good financial practice and budgetary balance.

In the 1850s and 1860s New Jersey placed its fiscal regulation of local governments directly in each city's charter. In the 1880s the charter provisions were replaced by laws that applied to all cities. These laws concerned the publication of annual financial statements, spending limits, borrowing in anticipation of revenues, and the unexpended balance of taxes collected. The legislation gradually became more comprehensive and detailed. In 1906, the middle of the Progressive period of governmental expansion, the state passed a law concerning tax anticipation loans; in 1907 it added legislation on unexpended appropriations; in 1908 the state passed legislation regulating the fiscal year (Shipman 1936).

In 1916, after the Progressive era growth in spending, pressures to control local finance were reflected in the creation of a commission to survey local government and make recommendations for its improvement. From 1917 to 1919 the state adopted the measures recommended by this commission, called the Pierson Commission after its chairman. The legislation in 1917 was called the Pierson Local Budget Act. Budgetary control was exercised through legislation that applied to all local governments.

The 1917 law and its major modifications through 1936 affected budgeting in format and process, but left some areas vague, to be filled in by local tradition and choice. The scope of the legislation was broad, including records and accounting procedures, planned revenues and expenditures, appropriation procedures, budget administration, and borrowing in anticipation of tax collections. A variety of requirements for reporting and auditing were also included.

The legislation emphasized balanced budgets, rather than low or reduced property taxes. Thus, while the Indiana law encouraged state boards to increase the estimates of miscellaneous revenues to hold down property tax levies, the New Jersey legislation tried to prevent overestimates of revenue sources other than property taxes, such as the balance left from the previous year and miscellaneous revenues. "The temptation to balance the budget by appropriating a convenient amount of surplus, regardless of the actual amount of cash available, has always been present" (Shipman 1936, 4). Similarly, the miscellaneous revenue estimates tended to be high, presumably with the intent of keeping property taxes low, since property taxes were calculated as the amount needed to balance the budget after all other revenues had been counted.

Cities generally budgeted in stages. First, they estimated revenues and found out from departments what their needs were. Then they combined the estimates in a single request that would be examined, balanced, and then passed by the local governing body. The state law specified three steps: the receipt of the proposed budget by the governing body, indicating that the budget was ready for publication; a public hearing; and the adoption of the budget by the governing body.

Changes could be made in the budget after it was approved, but under the Pierson budget laws, if these changes were extensive (extensive was defined as any item changed by more than 10 percent or any taxes to be collected changed by more than 5 percent), the changed amounts had to be republished and a new hearing held before final adoption.

The purposes of the state control included establishing budget deadlines, exposing the budget to public examination and comment, limiting changes in the budget after public hearing, and controlling the estimation of local revenues. The prevention of overspending the budget was left to the local governments, but borrowing in anticipation of taxes was closely regulated. Transfers between items after the final adoption of the budget were restricted to the last two months of the year. A transfer could be made only by a formal resolution adopted by a two-thirds vote of the local governing body. This rule also applied to spending down fund balances. The highly detailed Pierson act also regulated emergency appropriations. "Emergency" meant such events as storms, floods, and wars, but in practice the definition included state-mandated expenditures, the costs of special elections, and added requirements, "which could not have been anticipated" (Shipman 1936, 25).

State regulation of local budgeting was primarily legislative, rather than administrative. The scope of authority of the state auditor was limited, and he lacked enforcement power. The Pierson act required that a copy of the local budget go to the auditor, who could inquire into any item. He could order a correction if he found a mistake or if a mandatory item was missing or underbudgeted. But the state auditor had no authority to see if the budget was really balanced, that is, if the amount of surplus cash listed was really available and whether the miscellaneous revenues listed could really be collected. He could only offer advice.

The Fourth Period: The Great Depression

The Great Depression strengthened the willingness of states to control local government finance, through legislation and increased administrative supervision. During the early years of the depression, rigid tax limits were widely adopted through legislation and constitutional amendment. In addition, existing budget legislation and supervision were often strengthened. Some controls were loosened, however, to make it possible to borrow to pay off floating debt and handle emergencies.

State legislative control over budgeting in particular increased during the depression. Texas passed a Uniform Budget Law in 1931 (MacCorkle 1937, 13). Florida began to require all taxing districts to adopt annual budgets. New Jersey revised its local budget law to place all local units on a cash basis. Existing budgeting statutes were strengthened in Alabama, Colorado, Indiana, Nevada, and Pennsylvania. New Hampshire in 1935 enacted an optional town budgeting law under which sixty-eight towns were operating by the end of 1936. Kansas in 1935 passed legislation designed to improve local accounting methods and secure reliable audits; in 1937 it passed a cash-basis law and a budget law (McKay 1950, 33).

By the end of the depression, most states had adopted some form of state supervision or control over local budgeting and finance. By 1941 thirty-eight states required budgets from some or all local governments by statute, and an additional four states did so by administrative procedure. Of those forty-two states, twenty-eight specifically required budgets from cities. The states without statutory budgeting requirements were Delaware, Georgia, Maine, Maryland, Michigan, Minnesota, Rhode Island, South Carolina, Tennessee, and Vermont. While many states mandated budgeting, "the states' early interest in local budgeting was necessarily confined to setting in motion the initial procedure. Budget forms were elementary and the states were satisfied if something like a budget was enacted and presumably used" (Kilpatrick 1941, 23–24).

Two trends of the depression era—limiting taxes and improving budgeting—contradicted each other. Limitations on revenues made it difficult to plan for needs, encouraged the proliferation of tax districts, broke down the levies into watertight compartments and forbade transfers between funds, and reduced the discretion of locally elected officials. One observer argued that legislative and constitutional tax limits reduced the imagination and effort of local officials in putting budgets together, that millage maximums tended to become minimums, and that when the millage rates were tied to specific areas of expenditure, they encouraged dishonest distribution of expenditures.

> It is customary, when tax limitations exist, to charge many expenditures to the account or fund which has the largest available balance. In a city recently visited, I found thirty-nine tax funds. While these existed, they meant little because the payroll of the city was not distributed on a cost basis but was charged to the accounts where the most money was on hand. (Leet and Paige 1936, 30)

This pattern of charges was fairly common because "improper distribution of expenditures is encouraged in any city if it is not possible to make reasonable transfers between various items" (Chatters 1935, 30).

Chatters went on to describe such earmarking of revenues as analogous to a business that made separate budgets for each department without regard to the whole. In an automobile plant it was as if 10 percent were set aside for plant operations 15 percent for assembly costs, 3 percent for the chassis, and 20 percent for making the bodies. The result might be beautiful bodies and poor chassis. If the budget allocations could not be shifted to improve the quality, the result would be a poorly made car. Chatters was concerned not just with the existence of tax limits but with the impact on budgeting of earmarked tax limits for each function of city government. Such a system of earmarked tax limits still exists in some places.

In this section, New Jersey, Texas, Indiana, and Oklahoma are described. By and large, during the depression, these states continued moving along whatever path they had worked out in the Progressive and post-Progressive eras while paying particular attention to the problems raised by the Great Depression, sometimes creating new institutions to carry out the work.

The State of New Jersey.—The focus of New Jersey's extensive control during the post-Progressive period was on financial control and the avoidance of deficits. During the Great Depression, the legislation was extended to include more controls of the same nature, but the fact of depression was recognized in efforts to handle floating debt and in loosening the definition of financial emergency. A system of control that had been almost exclusively legislative gave a bit more authority to the administrative control structure.

The Pierson law regulating local finance and budgeting was revised in 1936. One emphasis was on limiting the estimates of miscellaneous taxes and fund balances to a realistic increase from the previous year. These estimates were to be reviewed by the auditor before the budget was approved. The goal was to prevent overestimates of nonproperty tax revenues. Overestimating nonproperty taxes could help maintain low property tax levies but could produce deficits.

The Pierson law had required that major changes in the budget must be reapproved by the public. The depression era amendment altered the definition of major changes so that even relatively small changes had to go back to the public for approval. The intent was to assure that the budget approved by the public was the budget that was in fact implemented.

One of the problems that occurred during the depression was borrowing in anticipation of taxes. Normally, such borrowing for cash-flow purposes was nonproblematic because all or nearly all of the anticipated tax revenues were collected, and the notes were paid off promptly. But during the depression, many people did not pay their tax bills on time, and others never paid them at all. Sometimes, there were not enough revenues to cover the tax anticipation notes, resulting in the accumulation of floating debt. To prevent borrowing against delinquent tax payments that were not collectible, the reforms of 1936 put the localities on a "cash basis." They were not allowed to borrow in anticipation of revenues that might not occur, but they could add to the initial levy a portion anticipated for delinquent taxes. If the delinquent taxes were paid, the cities could collect and spend the revenues; if they were not paid, the cities never collected or spent the money. Under the modified rules, the localities would get as much money in a year as they were entitled to without borrowing (Shipman 1936).

The 1936 act required local governments to move to a cash basis, but earlier in the depression cities had already built up considerable unfunded debt. This floating debt had to be converted into funded debt and paid off. The state guided the local governments in disposing of their floating debts by issuing new obligations to pay off the old ones.

In addition, the state helped local governments respond to the depression by loosening the definition of emergency. At the same time, lawmakers indicated they didn't want the new flexibility to be abused. Under the 1936 revisions of the budget law, an emergency was any unforeseen expenditure for which provision had not been made in the budget. But such spending required a two-thirds vote and was limited to $10,000, or 3 percent of the budget.

Under the 1936 revision, the state auditor's scope was expanded, but it remained advisory. He could examine appropriations for debt service, deferred charges, floating debt, uncollectible taxes, cash deficits, reserve for uncollected taxes, and estimates of anticipated revenues to determine whether the provisions of the law were met. But local governments were not required to comply with the auditor's recommendations to solve the problems. The low level of funding of the auditor's office limited even this consultative role. Thus the cities retained considerable discretion.

The State of Texas.—Texas passed a uniform budget law in 1931.[4] The law prescribed the contents of municipal budgets and set forth the procedure for their enactment and execution. The law required a complete financial statement that listed outstanding obligations and the cash on hand in each fund. The law also required enough itemization to make possible a comparison between expenditures for the coming year and corresponding expenditures of the past year (MacCorkle 1937). The executive was made the budget officer and was given the power to require information from other municipal officers. A public hearing was required. The city council became responsible for enacting the budget into law. A copy of each budget had to be filed with the state comptroller. Taxes were to be levied in accordance with the budget, and expenditures had to follow it.

The law had some problems. It lacked some of the refinements of budgeting, such as a budget message, a budget summary, and supporting schedules. There was no mention of allotments to keep spending within the budget limits and no discussion of transfers. But the most important problem was a complete lack of "teeth." There was no follow-up on the budget reports after they were filed. Many cities ignored the requirement to draw up and file the budget. For fiscal year 1932–33, 192 cities filed budgets; 137 filed for 1933–34; and only about 60 filed for 1934–35. Only about half the cities ever filed their budgets with the comptroller (MacCorkle 1937). The budgets that were filed left much to be desired. Some sizable cities did not have a budget.

Texas's law was much narrower in scope than New Jersey's and

---

4. McCorkle 1937 cites Martin 1934 on the Texas budget law.

relied less on existing law or tradition. The purely legislative approach had the difficulty of not being self-implementing.

The State of Indiana. — Before the Great Depression, Indiana had an integrated plan of financial controls, including state-controlled budgeting, accounting, auditing, and reporting systems (Tharp 1933). During the depression, Indiana exchanged a state-level budget review for a county-level review. These county boards were given extensive powers, and the State Board of Tax Commissioners had further powers. Local governments were left with relatively little fiscal authority.

The County Tax Adjustment Boards were appointed bodies. They had seven members. One member was a county councilman selected by the county council, and the other six were appointed by the circuit court judge. One of these six had to be a mayor or president of a town board, one a township trustee, one a member of a board of school commissioners, and three had to be resident freeholders not holding public office or related in any way to the head of a local government by closer relationship than second cousin (Sheppard 1936).

The County Tax Adjustment Boards' powers covered both taxes and appropriations. They had the power to revise, change, and if necessary reduce the levy of any or all taxing units so that the total levy on property within any municipal corporation would not exceed the tax rates fixed by law (Tharp 1933). They could revise, change, and reduce specific items of appropriation for any unit. They could decrease the amount allowed for salaries or food in any county institution. This appointed agency was the final appropriating body; the changes made by the board did not go back to the local appropriating agency (Sheppard 1936).

Any ten taxpayers could appeal the decision of the county tax board to the State Board of Tax Commissioners, and any local unit whose levy was reduced could appeal to the state board. The state board could affirm, change, revise, or reduce the rates and items in the budget, provided that it did not increase the rate for any unit above the total rate originally fixed by the unit or increase the combined rate as fixed by the County Tax Adjustment Board.

In 1935 the legislature amended the system to make it more effective. Before 1935, after the budget changes had been made by the county and state boards, the local governments could pass supplemental appropriations, bypass the reductions, and in some cases create deficits. The supplemental appropriations could be appealed to the state board, but because the amounts were small, few were appealed.

In 1934 and 1935 back taxes were sometimes paid; these were quickly appropriated, sometimes for unnecessary things. So the 1935 amendment required all supplementals to be approved by the state board. Any supplemental appropriations, including transfers from one account to another, in any amount—no matter how small—had to be approved by the state tax board. The operation of the law left "very little home rule to the local units of government in matters of financing" (Sheppard 1936, 53).

The State of Oklahoma. —Oklahoma's control over local finance and budgeting combined constitutional and statutory provisions with administrative controls, and tax limits with budget supervision. The Office of the Examiner created the budget forms. But their use was supervised by the county excise boards, which often did not understand the forms, and by the state tax court, which could not deal with general issues across the state, but only with appeals on a case-by-case basis, and without setting precedent. This so-called court did not keep records. Oklahoma had a comprehensive system of state control, but implementation was problematic.[5]

Oklahoma became a state in 1907. Maximum tax limits were written into its original constitution. The constitutional provision limited property taxes to a maximum of 31.5 mills for all local governments and specified the maximums for separate local units inside the limit. The state set up county excise boards in 1910, to oversee the budgeting system. These excise boards were granted considerable discretion, causing clashes with constitutionally based home-rule powers.

A county excise board was composed of five regular county officials: the judge, attorney, clerk, treasurer, and superintendent of public instruction. In 1917 this board was enlarged to seven members by the addition of the county assessor and one commissioner selected by the county commission. The board was authorized to increase or decrease items in the spending plan (Carr 1937).

In 1924 the state supreme court held that the constitutional tax limits improperly constrained local exercise of taxing power. In granting more taxing power to the local units, the legislature reduced the tax limits of the municipalities well below the maximums permitted in the constitution. If local estimates of revenue needs exceeded the prescribed statutory limits, and if the county excise boards thought that the additional requested appropriations were reasonable, they could

---

5. The material on Oklahoma is from Carr 1937.

authorize a special election in which the voters could approve extra levies up to the constitutional limits.

During the depression, tax limits were made much more severe. In 1933, as a result of massive public pressure, a constitutional amendment was passed, drastically reducing the maximum tax levy from 31.5 mills to 15 mills. This limit was not subdivided in the constitution; that task was left to the legislature or the county excise boards. The county excise boards then focused more narrowly on the goal of implementing the limitations on property taxes.

In 1931 the composition of the county excise board underwent a serious change. The new governor had campaigned on the issue of economy in government. "The time has come," he argued, "to apply to the spending of public money the same rules of economy and business administration that private individuals are required to apply to their own private affairs in these times of financial stress" (Carr 1937, 103). The governor blamed the existing county excise boards for allowing local governments to spend extravagantly. He argued that they would permit increased spending because they were public officials. The governor wanted the excise boards to represent the taxpayers, rather than government officials. The county board of equalization and the excise board were abolished and a new board that combined both functions was created, with three members. One of the members was appointed by the state tax commission, one by the district judge, and one by the county commissioners. Despite the political argumentation, the cities had not found the county excise boards particularly sympathetic to their spending requests. The earlier seven-member boards were composed primarily of farmers who had little sympathy for municipal spending.

Legislation adopted in 1917 and amended in 1933 spelled out the powers of the county excise board and prescribed the budgetary procedure for local governments. The local budget process was to begin in July, with the preparation of a statement summarizing the financial condition of the governmental unit for the year just ended and an itemized statement of needs for the current year by department. Local governments were required to calculate how much they needed to put into sinking funds for debt repayment and to estimate all nonproperty tax revenues. After the local governments made their estimates public, local officials were supposed to forward these tentative budgets to the county excise boards. The county boards could revise or correct any estimate, by eliminating, increasing, or decreasing any item. They were also empowered to add items. Then the excise boards were supposed to set property tax levies. The clerk in each governmental unit was then supposed to set up accounts to match the appropriations and was forbidden to pay any bills in excess of those amounts.

Additional emergency appropriations could be made, but only if the amount did not exceed the revenues for the year. The excise board could authorize transfers from the surplus revenue account (now called the year-end balance) to pay for the emergency. If there wasn't enough in the surplus account, the excise board could cancel or reduce other expenditures to cover the amount requested.

This system looked reasonable on paper, but in practice it had several weaknesses. First, some of the county excise board members were sufficiently motivated to reduce the size of government that they were willing to exceed their court-mandated authority. Second, the board members were generally not chosen for their knowledge of finances or their intellect and consequently were often of little help to local officials in filling out the complex budget forms prescribed by the state examiner. Many local governments left the forms incomplete or used incorrect numbers.

Beginning in 1928, the county excise boards were backed up by a special tax court. Though known as a court, it operated more like an administrative agency. The county excise boards and the tax court operated together to favor tax relief for big business. Part of the reason was that many tax cases never made it to the court but were settled at an earlier stage. The county excise board could revise the contested budget before it got to court, creating a pattern of compromises that encouraged large corporations to contest their payments.

The court consisted of three regularly elected district judges designated by the governor. The judges were good men but the proceedings were informal. The court had no fixed meeting place, did not keep records, and treated similar cases differently because of the tendency to compromise and arbitrate. Most of the compromises were not based on consideration of the local government's needs or on the citizens' ability to pay.

This bargaining process at both the county and the state level encouraged corporations to add more contested issues, with the expectation that some would be knocked out and others would be successful. By making tax protests, the big corporations could tie up the revenues of smaller governments. Because local governments feared having their revenues tied up, they often capitulated to the protesting corporations.

From the corporations' point of view, they were better off if they could minimize their tax burdens. Their chief executives did not live in the towns being denied revenues, and they would not have to deal with torn-up pavement or leaky sewer and water systems. They had little interest in supporting cities to provide relief or jobs during the depression. In contrast, taxpayers living in the community wanted to reduce the burden of taxation on themselves but also wanted particular projects and services.

The tax courts were based on appeals and therefore were unable to provide systematic examination of budgets for compliance to the state laws. Other agencies in the state tried to create some unity and comparability through the use of standardized budgeting and accounting forms. But budget forms alone, no matter how good, could not guarantee sound financial practice in all the local governments of a state. A single form could not adequately handle the complexity of the largest cities, for example. And if local officials did not know how to fill out the forms, the forms could not do a whole lot of good.

As in Indiana, the state government gave disproportionate power to businesses interested in reducing their tax burden and tried to reduce the role of government officials in implementing budgeting rules and tax limits. Antitaxers were supposed to hold the balance of budgetary power. By disproportionately empowering a minority that felt threatened by increased taxes, the state ensured the reduction of property tax yields and hence limited the scope of government services during the depression.

Conclusions

The impact of the states on cities' budgeting has been substantial but has not been uniform or all encompassing.[6] Some states have had minimal supervision of local governments' budgeting and financial management; other states have laws in place but have not enforced them. At the other extreme, some states prescribed the formats for municipal budgets, required that budgets be balanced, and laid out in fine detail requirements for accounting, reporting, and borrowing. There has been enormous variation in the scope of state controls and

---

6. As of 1977, thirty-seven states had statutes regulating local budgeting. See Petersen, Cole, and Petrillo 1977.

supervision, the degree and manner of the implementation of state regulations, and the nature of state goals.

States tended not to be leaders in designing and imposing the best budgeting models. They sometimes took the best models from cities and spread them across the state; sometimes they established minimal standards, or better than minimal standards, but they only minimally enforced them. At times, states actually contributed to the worsening of budgetary practices when they were so concerned about reducing taxes that they set unrealistically low revenue constraints or established enforcement procedures for tax limits that distorted budgeting information.

Where state controls were intense and centralized, those controls persisted nearly unchanged for many decades. Laws that had been useful became problematic. For example, requirements to levy taxes for specific purposes, which provided the basis for the rudimentary budget typical of the post–Civil War period, became problematic during the Great Depression when excessive rigidity prevented cities from legally spending money where they needed it the most. In most cases, however, state supervision of local budgeting has responded to changing conditions. For example, when cities borrowed too much, the states intervened to limit borrowing. In the post-Progressive and Great Depression periods, states sometimes stepped in to keep property taxes low.

As state control and supervision developed, it was sometimes difficult to find a balance between state supervision and local democratic control. As the next chapter points out, these problems were generally resolved, only to be reintroduced when states increased mandates to local governments without proportional financial aid. Local government fiscal crises highlighted the continuing need for state intervention, and tax revolts continued to occur, but solutions had to be worked out in the context of local government autonomy.

8

The States and Local Budgeting:
The Modern Period

THE SYSTEMS of state regulation of local budgeting that had been worked out and elaborated in the 1910s, 1920s, and 1930s remained in place during and after World War II. By the 1970s a number of factors had brought about changes in the nature of state supervision. The basic structure remained intact in most states, but the emphasis often changed.

In the mid-1970s New York City experienced a widely publicized and dramatic fiscal crisis in which the banks refused to lend the city any more money. Because the city had vast quantities of floating debt that was financed by rolling over short-term notes, the refusal of the banks to lend additional money to the city created an emergency situation. The State of New York had to help New York City regain entry to the financial markets by improving its fiscal condition. The state's role was obtrusive and uncomfortable for the city, but the city did ultimately win back the support of the financial community.

As a result of the tumult kicked up by New York City's fiscal crisis and the role of the State of New York, the National Council of State Legislatures and the Government Finance Officers' Association did a study summarizing the level and nature of state supervision (Petersen, Cole, and Petrillo 1977). The study was revealing because of the continuities it suggested and some of the discontinuities it hinted at. The rate of change accelerated in the late 1970s, after the study was completed, so the study understates the changes.

The 1977 report revealed that thirty-seven states had a statutory basis for monitoring or supervising local government budgets; twenty-four of those had devised uniform budget standards or guidelines for the preparation of local budget documents. Thirty-four out of thirty-seven collected the local government budgets. Most of the states that collected local budgets examined them for conformance to state tax and expenditure limits. In most cases, the report concluded, if a budget was found in violation of the law, state officials could alter the budget or disapprove it. In eight states, all or part of the local budget had to be approved by state officials (or by the county in Ohio) before funds could be disbursed. Indiana, Massachusetts, Nevada, New Hampshire, New Jersey, New Mexico, Ohio, and West Virginia required approval of the budget or certification of the tax rate before funds could be expended or revenues raised. Two other states, Colorado and Missouri, required the budget to be filed before expenditures could be made, but no permission or approval was necessary. In four other states—Louisiana, Tennessee, Michigan, and North Carolina—detailed control of local budgets was required under some circumstances.

The continuities suggested by this brief description are twofold. First, about the same number of states had statutory controls over local budgeting as had them at the end of the Great Depression. Second, many of the states that forged centralized systems of control before and during the depression still had such centralized control, states such as Indiana, Massachusetts, New Jersey, New Mexico, Ohio, and North Carolina.

The study also indirectly suggests some of the changes that occurred since the end of the Great Depression. First, the report notes that the purpose of state review of local budgets was in most cases to assure conformity with state law; that had not always been the clear intent of state supervision of local budgets. Second, some states, for example New Hampshire, had only optional controls in the 1930s but in the 1970s required state approval of local budgets. States such as Iowa, which would have been included on a list of those with centralized control in the 1920s and 1930s, were not on the 1977 list.

In fact, a considerable amount of change occurred within the overall framework of continuity. North Carolina modified its approach considerably in the 1970s, though it retained many features of the older system; Indiana eliminated some of the more controversial features of its system of control. A number of states increased their grants of home rule, simplified the administrative structure of state supervision, and began efforts to curtail or control the level of state mandating to local governments. These and other changes were adopted incrementally, but overall they had the impact of changing the direction of state supervision.

The causes of these changes were many. Some began as early as the 1930s, as the courts wrestled with the new centralized systems and their compatibility with home-rule legislation. Gradually, the more questionable systems were curtailed, especially those that relied on a board of appointed officials, rather than local elected officials, as the final arbiter of budget priorities. The states then took on a legally more acceptable function of reviewing local budgets for compliance with state laws, especially but not exclusively state tax and expenditure limits. The idea that it was the role of the state government to step in and reduce property taxes by altering local budgets yielded to other methods of controlling property taxes, including tax and spending limits, state aid given to substitute for property taxes, and permission from the state for local governments to raise nonproperty taxes.

Also, during the Great Depression, states adopted new sources of revenues, and as they did so, they increased the amount of aid they gave to local governments. After World War II, states continued to expand their revenue bases and shared more of their income with the cities. Twenty-one states adopted a sales tax between 1945 and 1970, and eleven states adopted individual income taxes during the 1960s and 1970s (ACIR 1988, 96). State aid to local government increased at a rapid rate, from $8.1 billion in 1958 to $36.8 billion in 1972 (Wright 1978). In 1962, 18.7 percent of state aid went to cities; in 1967, 21.3 percent (ACIR 1969). Cities were getting a slightly larger share of a vastly increased flow of funds from the states to the local governments. The increase of aid came not only with strings attached,[1] but

---

1. Not only did the states attach conditions to the grants they offered to local governments, they often attached additional requirements to federal grants passed through the states to the local governments. In a 1975 survey by ACIR and the International City Management Association, twenty out of thirty-four respondents indicated that they always attached procedural stipulations to grants, such as auditing and reporting requirements; fourteen out of thirty-three said they always added performance standards to federal pass-through grants (ACIR 1985).

also with a feeling that states now had more right to inspect and improve the quality of financial management of local governments.

The third cause of change also had its roots in the depression but was exaggerated by the effects of the Second World War. During the Great Depression, capital projects were often delayed unless they were funded by the federal government; during the war, almost all capital projects were delayed to allow capital to flow into the war effort. Cities were not allowed to accumulate capital for the inevitable and backed-up needs after the war, so long-delayed capital projects had to be debt funded. This postwar run-up of debt-funded projects combined with war-induced inflation to push up expenditures while suburbanization pushed up service demands. The result for local governments was an increase in property taxes that had in many cases been low and stable since early in the depression (see, for example, McKay 1950).

The growth in expenditures increased the pressure from local governments for more home rule, especially in terms of control over new nonproperty tax revenues. City officials complained they lacked the broad tax bases of the state and nation and could not produce the income required to satisfy growing demand for services (for Kansas, see McKay 1950). Urban riots in the 1960s put pressure on the states to facilitate local government responses and enhanced pressure for home rule. The states' response was more in the area of allowing cities to determine their own charters, including the services they would deliver and forms of organization they would use, than in granting more autonomy over finances (for Indiana, see Hojnacki 1983, 146).

Many states responded to the increased pressure for more home rule. For example, Illinois granted municipal home rule in 1970; Pennsylvania granted a home-rule option to cities in 1972; Indiana strengthened and codified its home-rule provisions in 1980 and 1981; Iowa granted home-rule constitutionally in 1969; Montana offered a home-rule option in 1976. Local officials continued to ask for more discretion over policymaking in the face of public demand for property tax relief, court- and referendum-mandated upgrading of assessment practices, and the trend toward state restrictions on local tax and spending powers (White 1979).

Another cause of change was the increased number of state mandates to local governments. States have always had the legal ability to mandate services and procedures for local governments, but these regulations multiplied rapidly from 1960 to 1978 (Lovell and Egan 1983; Lovell and Tobin 1981).

Reasons given for the increase in mandating include the growth of state activism and capacity, the desire for uniform services across the state, the ability of interest groups to influence the state to mandate service levels or benefit levels, and the states' efforts to pass on expensive burdens of service delivery to local governments (Kelly 1992; ACIR 1990).

Enhanced state activism ran into limited revenues, especially during recessions. "State governments are much more powerful policy engines than they were in the past, but the fiscal fuel needed to operate those engines is often in short supply. To some extent, therefore, to make use of their policymaking abilities and also to comply with federal mandates, states must commandeer the engines of their local governments" (ACIR 1990, 3).

State government became more professionalized in the 1960s and 1970s, and by the 1980s had taken on some of the functions reassigned by the federal government. The increased level of activation of the states was reflected in increased centralization of functions, in which the state picked up a larger share of state-local expenditures and performed more functions directly at the state level (Stephens 1974, 1985; Stonecash 1983, 1985).

At least in part because of these trends toward greater activity at the state level, interest groups shifted their pressure activities to the state capitals. If they could get their policies adopted by the governor and the legislature, the policies would have to be implemented at the local level statewide, a much more efficient strategy than trying to persuade cities, one at a time, to adopt particular policies. While some new state mandates for budgeting may have had the benign intent of improving budgeting processes and reporting requirements, some state mandates were simply expressions of interest-group pressure funneled through the state governments on to the cities.

By 1981 there were an overwhelming number of state mandates. Some stipulated a service to be performed or set requirements for the quality of services to be delivered, while others established procedures for local governments to follow. About 10 percent of the total number of mandates dealt specifically with budgeting or finance, but other mandates also affected municipal budgeting by setting performance standards for specific services or specifying the terms of pensions for employees. Mandates affecting local government were expanding rapidly in quantity, range, and scope and severely limited the choices local governments could make (Lovell and Tobin 1981).

As long as state aid more or less kept up with state mandates for increased or improved service delivery, the inherent stress was kept in limits, but during the 1970s a deep recession hit the cities, the federal government cut back on aid, and the states reduced the rate of growth in their aid to cities. These trends combined with a new round of tax and expenditure limits to put real pressure on cities' finances. Cities' long and loud complaints about unfunded mandates pressured the states to curtail or control them.

Mounting pressures broke through dramatically in New York City's fiscal crisis. The New York crisis demonstrated not only the impact of recession and increased services but also the consequences of financial mismanagement. Other states reacted to New York City's fiscal crisis in two ways. On the one hand, they sought to control mismanagement and keep costs down in the cities; on the other hand, they sought to help the cities by examining and withdrawing state regulations that had been making matters worse, rather than better. One way to keep taxes down and still keep cities financially healthy was to help cities improve their financial management. Thus some states responded by helping cities borrow at lower interest rates or by helping cities invest their cash in statewide pools.

Professional associations tried to forge constructive proposals for the states that would help the cities. For example, the Committee for Economic Development put out a statement in 1976 that argued for a larger state role in local finance but urged against treading on local autonomy.

> We believe the state governments should play a central role in providing leadership, incentives, and technical assistance for improving the productivity of their local governments and further should work toward removing state-imposed impediments to productivity, which in many states are numerous. This does not imply a diminution of local prerogatives; on the contrary, it suggests a need for states to update their traditional responsibility for providing foundations of local government that will permit cities and counties to manage their affairs more efficiently. (Committee for Economic Development 1976, 68)

The national-level Advisory Commission on Intergovernmental Relations (ACIR) in 1979 reiterated the responsibilities of states to help avoid fiscal crises in local government. "Obviously, states are critical actors and represent a necessary starting point in solving local financial management problems and in strengthening overall local financial management capacity" (White 1979, 22).

ACIR created a model agenda for state legislation, taken in part from experiments in the states. One set of proposals was intended to make states more aware of the costs they were imposing on local governments and to persuade the states either to pay for mandates or to curtail them. A second goal of the proposals was to increase citizen participation in budget processes, making budgets available for public examination and providing budget hearings for citizens. Other proposals dealt with ways the states could help the local governments manage pensions, insurance, investments, and debt issuance. Some of the proposals dealt with techniques for the states to prevent and control local government financial emergencies. Part of the thrust of the proposals was to advise the states to remove unnecessary shackles on local finance by removing from constitutions details on local government borrowing and taxing powers and substituting legislative controls. The intent of these proposals was to improve the flexibility and responsiveness of state regulation.

State governments have reacted in a piecemeal fashion. Some responded quickly, and others slowly; some made large changes, and others small ones. Some responded to a problem that was acute in that particular state. It is difficult to see among the variety of piecemeal changes what the trends have been. The following summary of the trends during the 1970s and early 1980s is therefore sometimes based on the experiences of only a few states.

- States changed the function of oversight of local budgeting away from holding down taxes and toward ensuring compliance with the law. Other techniques were used to hold down property taxes.
- There was increased (or renewed) interest in uniform systems of accounting and integrating such systems with budgeting. There was also more interest in generally accepted accounting principles (GAAP). In 1978 only six states expressly required conformance with generally accepted principles of governmental

accounting, but by the end of 1979 at least six additional states had adopted legislation affecting local accounting, auditing, and financial reporting. Provisions of these laws varied, but in general they imposed more stringent controls over local practices (ACIR 1985). States wanted to know how healthy their local governments were and wanted the bond market to know this as well. They could do so only if they had good and uniform accounting and budgeting data.

- A variety of new institutional arrangements sprang up in the 1970s and early 1980s to help implement a more cooperative attitude between state and local governments. In 1974 there were only four state-level Advisory Commissions on Intergovernmental Relations, but by 1983 eleven states had ACIRs that conformed to the national model, with representation from various local governments, the public, and state legislative and executive branches. Notable among the eleven were Iowa, North Carolina, New Jersey, Washington, and Massachusetts, which had centralized control over local budgeting and financial management. Ohio, which also had intense state supervision of local budgeting, set up a state and local government commission in 1978, but it was unfunded in 1983 because of state financial troubles (ACIR 1985, 352).

- There was more effort on the part of states to measure and control unfunded mandates and to recognize and withdraw controls and regulations that were harmfully restrictive.

- The trend continued toward making budgeting requirements increasingly sophisticated. At the same time, efforts were made to make regulation more flexible, differentially applying rules to those that needed it most and not overburdening smaller governments with high levels of detailed reporting.

- Some states began to offer services to local governments to improve their financial management and cash flow. This offered a path toward more revenues without raising taxes.

Some illustrations of these trends follow.

Oklahoma, Indiana, and Ohio

Oklahoma, Indiana, and Ohio had developed systems of state supervision of local budgeting that depended on appointees at the county level. These appointees often had considerable control over local budgeting decisions. Many members of these county budgeting commissions conceived of their role as holding down taxes regardless of popular will, especially during the Great Depression. In Ohio local officials were members of the county review boards, but in Indiana and Oklahoma the ability of the boards to overrule local officials raised questions not only about home rule but also about democratic governance. In Ohio the dominance of the county officials over other jurisdictions located in the county raised a related set of questions. The excesses of these systems were recognized as early as the depression years.

The problematic issues were resolved somewhat differently in each state. In Oklahoma the courts stepped in to curtail the scope of decision making of the budget review commissions in order to reconcile home rule with budget supervision. In Indiana local governments had less home rule to start with, so the discordance between strong budget control and home rule was less troublesome. But the county tax boards' practice of reducing the local government's levies below the legal limit brought about change. Also, the need for services during the depression created a group of activists working for public-sector funding. Opponents of county tax adjustment committees' decisions could appeal them to the state level, whether those opponents were individuals opposing their taxes or city officials opposing cuts. The state could increase the levy on appeal, so there was a way around the county budget commissions. In Ohio the powers of the county budget commission were gradually curtailed, and the ability of the county to dominate the allocations of state aid was reduced. The basic structure remains in each of these states, but its operation has changed.

In Oklahoma the courts sought over a long period to curtail the inherent clash between autonomous county excise boards and home-rule powers. Ultimately, the court reinterpreted the functions of the county excise boards so that they would be compatible with home rule (Carr 1937).

The initial response of the state courts was to limit the county excise boards to reviewing the budgets for compliance to state law. The courts stripped the county excise boards of the power to revise the budgets. But the political thrust behind the boards changed in 1931 with the election of a new governor. The newly created state tax commission considered the new excise boards' powers more extensive than the old. The state tax commission directed the new county excise boards to cut any unnecessary taxes. The state courts continued to rule that the powers of the county excise boards were limited and not discretionary. The boards could increase or add items if the local government failed to provide adequately for some item mandated by state law; it could strike items if they were illegal or unauthorized; and it could decrease items if the total appropriation was above the legal levy limit. Other than those exceptions, the boards were to levy the property tax as the local governments requested.

Indiana's system clashed more with democracy than with home rule. The pattern of supervision and control changed from direct intervention in local budgets toward a review of budgets for compliance with the law. The system bias favoring those who opposed taxation was altered, within the basic framework of supervision worked out before and during the Great Depression.

One of the earliest major changes in the Indiana system occurred in 1927 when the state allowed the state tax board to increase the levy allowed by the county tax adjustment board up to the limit of the request of local officials. Further flexibility was introduced in 1932 and 1937 when the county tax adjustment boards were allowed to declare an emergency that required taxation above the state tax limits; the state board was required to review these requests.

The flexibility and responsiveness of the Indiana system may have helped keep the basic structure intact. After all these years, Indiana's system still has not changed much. The county board of tax adjustment still exists. It is composed of seven members, no more than four from one party, and four of whom may not have held office or been employed by a local government in the previous year. The county board of tax adjustment still is required to review the budget, tax levy, and tax rate of each local jurisdiction. The board is empowered to revise or reduce, but not to increase, the budget, levy, or rate. But the judgment of the board can be appealed by citizens or by the local government that devised the proposal; the appeal is to the state tax commission, a three-member board appointed by the governor. The state tax commission can increase or decrease the levy and tax rates.

The Division of Appropriations and Budget review of the State Board of Tax Commissioners prescribes uniform and mandatory standards for budgeting, including requirements to advertise budget hearings and dates for each stage of budget adoption. The division reviews every local government's proposed budget for compliance with procedural and statutory requirements. The division also calculates the amounts of miscellaneous revenues from cigarette, liquor, and gasoline taxes that the state distributes to the local governments by formula (Petersen, Cole, and Petrillo 1977). This procedure emphasizes both uniformity of budgetary reporting and state supervision for compliance with laws.

Indiana gave local governments very limited home rule, and so the clash between the old county boards of tax adjustments and local government autonomy was not as clear in Indiana as it had been in Oklahoma. Local pressure for home rule increased in the 1960s and 1970s, resulting in a new home-rule measure in 1980. But the new measure dealt primarily with the ability of local governments to organize themselves and adopt new functions; the law helped clarify but did not increase the authority of local governments over budgeting.

In the 1970s the state was still concerned about holding down property taxes, but its approach had changed. Tax caps were put in place, limiting property tax yields. The state set aside a fund to reimburse local property taxpayers for a portion of their property tax bills. The state also granted the counties permission to raise an income tax to offset the property tax. This option was not widely utilized but represents the change in approach toward giving local governments ways of reducing property tax without determining in advance that services must be curtailed.

Indiana's system of state supervision of local finances remained centralized and comprehensive, but it edged away from a model of intervention in local government priorities on the petition of ten taxpayers toward an across-the-board examination of local finances for compliance with state law. The county board of tax adjustments could still reduce the levy or the tax rate proposed by local officials, but its decisions became subject to appeal by the local jurisdiction affected by the decision. The greater emphasis on conformance with law resulted in a standardized budget proposal issued by the state and a uniform budget process embodied in statutes. Without such standardization, there was no way to compare across government units.

The Indiana code specified the budget process in detail, beginning with a line-item budget proposal from the department heads, which included estimated revenues from different sources by the budget office, estimated nondepartmental spending, an examination and possible reduction of the departmental estimates by the executive, and presentation of the proposal to the council. The council was required to act on the budget proposal and was allowed to reduce any estimated item, but it was not allowed to increase items unless the executive recommended an increase.

Ohio's system of supervision of local taxation and budgeting has also gradually changed. One very important change occurred during the Great Depression when the state began to allocate revenues other than the property tax to local governments in order to take some of the burden off the property tax while allowing local governments to continue to perform essential functions. The allocation of these funds was to be based on need, as determined by the county budget commissions (Ohio Legislative Service Commission 1969). This function turned out to be far more controversial than the commission's role in supervising budgeting and taxation. The county budget commissions have continued to supervise local government budgeting and taxation, but their powers have been gradually circumscribed.

As in Indiana and other states with centralized budget supervision, Ohio mandates virtually the entire budget process for local governments, including what the budget must contain. The list of items that must be in the budget includes necessary operating expenses of each department, expenditures necessary for permanent improvements, amounts required for payment of final judgments, expenditures supported by special levies, comparative statements of expenditures from preceding years, estimates of receipts from other than the general property tax, estimates of debt charges and anticipated receipts for their payment, and a statement of the amount each subdivision fund requires from the general property tax. The county budget commissions adjust the tax rates to ensure compliance with the 10 mill tax limit and certify that the tax rates are not higher than they need to be to produce the required amounts of revenues. If a reassessment increases the levy, the budget commission can reduce the tax rate proportionally.

As in Indiana, the local government can accept the decision of the county budget commission or appeal it. The local government can reduce expenditures to get under the 10 mill limit or ask for a referendum to increase the legal tax rate. If a new levy is approved, the commission must meet again to consider the revisions.

While the budget commissions continue to play a role in local finance, the powers of the county budget commission have been curtailed, not only by an appeal process but also by statutory limits and court judgments. The budget commissions were forbidden to make an independent judgment of the cities' needs as a basis for allocation of the state-provided local government funds. A court decision in 1942 held that neither budget commissions nor boards of tax appeals were authorized to go behind local governments' findings of need to determine whether faulty financing or administration contributed to the need. Budget commissions were forbidden to consider balances in local governments' current expenditure or special levy funds in determining need unless they deducted from the fund balance revenues received from voter-approved taxes or service charges. The commissions were caught between two requirements of the courts: on the one hand, they were forbidden to look behind the local governments' estimates of need, and on the other hand, they were required to allocate the funds based on actual, rather than claimed, need (Ohio Legislative Service Commission 1969).

The county budget commissions were limited in how much of the local government fund they were permitted to allocate to the county. Because the county budget commission was accused of favoring the county over municipalities, maximum percentage allocations to the county were written into the legislation. This curtailment of the county budget committee's authority was passed in 1957 (Ohio Legislative Service Commission 1969, 9). In 1985 a change was made to allocate the state funding to each jurisdiction in the county based on its percentage of the total classified property taxes in the county. Local officials could make a presentation to the county budget commission to alter their formula-based allocation, justifying their request by describing their needs (Ohio Tax Levy Law, sec. 5705.32, November 1991).

Another limit on the powers of the county budget commission was the requirement that it approve without modification several types of levies whenever they conformed to statutory provisions governing the adoption of taxes. Commissions were also limited in the amount they were allowed to reduce levies of certain taxing authorities such as schools. No levy was to be reduced below a minimum fixed by law. If a city won an increase over 10 mills in a referendum, as long as the limit was legally implemented the budget commission had to approve the amount; the commission was also required to approve levies for debt outside the 10 mill limit and for police and fire relief and pension funds, for health districts, and for municipal universities. The commissions had to approve a guaranteed millage levy for all subdivisions that were in existence since before 1933 (Ohio Legislative Service Commission 1969, 3).

A court case in 1984 summarized the powers of the Ohio budget commissions. In judging whether a levy was properly authorized, the county budget commission had to determine whether the tax rate increase was clearly required, that the levy would not generate more funds than the budgeted expenses, and that the funds were budgeted as voted by the electorate. The commission was not to judge the necessity or desirability of the budgeted expenses (Ohio Tax Levy Law, sec. 5705.31, November 1991). The case was *South Russell* v. *Geauga County Budget Commission.*

Though the same machinery for oversight of budgeting persisted in Ohio from 1910 through the 1990s, it had evolved from a very powerful body that could rewrite local budgets nearly at will to a system in which local budgeting procedures are prescribed by the state and the county budget commissions' powers to intervene in local priorities have been curtailed. The current functions of the county budget commissions are much less discretionary.

North Carolina

North Carolina, which had centralized its state control over local finance, especially local borrowing, during the Great Depression (Betters 1932), maintained its system of control nearly intact until the early 1970s. Then it made a few changes while keeping most of the system the same. These modifications are highly suggestive of the ways that state control and supervision of local budgeting were evolving in the 1970s and early 1980s. One set of changes required more focused attention on cities that were experiencing fiscal stress, rather than a scatter-gun control over all cities, whether they were at fiscal risk or not. A second set of changes included a loosening up of detailed control over funds to allow some flexibility in the expenditure of funds. This second set of changes was emblematic of states' efforts to roll back regulations that had become excessively burdensome to local governments, as well as out of date. Other, less burdensome controls could be substituted. A third set of changes made the budget easier to read and hence more accessible to the public.

In 1971 the North Carolina General Assembly revised its local government control act, consolidating in it the law regarding local government budgeting and accounting and the law regarding the borrowing of money by local governments. The new law gave more prominence to budgeting, while its predecessor, written during the

Great Depression, paid more attention to managing debt and avoiding deficits. The most important policy innovation was the extension of the law from cities and counties to all local governments, including special districts and authorities (Lawrence 1974). The requirement for a balanced budget remained unchanged, but the requirement for appropriation of all money was new. It had been the practice not to appropriate federal grants or special assessments.

In an effort at modernization, accounting responsibilities were shifted to a budget officer, who was allowed to ask for information from the departments in whatever form he or she chose; the board was allowed to present the ordinance in whatever format made sense for policymaking. These changes allowed budgeting to take forms other than line-item budgeting.

In an apparent effort to make the budget more comprehensible for the public, the new law required, rather than allowed, a budget message and suggested the contents of the message. The new law also specified that there had to be a hearing on the budget proposal before adoption of the ordinance, to allow citizens to speak on the proposal.

In some cases, the revision tightened up loopholes that were contributing to financial problems, but more generally, the thrust of the revisions was to loosen many of the constraints that the state had placed on budget making, to make budgeting easier in a time of fiscal stress. For example, contingency appropriations greater than 5 percent in public assistance funds and the expenditure of contingency funds on the authority of the budget officer were explicitly permitted.

The new freedom in budgeting was especially visible in interfund transfers. Former law prohibited all interfund transfers except from the general fund to other funds. This prohibition was a result of efforts to control depression-era transfers to balance the general fund. In the revised law, such transfers were allowed, but controlled, so that earmarked money would not be misspent. Explicit permission was granted to charge each fund for costs of revenue collection and for general overhead. Local governments were also granted the ability to set up capital revolving funds that could transfer revenues from a variety of funds to a capital fund, as long as the source of the transfer was made clear. Regulations concerning budget amendments were also loosened because interfund transfers were allowed during the year.

Under the old law, the Local Government Commission had to approve all capital spending, including withdrawals from the capital reserve fund. Under the new law, such permission was no longer needed, but a different (and more contemporary) control was substituted. Disbursements could no longer be made directly from the capital fund but had to be appropriated to an operating fund and disbursed from there.

The revised law also paid attention to how to deal with local governments that were not paying principal and interest on loans. A new section allowed the local government commission to step in and levy taxes to pay debt service if a community failed to do so. The commission was allowed to take over the financial direction of a unit or authority if the unit defaulted or was about to default on debt service or when the unit or authority persisted, after notice from the commission, in violating the chapter. Thus North Carolina eased up on its control of the majority and at the same time maintained sufficient control over the few communities that were in genuine trouble.

While the North Carolina revisions did not represent a major restructuring of state supervision and control over the local governments, they did suggest that the state had seriously examined its regulations, modernized them in places (substituting a budget director for an accountant), eliminated the most constraining and inappropriate regulations (it allowed for non-line-item budgeting and transfers between funds), and shifted focus more to the troubled localities instead of constraining all governments equally. In making this shift, the state focused more on budgeting and less on debt control or limitation.

Other States

Many other states made piecemeal changes to their system of state supervision and control during the 1970s and 1980s. In response to the New York City fiscal crisis, many states focused on improvements in accounting and integration of the accounting, budgeting, and reporting systems. Such changes could provide an early warning system to the states to prevent budget emergencies; they could also provide better information to the local governments to improve their financial management. A second response was to improve the budgeting forms that states imposed on local governments while allowing local governments more discretion within the standards. North Carolina decided to let local governments decide on their own budget formats—an extreme in tolerating differences between cities. Other states continued to require uniformity, but they built increasing sophistication into their budget forms. In addition, there was a tendency to make the more sophisticated forms adaptable to a greater variety of circumstances. Third, states began to adopt a more cooperative model of designing regulation and supervision over local governments.

In the late 1960s and early 1970s, Washington State introduced its budgeting, accounting, and reporting system (BARS), an integrated system for local government (Petersen, Stallings, and Spain, n.d.). Washington has long had a centralized system of state control over local government finance. The state policy role required a level of information about local governments that the state did not have, and so the legislature instructed the state auditor to come up with a system of uniform accounting and reporting. The result was a system that required local governments to use a program format, but otherwise left considerable flexibility to local governments.

Though the initial purpose of the BARS system was to aid state policymaking, the design of the system was intended to meet both state and local management needs. The system consequently became fairly sophisticated. Small units of government have complained that the accounting structure is more elaborate than they need. The state has been flexible, however, in allowing smaller jurisdictions to operate on a cash basis, use single-entry bookkeeping, and report to the state with less detail than larger jurisdictions.

The level of detail in the budget forms is greater at lower levels of the organization and less so at the higher levels. This distinction allows the managers the detailed information they need to manage, while giving boards the broad information they need for planning. Budget forms provide space for data on the current fiscal year, the next budget year, and the four succeeding years. This five-year operating budget is expected to link the goals and objectives of each department with cost estimates for the various services. To help in the planning, the state strongly recommended that the operating budget be presented on a program basis to the top management. The flexibility allowed in local budget preparation helped gain acceptance for the system among local governments.

Efforts to improve accounting and reporting increased as a result of the New York City fiscal crisis as states struggled to determine their cities' financial status. Some states that had had minimal state supervision over budgeting began or intensified their oversight as a result of cities' financial problems in the mid-1970s.

For example, Minnesota tightened up its financial reporting in reaction to the problems New York City was experiencing. In 1976 the legislature directed the Office of Local and Urban Affairs to investigate local government fiscal problems, debts, and fiscal management. The researchers reported back that the state reporting process was inadequate for the analysis the legislature wanted. With the concurrence of local interest groups, the legislature passed a new law affecting city financial reports. The act required strict enforcement and allowed the auditor a better postaudit review of cities.

Rhode Island had traditionally had minimal supervision of local finance, but in 1976 the legislature empowered the state auditor general, a legislatively appointed official, to promulgate financial reporting standards in conformity with generally accepted accounting principles and to monitor compliance. These standards were part of a package of legislative proposals intended to improve municipal accountability and regulate and strengthen local financial practices. The auditing standards, the only part of the package that passed, were intended to increase investor confidence and reduce the cost of municipal borrowing.

State supervision in Tennessee was minimal until 1970, when the comptroller was given authority to establish accounting and reporting standards for cities and to oversee the municipal audits. In the mid-1970s the comptroller was granted authority to approve municipal short-term borrowing and review and approve municipal budgets during the period when short-term debt is outstanding. The purpose of controlling short-term debt was to ensure that the short-term borrowers maintained a balanced budget during the period when they were repaying short-term debt. This requirement for state examination of municipal budgets that have outstanding short-term debt became effective in 1977. The rationale for this unpopular state intervention in local budgeting was that abuse of short-term debt was an early indicator of much broader problems. The discovery of misuse of state funds in some cities in 1973 gave additional rationale for increased state supervision.

Even in states that were increasing their regulation in response to the fiscal stress of the 1970s, there was a greater understanding that controls could not simply be imposed by the state on the local governments but had to be negotiated and had to serve the purposes of the local governments as well as the state. The implementation of BARS in Washington State demonstrated the trend toward including local government perspectives and needs into state supervision systems.

The goals in Washington and in other states that have adopted

BARS-type systems have been as much to provide information for local decision making as to provide information for state control. For example, in the mid-1970s Montana developed a budgeting, accounting, and reporting system for cities and counties more in response to local demands than from state initiative. The aim was to help create day-to-day financial reports to assist local government managers in financial decision making (Council of State Community Affairs Agencies 1978, 6).

Iowa, which had adopted a pattern of supervision similar to Indiana's, altered its pattern of supervision in 1969 when it adopted a home-rule provision in its constitution. Legislation implementing the constitutional amendment set up a city finance committee composed of both state and municipal representatives. The committee was empowered to direct the development and establishment of various legislative mandates, including program performance budgeting and capital improvement programming. The committee can specify budgetary formats, provide rules for interfund transfers and budget amendments, and establish uniform accounting practices. While still maintaining much of its central control, the state delegated to an administrative unit composed of both city and state officials the creation of further regulation (Council of State Community Affairs Agencies 1978). The clear implication was that legislation would not be formulated or presented to the legislature unless the cities had examined it and agreed to it.

The idea that new financial controls should not be imposed without extensive discussion and agreement with local governments was stated as policy by the New York State Assembly's Ways and Means Committee in 1979.[2] The committee was wrestling with appropriate regulatory procedures to recommend so that the state could identify and help local governments in financial trouble. The committee noted that traditionally changes in state supervision of local finance have been top-down, but that in recent years, this approach has created increasing resentment, especially in terms of the burden of unfunded mandates. Therefore the committee attempted to generate legislative proposals by presenting particular recommendations to local officials for discussion and approval or disapproval (Billingsley and Moore 1979).

---

2. The committee's report was entitled "New York's Role in the Fiscal Affairs of Its Local Governments—New Directions for an Old Partnership."

Responses to the New York City fiscal crisis had not completely worked their way through the legislatures when, in 1978, Proposition 13 in California brought the tax limitation movement to a fever pitch. Widespread tax limitations brought local government protests against state unfunded mandates. States increasingly recognized and accepted that their unfunded mandates were contributing to the fiscal stress they were trying to avoid.

As long as federal aid was growing and state aid was increasing, unfunded state mandates were not terribly problematic for local governments; some of their autonomy might have been curtailed, but the states were providing enough revenue to cover some of the costs. "Many state legislatures see state revenue sharing as form of compensation for revenue restrictions and mandates.... But no state level study has ever concluded that shared revenue was sufficient to compensate the localities for state mandates. Several have concluded that state shared revenue could only compensate for a small percentage of the state mandates" (Kelly 1992, 16–17). After 1975, when federal aid was reduced and state aid began to decline in proportion to municipal budgets, these mandates remained, creating what is now known as the mandate problem. A handful of states compensated local governments for mandates that required them to make expenditures, but most did not, creating an increasing fiscal burden on local governments.

To make matters worse, decreasing reliance on property taxes and increased reliance on sales and income taxes made cities more vulnerable to recession. From the 1950s to the 1980s, both state and local taxes became more elastic with respect to the economy, changing from .93 percent in 1951 to 1.03 percent in 1981. During recessions, the states often reduced their spending levels (Stonecash 1986). Cities wounded by recessions have sometimes been struck simultaneously with cutbacks in state spending and unfunded mandates.

From the late 1960s to the mid-1980s states responded to the need to curtail unfunded mandates. The most common response was to add a fiscal note to proposed legislative mandates, estimating the costs to local governments. By the end of 1979, twenty-five states had adopted some form of fiscal noting for mandates, and others were considering such action (White 1979). By 1991 the number had increased to twenty-eight (Kelly 1992). The idea behind fiscal noting is that if state policymakers are required to calculate the costs they are imposing on local governments, they might be more restrained in imposing unfunded mandates. The costs of mandating, which had been hidden, would be more apparent. In addition to fiscal notes, fourteen states adopted some form of reimbursement to local governments for mandated costs.

Neither fiscal noting nor reimbursement legislation has been completely successful in curtailing state mandates. The legislation is too easy to ignore or bypass, and estimates of costs are crude, especially before legislation has passed. Florida's constitutional amendment to control unfunded mandating, a strong provision, is still relatively easy to evade by declaring an important state interest in the provision.[3] Also, it has been difficult to track down the financial impact of many bills. In 1993, of forty-five laws passed that contained mandates on cities and counties, the Florida Advisory Council on Intergovernmental Relations was able to find estimates of impacts for six of them. The state also passed twenty-one laws with new or expanded revenue opportunities for cities and counties. The Florida ACIR was able to track estimates of impacts for seven of them (Florida ACIR 1993).

Regardless of the effectiveness of particular measures, states are trying to improve relations with local governments, have increased their awareness of the impacts of unfunded mandates, and are changing the legislative process to include more consultation with local governments before regulatory actions are proposed.

Despite their goodwill, states were caught between pressures to keep taxes down and pressures to help local governments survive financially and provide services at the level demanded by organized interests. One way out of this box has been for the states to help local governments, especially smaller ones, borrow less expensively, invest at higher rates of return, and generally improve their financial management. Efforts to improve cash management, risk management, and borrowing promised to free up funds for local governments without increasing taxes. By 1988 twenty-two states reported that they had created local government investment pools. Massachusetts required local governments to bid for their banking services; Texas and California required all local governments to adopt a model investment policy. North Carolina adopted a program in 1985 to evaluate local governments' investment practices and suggest shortcomings (Coe 1988).

Overall, the 1970s was a period of change in patterns of state

---

3. For information on Florida's amendment and how it is working, see Florida ACIR 1993.

supervision. There has been a relatively clear direction to the recent changes as states wrestled with a common set of conditions. Yet a set of contradictory pressures remains in place generating outcomes that have not yet precipitated out into recognizable patterns. States increased their policy capacity and involvement in the 1950s and 1960s, attracting more interest-group participation. The states seemed to say yes to a variety of interest groups. They said yes to the homeowners and large property taxpayers who wanted reduced tax rates; they also said yes to public-sector unions lobbying for higher salaries and pensions; they said yes to interest groups lobbying for more and better services; and they said yes to local governments pleading for relief from unfunded mandates.

As long as there was considerable new money coming into the state treasury, many apparently contradictory demands could be met, but when the states' financial picture deteriorated, the outcomes became unpredictable. If states reduce or stop unfunded mandates, how will they deal with the interest groups demanding more or better services or forbidding their services to be cut? If the states reimburse local governments for mandated expenditures, where will the money come from? What services will be cut or whose taxes raised? Will states grant more freedom to local governments to set their own taxes? How will the states deal with the pressures to keep taxes down? Presumably states will forge their own balance of answers, but the pattern of those outcomes may take years to emerge, during which time the economy, and state budgets, may improve. In the meantime, the philosophy seems to be to do as little harm as possible, to avoid making matters worse with ill-considered or overly extreme or rigid controls, and to concentrate on the areas where local governments welcome assistance, such as state investment pools and efforts to lower borrowing costs.

Conclusions

The impact of state control and supervision over municipal budgeting has varied from state to state. Some states have played a minor role in local budgeting. Either there was no state statute regulating municipal budgeting or the existing statutes were unenforced and circumvented. In states that have taken a more active role, the consequences have often been benign if not stellar. As Wylie Kilpatrick observed during the Great Depression:

The gains from budgetary supervision have been substantial, probably not so much in employing advanced technique as in ensuring the
observance of minimum standards in the majority of subdivisions.
While the actual budgetary operations often bear slight semblance to
adequate budgeting, a foundation is laid on which improvements can
be and have been effected. (Kilpatrick 1936, 342–43)

In support of the argument that state regulation has generally been
helpful, one might note that New York City's fiscal crisis was related
in part to the city's exemption from New York State's requirement for
uniform accounting standards in accordance with generally accepted
practices (Silverman 1981).

But the effects of state controls and supervision have not always
been good. States frequently required each local government to file a
copy of its budget. State officials could analyze these documents only
if they were uniform across local governments. Consequently, states
that regulated local finance often issued uniform requirements for
budget formats. That uniformity meant that smaller cities often had
requirements beyond their capacity or needs, while larger cities were
handicapped by systems that were too simple. Also, the requirement
of including information that was necessary to judge whether the city
was in compliance with state laws meant that other information was
often excluded.

Writing in the 1930s, one observer described the limitations of
Oklahoma's budget forms:

As mere budgetary forms go, they are quite complete. On the other
hand, they hardly constitute comprehensive accounting or bookkeeping systems for the use of local governments. These forms are detailed, but hardly adequate for needs of the very largest and most
populous units, expert opinion being that they are not sufficiently detailed to reflect fully the financial programs of these units. Since the
law does not require some pieces of information, the examiner cannot request them, even though they would make the budgets more
complete. Under present law, home rule cities could probably ignore
the examiners' forms and use their own. But only two cities, Oklahoma City and Tulsa, do make use of their own forms. The forms
used by the two large cities do not vary to any considerable extent
from those prepared by the examiner, they are just more fully itemized. (Carr 1937, 218–19)

Some states got around the difficulty of one size fits all by exempting first-class cities or home-rule cities. More recently, some states have allowed smaller cities to use simpler accounting and reporting procedures. But the problem of designing the budget forms so that examiners could tell if the local governments complied with the law was more troublesome. In Ohio, when there were several different limits on property taxes, budgetary items that would normally have been grouped together had to be separated to show compliance or lack of compliance with different limits, making the budgets fragmented and difficult to understand.

Another problem was that state-mandated budget forms did not change often enough to represent state of the art. In the 1910s, some degree of line-item budget control was considered a major advance over rough descriptions like $200,000 for the horse stable and horses. Many states included line itemization in their requirements for local budgets as a financial control measure. State requirements for line itemization have been slow to change, even long after financial control ceased to be a major problem for cities, and other issues, such as the ability of the budget to explain the city's finances to the public, became more urgent.

While states have generally not taken the lead in experiments with budget formats and reforms, they have adapted over the years, responding, sometimes too intensely, to perceived problems such as excessive debt burdens, municipal bond defaults, or unbalanced budgets. Especially when problems seemed widespread, states have placed controls or limits on all cities, rather than just the ones that seemed to need extra assistance. Across-the-board policy, once forged and accepted, has often stayed in place for decades.

The problem has been not so much that the states have ignored financial problems of local governments as that they have failed to modify or withdraw their controls in a timely way when the problem was resolved. The states did allow the erosion of overly tight legislative limits on borrowing and property taxes, but they were much slower to withdraw the extremes of their mandated budget procedures, layout requirements, and approval provisions. Constitutional controls are notoriously hard to change. Budget controls have therefore tended to accrete, with one overlaid on another. Only in the recent period has there been a major effort to examine the system of control, pare it back, and make it more flexible.

State policies toward control and supervision of local governments have been shaped by the problems themselves and by interest-group pressures. The states have not always responded equally to all interests and sometimes have yielded to pressure groups instead of focusing on improving local finance and budgeting. In responding to pressures to hold down property taxes during the Great Depression, for example, some states structured their supervision and control procedures so that those favoring low taxes would have a disproportionate influence on the outcomes.

In their efforts to address problems in local government finance, the states often established minimum standards, but they seldom held back innovations from cities that were inclined to improve their own budgeting and finance. Even in states that set the budget formats for local governments, municipal budgeting has often gone beyond the state's minimum requirements.

Although the state governments generally did not mandate reforms in budgeting such as program budgeting or ZBB, many cities adopted such innovations during the late 1970s and early 1980s. A study comparing municipal budgeting in 1976 and 1983 found that the use of program, zero-based, or target-based budgeting had increased from 50 percent to 77 percent of the sample. The use of management-by-objectives increased from 41 percent to 59 percent, and performance monitoring was up from 28 percent to 68 percent (Poister and McGowan 1984). Cities adopted these changes on their own.

Cities felt an immense need to make budgeting more responsive to the public. As during the Great Depression, a wave of restrictive tax limits was followed by efforts to improve budgeting and make it more accountable, to give the public a greater sense of control. In recent years, professional associations such as the Government Finance Officers' Association have emphasized the ability of the budget to explain to the public certain features of the city's finances, including spending and taxing decisions, and have encouraged cities to improve the appearance and layout of budgets. State supervision did not have public communication as a goal, although it did emphasize accountability to financial markets. Cities fashioned a response to the tax limitation movement themselves, dealing on the one hand with increased uncertainty and the need to make tradeoffs in limited budgets and on the other hand with increased need to communicate with the public and give citizens more sense of control over the budget.

9

Conclusion

BUDGETING HAS changed dramatically since its origins after the Civil War, responding to the growth of cities, to cycles of boom and bust in the economy, to ethnic and class splits, variously defined, and to the proportion of the voters who owned their own homes. Budgeting has also responded to guidance from state governments and to across-the-board tax limits. And, as the city manager in Phoenix argued, budgeting has responded to the degree of public trust in government.

Budgeting has changed in bursts. Each major period has been marked by its own distinctive problems and budgetary solutions. The earliest budgets addressed themselves to overspending by departments and changes in budgets during the year, as well as to the need to justify taxes and expenditures. Earmarking property taxes for specified purposes formed the rudiments of a budget; the appropriation ordinance, with its legislative approval of ceilings for spending by departments, was a second step in this direction. The gathering and reviewing of requests from the departments by the controller or the mayor before handing over to the council represented a third step. All three developments were in place by the turn of the century.

At the same time that the budget process was improving, the political structures that were drawing up the budgets were changing. Beginning in the 1870s, Boards of Estimate and Apportionment gave power initially to neither the council nor the mayor, but to a board whose members had to negotiate with each other. This structure was intended to curtail expenditures, which it did, but it did not lead to good government, and so gradually the mayor was granted dominance over this fragmented body.

Control of spending dominated budgeting until the beginning of the Progressive era. The Progressive era was a period of growth and governmental activism. The emphasis in budgeting shifted to efficiency, getting the most out of every dollar. It was in this environment that executive-dominated budgeting emerged and spread. Program and performance budgeting began but did not take deep root.

After the Progressive period, with the First World War and rapid inflation, the spending habits of the Progressive era became problematic, and budgeting focused more on curtailing taxes. Tax limits were passed at the state level, and some states set up oversight of local budgeting to assure that tax limits were complied with and that taxes were as low as they should be. Line itemization was introduced to help control expenditures.

The post-Progressive era blended into the Great Depression of the 1930s. More tax limits were passed, some were embedded in constitutions, and existing tax limits were often tightened. States increasingly mandated local government budgeting, with various degrees of success. Some states substituted appointed commissions for locally elected officials and imposed preferences for low taxes and low services even when the voting public preferred other choices.

After the depression and World War II, delayed capital projects and inflation pushed up expenditures and property taxes. States that had diversified their tax bases during the depression and helped local governments with aid found themselves more subject to fluctuations in the economy. The growth of aid halted, while the unfunded mandates from the states grew. Suburbanization began to deplete the populations of older central cities, while migrations swelled the cities of the Southwest and strained services. The long-term trend toward homeownership among larger segments of the population continued.

These trends affected politics, taxation, and budgeting. Property tax limitation movements were often successful in the 1970s and early 1980s. The planning orientation that marked the period of growth after World War II yielded to a variety of techniques to cut back the budget, including zero-based budgeting and its more popular cousin, target-based budgeting. Taxpayer revolts led some cities to broaden access to the budget process. Many budget officers designed budgets that were easier to read, and mayors brought them to the neighborhoods to discuss, while some cities brought citizens into the budget process and solicited project ideas from them. Performance budgeting finally took root in some cities, though it was not as widespread as target-based budgeting and was sometimes only partially implemented.

The states began to see themselves as part of the financial problem of cities and began to reexamine their regulations and create committees of state and local officials to examine future legislative proposals. While unfunded mandates have not been eliminated, the costs are now more visible, and both state and local governments are more wary of them.

Putting matters schematically, budgeting has shifted over a century from (1) property-owning elites taxing themselves for projects they wanted to (2) these elites buffering themselves from the demands of the poor and those who did not pay taxes (or as much taxes as elites did), to (3) the business elites taxing everyone, including the poor, for projects the elites wanted such as downtown renewal, to (4) the current period, in which a broadened base of taxpayers are saying no, we will not pay taxes for huge renewal projects, we will pay taxes only for the projects and services that benefit us, or we will not approve tax surcharges or increases.

The city manager of Phoenix described the budget process as sensitive to cycles of popular distrust. The city opened up the budget process to some extent to the neighborhoods and ethnic groups, but some politicians see the chamber of commerce as coming back into influence at city hall. They envision that the crisis of responsiveness is over and that the business community can resume its prior dominance. But the pattern of political influence is unlikely to go back to where it was. It is not only that the control of the business community was too extreme and narrow, but circumstances have changed.

Across the country, homeownership is more widely distributed than in earlier years. As fiscal stress hit individual homeowners, they became as concerned about expenditures at city hall as the former large taxpayers used to be. Responding to their fears and complaints, cities became less dependent on property taxes. Consequently, the burden of taxation now falls on a broader base of taxpayers, through sales taxes and user fees. There are thus more players in the game who feel they have a stake in how cities spend their money and what they spend it on. The current mood of rejection of government and taxes may lessen in years to come, but the simple structure of taxation that led to a certain legitimacy of dominance of city government by a property taxpaying elite is gone.

City budgeting has adapted to these changes in a variety of ways. The outlines of those adaptations are clear from the cities in the study. They include developing a broader base of support for city budgets and more two-way communication. The definition of professionalism has begun to change, from experts who do something for the city to managers who figure out how to translate public and political demands into services in an efficient manner.

Yet to be worked out in many cities is the limit of how much politicians can ask for, how to curb their tendencies to try to get something for nothing. Sometimes the public wants something for nothing, and the appearance of achieving it makes elected officials look good. Professional bureaucrats cannot deliver something for nothing, however, and continuing pressure to do so is likely to erode the quality of management and the quality of information in the budget.

While budgeting has decidedly changed over time and adapted to current problems, it has often retained solutions worked out in the past. Some Illinois cities still use the appropriation ordinances designed in the 1800s, despite the existence of vastly improved budgeting systems. Many states and cities still mandate line-item formats for their budgets, although line-item budgeting was considered a major innovation early in this century and is now considered somewhat of a hindrance to good budgeting. New York City only recently gave up its Board of Estimate and Apportionment, initially adopted in 1873. Equally important, many cities adopted the Board of Estimate form decades after its invention, presumably because it helped keep taxes down, though it had proven an inefficient form of government. Most of the cities with the commission form of government changed to council-manager form, but a few cities retained the commission form, or a semblance of it, for years. Ohio still has its county budget commissions, though their functions have changed over the years.

Part of the problem has been that some states have had very detailed budget laws and have not changed them in many years. When they examine their laws, they find that depression era rules still guide the budget, forbidding transfers into the general fund, for example. Or they find that their laws specify line-item budgets and thereby forbid more modern program budgets, or require examination of the budget by the controller, when more modern cities have a budget director do that task. The states are gradually catching up, examining their laws and making efforts to modernize them, but there has been a lag time. Cities less burdened by state regulations have been freer to come up with their own budgeting solutions. But even cities wrestling with charter provisions and state-mandated requirements have added newer budget formats to older forms.

Budgeting has been adaptive, but it has grown by accretion and is clumsy and hard to explain. Making the budget process transparent to the public often means laying out the budget as if the rules and earmarking do not matter. Citizens reading such a budget cannot understand the constraints under which a city is operating. It would be better for state and local governments to stop and figure out which controls work best and are least obtrusive and drop the rest. It is not necessary to control property taxation by earmarking the property tax for different purposes, and by estimating all other taxes first and using property taxes only to fill the gap, and by passing tax limitations, and by having county budget commissions trying to assure that the property tax is as low as it can be. It probably is not necessary to have both input and output controls, or at least not nearly so many controls as currently exist. The trend toward isolating those cities having trouble and focusing state solutions on them is much wiser than the older across-the-board approach. Budgeting can not only look simpler, it can be simpler. Budgets must be not only understandable but acceptable to the public if cities are to renegotiate citizen's willingness to be taxed. Periodic renegotiation of what citizens are willing to pay and what governments can provide underlies governance in a democracy.

References

(ACIR) Advisory Commission on Intergovernmental Relations. 1969. *State Aid to Local Governments*. Washington, D.C.: Government Printing Office.

———. 1985. *The Question of State Government Capability*. Washington, D.C.: Government Printing Office.

———. 1988. *Significant Features of Fiscal Federalism, 1988*. Washington, D.C.: Government Printing Office.

———. 1990. *Mandates: Cases in State-Local Relations*. Washington, D.C.: Government Printing Office. September.

Allen, W.H. 1908. "The Budget as an Instrument of Financial Control." *Government Accountant* 2 (September): 192–200.

———. 1917. "The Budget Amendment of the Maryland Constitution." *National Municipal Review* 6, no. 4: 485–91.

Anderson, A.D. 1977. *The Origin and Resolution of an Urban Crisis: Baltimore 1890–1930*. Baltimore: Johns Hopkins University Press.

Atkinson, R.C. 1923. "The Effects of Tax Limitation upon Local Finance in Ohio 1911–1922." Ph.D. dissertation, Columbia University.

———. 1936. "Stringent Tax Limitation and Its Effects in Ohio." In *Property Tax Limitation Laws*, 69–74, ed. G. Leet and R. Paige. Chicago: Public Administration Service.

Barclay, T.S. 1943. "The Movement for Municipal Home Rule in St. Louis." *University of Missouri Studies* 18, no. 3. Columbia: University of Missouri Press.

———. 1962. "The St. Louis Home Rule Charter of 1876." *University of Missouri Studies* 38. Columbia: University of Missouri Press.

Beito, D.T. 1989. *Taxpayers in Revolt: Tax Resistance during the Great Depression*. Chapel Hill: University of North Carolina Press.

Bernard, R.M. 1990. "Introduction: Snowbelt Politics." In *Snowbelt Cities: Metropolitan Politics in the Northeast and Midwest since World War II*, ed. R.M. Bernard. Bloomington: Indiana University Press.

Betters, P.V., ed. 1932. *State Centralization in North Carolina*. Washington, D.C.: Brookings Institution.

Billingsley, A.G., and P.D. Moore. 1979. "Defining New York State's Role in Monitoring Local Fiscal Affairs." *Governmental Finance* 8 (December): 12–16.

Boston Municipal Research Bureau. 1939. *Budget Procedure in Boston and Other Cities.* Working material prepared for special commission appointed by legislative resolve of 1939. Boston.

Bruere, H.J. 1912. *The New City Government: A Discussion of Municipal Administration Based on a Survey of Ten Commission Governed Cities.* New York: D. Appleton.

Buck, A.E. 1929. *Public Budgeting.* New York: Harper.

———. 1934. *The Budget in Governments of Today.* New York: Macmillan.

———. 1943. *Wartime Problems of State and Local Finance.* Symposium conducted by the Tax Institute, 27–28 November 1942. Philadelphia: Tax Institute.

Burns, C.K. 1984. "The Irony of Progressive Reform: Boston 1898–1910." In *Boston, 1700–1980: The Evolution of Urban Politics,* ed. R.P. Formisano and C.K. Burns. Westport, Conn.: Greenwood Press.

Carr, R.K. 1937. *State Control of Local Finance in Oklahoma.* Norman: University of Oklahoma Press.

Carroll, B.H. 1912. *Standard History of Houston, Texas, from a Study of the Original Sources.* Knoxville: H.W. Crew and Co.

Chatters, C. 1935. "Municipal Finance." In *What the Depression Has Done to Cities: An Appraisal by Thirteen Authorities on the Effects of the Depression on Municipal Activities,* ed. C.E. Ridley and O.F. Nolting. Chicago: International City Managers Association.

City of St. Louis. 1988. *Fiscal Year 1988–89 Budget Summary.*

Cleveland, F.A. 1913. *Organized Democracy: An Introduction to the Study of American Politics.* New York: Longman, Green.

Clow, F.R. 1901. *A Comparative Study of the Administration of City Finances in the United States, with Special Reference to the Budget.* Sponsored by the American Economic Association. New York: Macmillan.

Clute, W.K. 1920. *The Law of Modern Municipal Charters and the Organization of Cities on Commision, City Manager and Federal Plans.* Vol. 1, *Special Treatment of Home Rule Laws.* Detroit: Fred S. Drake.

Coe, C.K. 1988. "The Effects of Cash Management Assistance by States to Local Governments." *Public Budgeting and Finance* 8, no. 2 (Summer): 80–90.

Committee for Economic Development. 1976. *Improving Productivity in State and Local Government: A Statement on National Policy.* New York: Committee for Economic Development.

Council of State Community Affairs Agencies. 1978. *DCA Roles in Local Financial Management: Ten State Profiles.* Washington, D.C.: DHUD, Office of Policy Development and Research. December.

Crooks, J.B. 1968. *Politics and Progress: The Rise of Urban Progressivism in Baltimore, 1895–1911.* Baton Rouge: Louisiana State University Press.

Durand, E.D. 1898. *The Finances of New York City.* New York: Macmillan.

Eghtedari, A., and Frank Sherwood. 1960. "Performance Budgeting in Los Angeles." *Public Administration Review* 20 (Spring).

Fairlie, J.A. 1904. "State Supervision of Local Finance." In *Proceedings of the American Political Science Association,* Chicago.

Florida (ACIR) Advisory Council on Intergovernmental Relations. 1993. *1993 Intergovernmental Impact Report.* Tallahassee.

Glaab, C.N., and A.T. Brown. 1983. *A History of Urban America,* 3d ed. New York: Macmillan.

Goodnow, F.J. 1904. *City Government in the United States.* New York: Century Company.

Griffith, E. 1974. *A History of American City Government: The Progressive Years and Their Aftermath, 1900–1920.* New York: Praeger.

Hall, J.S. 1982. "Phoenix, Arizona." In *Decentralizing Urban Policy: Case Studies in Community Development,* ed. P.S. Dommel. Washington, D.C.: Brookings Institution.

———. 1986. "Retrenchment in Phoenix, Arizona." In *Reagan and the Cities,* ed. G.E. Peterson and C.W. Lewis. Washington, D.C.: Urban Institute Press.

Hays, S.P. 1964. "The Politics of Reform in Municipal Government in the Progressive Era." *Pacific Northwest Quarterly* 55 (October): 157–69.

Hojnacki, W.P., ed. 1983. *Politics and Public Policy in Indiana: Prospects for Change in State and Local Government.* Dubuque, Iowa: Kendall/ Hunt.

Hollander, J.H. 1899. *The Financial History of Baltimore.* Johns Hopkins University Studies in Historical and Political Science. Baltimore: John Hopkins University Press.

Huse, C.P. 1916. *The Financial History of Boston from May 1, 1822, to January 31, 1909.* Cambridge, Mass.: Harvard University Press.

Jamison, J.H. 1928. "How Berkeley Controls Its Municipal Expenditures." *Tax Digest,* October, 331–35.

Johnson, C.M. 1932. "State Supervision of Local Finance." In *State Centralization in North Carolina,* ed. P.V. Betters. Washington, D.C.: Brookings Institution.

Kelly, J.M. 1992. *State Mandates: Fiscal Notes, Reimbursement, and Antimandate Strategies.* Washington, D.C.: National League of Cities.

Kilpatrick, W. 1927. *State Administrative Review of Local Budget Making: An Examination of State Supervision of Local Taxes and Bonds in Indiana and Iowa.* New York: Municipal Administration Service.

———. 1936. "State Administrative Supervision of Local Financial Processes." In *Municipal Yearbook* 3: 340–66.

———. 1939. *State Supervision of Local Budgeting.* New York: National Municipal League.

———. 1941. *State Supervision of Local Finance.* Chicago: Public Administration Service.

Koren, J. 1923. *Boston, 1822–1922: The Story of Its Government and Principal Activities.* Boston: City of Boston Printing Department.

Lawrence, D.M., annotator. 1974. *The Local Government Budget and Fiscal Control Act.* Rev. ed. Chapel Hill: Institute of Government, University of North Carolina. Photo offset.

Leet, G., and R. Paige, eds. 1936. *Property Tax Limitation Laws.* Public Administration Service, No. 36. Chicago: Public Administration Service.

Lewis, V. 1988. "Reflections on Budget Systems." *Public Budgeting and Finance* 8, no. 1 (Spring): 4–19.

Lo, C.Y.H. 1990. *Small Property versus Big Government: Social Origins of the Property Tax Revolt.* Berkeley: University of California Press.

Lovell, C., and H. Egan. 1983. "Fiscal Notes and Mandate Reimbursement in the Fifty States." *Public Budgeting and Finance* 3, no. 3 (Autumn): 3–18.

Lovell, C., and C. Tobin. 1981. "The Mandate Issue." *Public Administration Review* 41, no. 3 (May/June): 318–31.

Luckingham, B. 1989. *Phoenix: The History of a Southwestern Metropolis.* Tucson: University of Arizona Press.

MacCorkle, S.A. 1937. *State Financial Control over Cities in Texas.* Arnold Foundation Studies in Public Affairs, vol. 6. The George F. and Ora Nixon Arnold Foundation, Southern Methodist University. Dallas. Pamphlet.

MacManus, S.A. 1983. "State Government: The Overseer of Municipal Finance." In *The Municipal Money Chase: The Politics of Local Government Finance,* ed. A.M. Sbragia. Boulder, Colo.: Westview Press.

Martin, R.C. 1934. *A Budget Manual for Texas Cities.* University of Texas Bulletin No. 3445, 1 December.

Matthews, N.J., Jr. 1895. *The City Government of Boston: A Valedictory Address to the Members of the City Council, January 5, 1895.* Boston: Rockwell and Churchill.

McDonald, T.J. 1986. *Parameters of Urban Fiscal Policy: Socioeconomic Change and Political Culture in San Francisco, 1860–1906.* Berkeley: University of California Press.

McKay, J.F. 1950. *Recent Trends in City Finance: A Survey of Ten Cities in Kansas.* Lawrence: Bureau of Government Research, University of Kansas.

McKelvey, B. 1973. *Rochester on the Genesee: The Growth of a City.* Syracuse, N.Y.: Syracuse University Press.

Merriman, D. 1987. *The Control of Municipal Budgets: Toward the Effective Design of Tax and Expenditure Limits.* New York: Quorum.

Mosher, F.C. 1940. "City Manager Government in Rochester, New York." In *City Manager Government in Seven Cities,"* F. Mosher, A. Harris, H. White, J. Veig, L. Bolling, A.G. Miller, D. Monroe, and H.O. Wilson. Chicago: Public Administration Service.

Mushkin, S.J., director. 1969. *Implementing PPB in State, City, and County: A Report on the 5-5-5 Project.* Published in cooperation with the Council of State Governments, the International City Managers Association, the National Association of Counties, the National Governors Conference, the National League of Cities, and the U.S. Conference of Mayors. Washington, D.C.: State-Local Finances Project, George Washington University.

Ohio Legislative Service Commission. 1969. *County Budget Commissions in Ohio.* Report No. 91. Columbus, Ohio: Columbus Blank Book Company.

Petersen, J.E., L.A. Cole, and M.L. Petrillo. 1977. *Watching and Counting: A Survey of State Assistance to and Supervision of Local Debt and Financial Administration.* National Council of State Legislatures and the

Municipal Finance Officers Association, n.p.

Petersen, J.E., C.W. Stallings, and C.L. Spain. 1979. *State Roles in Local Government Financial Management: A Comparative Analysis.* Washington, D.C.: Government Finance Research Center.

———. n.d. *State Roles in Local Government Financial Management: Nine Case Studies.* Washington, D.C.: Government Finance Research Center.

Platt, H.L. 1983. *City Building in the New South: The Growth of Public Services in Houston, Texas, 1830–1910.* Philadelphia: Temple University Press.

Poister, T., and R.P. McGowan. 1984. "Use of Management Tools in Municipal Government: A National Survey." *Public Administration Review* 44 (May/June): 215–23.

Rea, L.O. 1929. *The Financial History of Baltimore 1900–1926.* Johns Hopkins University Studies in Historical and Political Science. Baltimore: Johns Hopkins University Press.

Ridley, C.E., and O.F. Nolting, eds. 1935. *What the Depression Has Done to Cities: An Appraisal by Thirteen Authorities on the Effects of the Depression on Municipal Activities.* Chicago: International City Managers Association.

Ridley, C.E., and H.A. Simon. 1938. *Measuring Municipal Activities.* Chicago: International City Managers Association.

Rightor, C.E., D.C. Sowers, and W. Matscheck. 1919. *City Manager in Dayton: Four Years of Commission-Manager Government, 1914– 1917; and Comparisons with Four Preceding Years under the Mayor-Council Plan, 1910–1913.* New York: Macmillan.

Rocca, H. 1935. *Council-manager Government in Berkeley, California, 1923–1935.* Berkeley: James J. Gillick Co.

Rochester Bureau of Municipal Research. 1923. *Report of a Study of the Financial Condition and Practices of the City of Rochester, New York.* Rochester.

Rubin, I.S. 1991. "Budgeting for Our Times: Target Based Budgeting." *Public Budgeting and Finance* 11, no. 3 (Fall): 5–14.

———. 1992. "Budget Reform and Political Reform: Conclusions from Six Cities." *Public Administration Review* 52, no. 5 (September/October): 454–66.

Rubin, I.S., and L. Stein. 1990. "Budget Reform in St. Louis: Why Does Budgeting Change?" *Public Administration Review* 50, no. 4 (July/August): 420–26.

Sbragia, A.M. 1983. *The Municipal Money Chase: The Politics of Local Government Finance.* Boulder, Colo.: Westview Press.

Schick, A. 1966. "The Road to PPB: The Stages of Budget Reform." *Public Administration Review* 26 (November/December): 243–58.

Schiesl, M. 1977. *The Politics of Efficiency: Municipal Administration and Reform in America, 1800–1920.* Berkeley: University of California Press.

Sealander, J. 1988. *Grand Plans: Business Progressivism and Social Change in Ohio's Miami Valley, 1890–1929.* Lexington: University of Kentucky Press.

Sears, D.O., and J. Citrin. 1985. *Tax Revolt: Something for Nothing in California*, 2d ed. Cambridge, Mass.: Harvard University Press.

Sheppard, V. 1936. "Indiana Tax Limitations." In *Property Tax Limitation Laws: The Evidence and the Arguments for and against Them by Twenty-Four Authorities*, ed. G. Leet and R.M. Paige. Chicago: Public Administration Service.

Shipman, G.A. 1936. *The Budget Process in New Jersey Local Government*. Princeton Local Government Survey. Princeton, N.J.: Princeton University Press.

Silverman, E.B. 1981. "New York City's New Integrated Financial System." In *Contemporary Public Budgeting*, ed. T.D. Lynch. New Brunswick, N.J.: Transaction Books.

Slavet, J.S., and R.G. Torto. 1985. *Boston's Recurring Crises: Three Decades of Fiscal Policy*. Boston: John McCormack Institute of Public Affairs, University of Massachusetts.

Stein, L. 1991. *Holding Bureaucrats Accountable: Politicians and Professionals in St. Louis*. Tuscaloosa: University of Alabama Press.

Stephens, G.R. 1974. "State Centralization and the Erosion of Local Autonomy." *Journal of Politics* 36 (February): 44–76.

———. 1985. "State Centralization Revisited." Paper presented at the annual meeting of the American Political Science Association, New Orleans, 29 August–1 September.

Stonecash, J. 1983. "Fiscal Centralization in the American States." *Publius* 13: 123–37.

———. 1985. "Paths of Fiscal Centralization in the American States." *Policy Studies Journal* 13 (March): 653–61.

———. 1986. "Incremental and Abrupt Change in Fiscal Centralization in the American States, 1957–1983." In *Intergovernmental Relations and Public Policy*, ed. J.E. Benton and D.R. Morgan. Westport, Conn.: Greenwood Press.

Taylor, R. Emmett 1925. *Municipal Budget-Making*. Chicago: University of Chicago Press.

Terhune, G.A. 1954. *An Administrative Case Study of Performance Budgeting in the City of Los Angeles*. Chicago: Municipal Finance Officers Association of the United States and Canada.

Tharp, C.R. 1933. *Control of Local Finance through Taxpayers' Associations and Centralized Administration*. Indianapolis: M. Ford Publishing.

Trout, C. 1984. "The Search for Irish Legitimacy." In *Boston 1700–1980: The Evolution of Urban Politics*, ed. R.P. Formisano and C.K. Burns, 133–64. Westport, Conn.: Greenwood Press.

Van De Woestyne, R.S. 1935. *State Control of Local Finance in Massachusetts*. Harvard Economic Studies. Cambridge, Mass.: Harvard University Press.

Wendel, G., and R. Cropf. 1993. "Municipal Debt and the Politics of Development." Paper delivered at the 1993 Midwest Political Science Association annual meeting, Chicago, 15–17 April.

Wenz, T., and A. Nolan. 1982. "Budgeting for the Future: Target Base Budgeting." *Public Budgeting and Finance* 2, no. 2 (Summer): 88–91.

White, M.E. 1979. "ACIR's Model State Legislation for Strengthening Local Government Financial Management." *Governmental Finance* 8 (December): 22–26.

Wilcox, C. 1922. "Rate Limitation and the General Property Tax in Ohio." Master's thesis, Ohio State University, Columbus.

Wright, D.S. 1978. *Understanding Intergovernmental Relations.* North Scituate, Mass.: Duxbury Press.

Index